THE
OXFORD BOOK OF
POLITICAL
ANECDOTES

EDITED BY
PAUL JOHNSON

Oxford   New York
OXFORD UNIVERSITY PRESS
1986

Oxford University Press, Walton Street, Oxford OX2 6DP

Oxford New York Toronto
Delhi Bombay Calcutta Madras Karachi
Petaling Jaya Singapore Hong Kong Tokyo
Nairobi Dar es Salaam Cape Town
Melbourne Auckland

and associated companies in
Beirut Berlin Ibadan Nicosia

Oxford is a trade mark of Oxford University Press

British Library Cataloguing in Publication Data
Johnson, Paul
The Oxford book of political anecdotes.
1. Political science—Anecdotes,
facetiae, satire, etc.   2. English wit
and humour
I. Title
828'.02   PN6231.P6
ISBN 0-19-214121-X

Library of Congress Cataloging in Publication Data
Main entry under title:
The Oxford book of political anecdotes
Includes index.
1. Great Britain—Politics and government—
Anecdotes, facetiae, satire, etc. I. Johnson,
Paul, 1928–
DA44.094 1986   941'.00207   85-31022
ISBN 0-19-214121-X

Set by Promenade Graphics Ltd.
Printed in Great Britain by
Richard Clay (The Chaucer Press) Ltd.
Bungay, Suffolk

CONTENTS

INTRODUCTION

ANECDOTES are a valuable source of historical truth. Inaccurate in detail they may be, but more often than not they convey an essential fact about a great personage which more formal records ignore—a characteristic which struck contemporaries, so that it became embedded in stories which they told among themselves, then passed on to their children and grandchildren. I am always inclined to give an anecdote the benefit of the doubt: true (at least in spirit) until proved false. Take, for instance, one of the earliest and most famous of stories: King Alfred and the Cakes. It is not found in Bishop Asser's *Life of Alfred*; or, rather, it did not become part of the *Life* until the antiquarian collector Archbishop Parker inserted it into his sixteenth-century edition of the text. It is first found in a twelfth-century life of St Neot, who is supposed to have been a kinsman of Alfred, perhaps his half-brother. Family tradition is nearly always a guarantee of substantial truth, in my view, and in this case the story fits what we know of Alfred's personality from other sources: that he was a man of powerful intellectual interests as well as a warrior and lawgiver, habitually inclined to probe some of the deepest aspects of human existence, and no doubt often abstracted. What more likely than that he was lost in his thoughts while the cakes smouldered?

Again, the rebuke King Canute administered to his flattering courtiers, who told him the tide would cease to rise at his command, is surely plausible. The source, Henry of Huntingdon, is late but the story doubtless embodies authentic tradition. Henry says that, after this episode, Canute never again wore his crown but 'hung it on the head of the crucified Lord'. This accords well with what we know of the King's religious fervour in his later years. The Ely chronicler says that, while being rowed in his barge to Ely Abbey, to keep the feast of the Purification there, Canute caught the distant sound of the monks singing the office, and bid his watermen pause and listen; and that to mark the occasion, he wrote a quatrain, which the chronicler quotes. I believe this tale, and another, from the same source, which describes the generous reward Canute bestowed on an immensely fat peasant who walked the fenland ice to see if it was safe for the King's sledge.

Naturally, most of our earliest political anecdotes centre around the Court and usually concern the king. We find them in royal biographies, chronicles, and occasionally in more objective documents, such as letters, financial records, and charters, which give us precious glimpses of our early rulers. Thus we see the notorious William II, called Rufus from his red face and orange hair, shocking the clergy with his oaths and especially his favourite imprecation 'By the Holy Face of Lucca!' Or his younger brother, Henry I, called Beauclerk because he could read and write Latin, who 'never smiled again' after his only son was drowned in the White Ship. Henry II, says Gerald of Wales, was so hyperactive that he would scarcely sit down even to eat: he stood, and kept his courtiers standing, 'before and after dinner'; but in his last years we have a vignette of him, tired after a long day in the saddle, sitting by candlelight, a page massaging his bare feet, while urgent dispatches were read to him. Sometimes the information is given graphically: in his *Lives of the Offas*, Matthew Paris, who was a gifted artist as well as a chronicler, inserts a little drawing of Henry III, a connoisseur and aesthete, giving orders to his architects. His son Edward I, a more martial figure, is illuminated by an entry in his household accounts, recording payment for repairing the crown, 'which the King in his rage did hurl into the fireplace'. We see *his* son, Edward II, a homosexual and pathic, engaging in the 'unkingly' sport of rowing, and (according to his biographer) consorting with unsuitable people such as 'singers, actors, grooms, sailors and others of this kind, artists and mechanics'. No marks were found on his murdered body in Berkeley Castle; but John Trevisa, who was a child living in the little town of Berkeley at the time, later translated Higden's account of the reign in his *Polychronicon*, and interpolated the information that Edward was killed 'with a hoote broche putte thro the secret place posterialle'.

Nowadays historians are more inclined than formerly to accord weight to traditional anecdotage, which gives, for instance, Henry VII a reputation for avarice. We know astonishingly little about this King from contemporary sources (Francis Bacon's *Life* was written three generations later), though I have always thought it significant that he initialled every line of his household accounts (as did his granddaughter, Elizabeth I). A quarter of a century ago, Professor G. R. Elton argued vehemently that Henry was not mean at all: it was 'a false view which speaks of rapacity and oppression'. Then, in 1972, C. J. Harrison of Keele University discovered, among the Anglesey Papers at Plas Newydd, a document written by Henry's financial factotum, Edmund Dudley, shortly before his execution in 1509, in which he confesses no less than eighty-four cases of unjust exactions, described in detail, and carried out by him on the King's instructions. So here is a case of the records confirming the impression which the old stories provide.

From the time of Henry VIII, and the beginnings in England of the Renaissance, with its far more intensive interest in human character and motive, the number of reliable political anecdotes increases sharply. We can build up quite a detailed picture of the King's relations with his ministers. He was a niggler, a nit-picker, a tireless amender of his secretaries' work. He 'crossed and blotted out many things' in the letters Secretary Petre drafted for him, and when the latter grumbled Henry said 'It is I that made both Cromwell, Wriothesley, and Paget good secretaries, and so must I do to thee.' Princes, he added, 'know best their own meaning, and there must be time and experience to acquaint [their secretaries] with their humours before a man can do any acceptable service'. He ordered that drafts have two-and-a-half-inch margins and inch-wide spaces between the lines to leave room for his changes. Sir Thomas More said he had seen one of Henry's letters with four separate layers of corrections, all in the King's handwriting. His daughter Elizabeth had the same propensity; her clerk of the Council, Robert Beale, left a note giving guidance to colleagues about doing business with her: 'Be not dismayed with the controlments and amendments of such things which you shall have done . . . avoid opinion of being newfangled, a bringer-in of new customs.'

Scores of fine political anecdotes survive from Elizabeth's Court, but about this time interest begins slowly to shift to parliament, and the first anecdotes of incidents in Commons debates reach us: Sir Walter Ralegh arousing the wrath of Members when he admitted he often 'plucked at a man's sleeve' to prevent his voting in the wrong lobby; the row over Monopolies in the 1601 parliament; the delivery of Elizabeth's famous 'Golden Speech' in the Whitehall Council Chamber. As the seventeenth century progresses, parliament gradually occupies the centre of the stage and becomes the prime theatre of political anecdote, though the Court, thanks to Bishop Burnett, Harvey, Fanny Burney, Creevey, Greville, Ponsonby and many others, remains a rich quarry.

Parliamentary anecdotes inevitably centre around speeches. There was, is, nothing like a good maiden. Chatham made his reputation by his spirited reply to Walpole's rebuke to his youth ('the atrocious crime of being a young man . . . I shall neither attempt to palliate nor deny');

though another story is that he began his first speech with the word 'Sugar', which provoked titters, then repeated it three times in an ever-louder voice and with ferocious scowls, until the House was reduced to silence. Disraeli had a disastrous maiden, ending 'Though I sit down now, the time will come when you *will* hear me', which seemed lame at the time. Lord Liverpool too made a poor maiden, but Pitt the Younger gave him a seat on the India Board on the strength of it, and thereafter Liverpool (who entered the House for Appleby, aged twenty) served in office for all but thirteen months of his thirty-six years in parliament, fifteen as Prime Minister.

F. E. Smith made his reputation with perhaps the most celebrated maiden of all. Grey, too, made a famous maiden, raising 'an eclat that has not been equalled in my recollection' (Addington). But such triumphs do not guarantee a successful career of oratory. The best maidens of the present time were made by Ian Gilmour (1962) and Bernadette Devlin (1969), but neither made major speeches thereafter. In 1755, William Hamilton attracted enormous attention with a three-hour speech which Horace Walpole called 'perfection'. We now know it was written for him by Dr Johnson, and Hamilton never again found a worthy speech-writer and ended his career many years later as 'Single-Speech Hamilton'. Among those he employed was Burke; but Burke, though hailed by posterity as the finest orator of all, was not a success in the Commons, being known as 'the Dinner Bell' for the speed with which he emptied the House.

Oratory never had much to do with political success. Bute spoke in halting bursts, punctuated by silences, 'like a minute gun'. North, a great parliamentary manager, had no oratorical skill at all and was so undistinguished that he evoked Johnson's laconic dismissal, 'He fills a chair.' Castlereagh could scarcely put two words together but retained the respect of the House where the ultra-articulate Canning failed. Parnell was a poor speaker, but the absolute master of his golden-tongued Irish party. Some Prime Ministers have been notorious bores. George III said of George Grenville: 'When he has wearied me for two hours, he looks at his watch to see if he may not tire me for an hour more.' His favourite reading was said to be an Act of Parliament. His son, Lord Grenville, was the opposite: 'He possessed in an eminent degree the talent of total silence.' He fell asleep in cabinet meetings, which were often held without him or even without asking him. Another sleeper was the Duke of Grafton, of whom Chatham said: 'The natural cloud of his understanding . . . made his meaning as unintelligible as his conversation was uninteresting.' (Two more statesmen who slept in cabinet were the Duke of Portland and Lord Hartington.)

Next to speeches it is personal characteristics and appearance which attract the anecdotes. James I was small, never washed, had a tongue too big for his mouth, and an unfortunate habit of scratching his genitals. His grandson, Charles II, was enormous, about 6 foot 3 inches, and probably the tallest of all our monarchs. When he was on the run from the Ironsides, parliamentary 'Wanted' posters described him as 'a tall black man, over two yards high'. A similar poster, issued by the Boers in 1900, gives us a police picture of Winston Churchill: 'walks with a forward stoop, reddish-brown hair, hardly noticeable moustache, talks through his nose and cannot pronounce the letter "s" properly'. His father, Lord Randolph Churchill, was generally reputed to be small, but it seems he merely looked small. Two Yorkshire gentlemen, disputing about his height, had the nerve to write to him and received the reply:

Dear Sir: Lord Randolph Churchill desires me to say, in reply to your letter of the 21st inst., that his height is just under 5ft 10in.

I am, Yours faithfully,
Cecil Drummond-Wolff, Secretary.

Lord John Russell, by contrast, really was small: 5 foot $4\frac{3}{4}$ inches, and weighed less than eight stone. Spencer Perceval was even smaller. It was the cartoonists who tended to notice such things. Harry Furniss counted the number of Sir William Harcourt's double chins and pronounced John Walter, proprietor of *The Times*, as possessed of 'the largest feet ever seen in the House of Commons'. The ugliest Member, he wrote, was Joseph Biggar, who invented obstruction and so brought about the guillotine. When he rose to make his maiden, a startled Disraeli turned to Lord Barrington and said 'What's that?' Biggar was a pork butcher, with a hunch back, a grating voice, a 'face like a gargoyle', bony hands and huge feet. Punch's parliamentary sketch-writer, Sir Henry Lucy, who wrote under the name 'Toby MP', described Biggar's waistcoat as 'a fearsome garment which, at a distance, might be taken for sealskin, but was understood to be of native manufacture'.

Ambitious politicians, in fact, often wore peculiar clothes precisely to catch the cartoonists' eye. Henry Broadhurst, MP for Stoke, delighted them with his huge boots. During his introduction on a public platform, the crowd roared: 'We know 'im, we know 'im, we've seen 'is boots in *Punch*!' Gladstone's high collars were world famous. Churchill confessed that, when he noticed the cartoonists were exaggerating the size of his hats, he deliberately bought them several sizes too big, to ram home the point. I have never forgotten the glee of the cartoonist Vicky when Harold Macmillan, a specialist in antique, strange, and notable gear, wore a white astrakhan hat on a visit to Moscow. He also sported old-fashioned shooting-breeches, complete with gaiters. All this was half-unconscious, half-deliberate, as was Lord Hailsham's adoption of a cloth cap when, as minister in charge of science and technology, he visited the industrial north. This, too, became part of his cartoon stock-in-trade.

Sometimes the cartoonists got it wrong. John Bright was mistakenly shown, at the beginning of his career, with an eyeglass, and this always appeared thereafter, though he never used one. But cartoonists also suppressed deformities. They never, for instance, indicated the missing finger Gladstone lost in a shooting accident, though I possess a presentation plate of him which clearly shows the fingerstall he wore in consequence. Gladstone was also famous for his umbrella, as were two other personalities: Sir William Joynson-Hicks ('Jix'), Home Secretary in the 1920s, and Neville Chamberlain. Some politicians have sought to alter their appearance in order to be more 'democratic'. After his fall from grace in 1890, Parnell changed his tall silk hat for a bowler, though it looked incongruous, as he continued to wear a frock-coat. Aneurin Bevan refused to wear a dinner jacket even at a Buckingham Palace dinner; so did Anthony Crosland, who also wore carpet slippers both in the Commons and at the Foreign Office, when Secretary of State. Tony Benn took to shirt sleeves on all but the most formal occasions, and gradually reduced his *Who's Who* entry to nothing. But one of the most celebrated political garments, Keir Hardie's 'cloth cap', was eccentric rather than demotic, being a Sherlock Holmes bit of headgear, more common among middle-class intellectuals than dockyard workers.

Political nicknames have abounded from the earliest times. Elizabeth I had names for all her ministers and courtiers: Essex was 'the Wild Horse', Sir John Pakington 'Lusty', Leicester was 'Eyes', Burghley 'Spirit', Walsingham 'the Moor', Sir Christopher Hatton 'Mutton', the small and deformed Sir Robert Cecil 'Pigmy' (she inherited this rather cruel taste from her father, who addressed one of his gentlemen, George Blagge, as 'Pig'). There are literally hundreds of political nicknames in English political history. Both the 1st and the 11th dukes of Norfolk were 'Jockey'. Strafford was 'Black Tom', Coke of Norfolk 'King Tom'. Lord Sandwich was 'Jeremy Twitcher' or 'Twitch', Shelburne 'Malagrida', after the sinister Portuguese Jesuit, a name which occasioned one of Oliver Goldsmith's worst lapses in tact: 'I never could understand', he said to Shelburne, 'why they called you Malagrida, as he was a rather good sort of fellow.' Godolphin was 'Volpone', a nickname he hated. Goderich was 'Snip' or 'Goody', Wellington 'Beau', Addington 'the Doctor', Brougham was variously known as 'Bruffam', 'Wickedshifts', and 'Beelzebub'. George Lambton, Lord Durham, was called 'King Jog' from his saying 'A man can jog along on £40,000 a year.' Lord John Russell was 'the Widow's Mite'; Greville, the diarist, was 'Punch', Palmerston 'Lord Cupid'. A. J. Balfour was 'Fanny' or 'Pretty Fanny', Lloyd George 'the Goat', Asquith 'Squiff' or 'Perrier Jouet'. Baldwin had many nicknames. To younger Tories he was 'Bonzo'; cabinet colleagues referred to him, sardonically, as 'God'; to his wife he was 'Tiger'—R. A. Butler testified in his memoirs: 'I have heard her say to him in a moment of indecision, "Go on, Tiger!" '

Many of these names refer to reprehensible habits, of course. Palmerston was a *coureur des dames* almost to the end of his life. Of the seven great hostesses 1815–35 who could get a Commons debate changed if it conflicted with one of their parties—Lady Cowper, Lady Jersey, Lady Tankerville, Lady Sefton, Lady Willoughby, Princess Lieven, and Princess Esterhazy—'Pam' had had affairs with three, and he was cited as a co-respondent in his seventy-ninth year. Melbourne was also cited in divorce actions, by Lord Brandon and the Hon. George Norton. Neither Prime Minister suffered the slightest damage in consequence. But later in the century, adultery was fatal, if discovered. Gladstone finished Parnell in 1890 by means of a famous public letter addressed to Morley, in which he alluded covertly to Parnell's affair with Mrs O'Shea, and he ended the ministerial career of Sir Charles ('Three-in-a-Bed') Dilke by writing against his name in the cabinet list the one word, 'Unavailable'.

Wives were generally more important than mistresses, however. 'Pam's' wife, the former Lady Cowper, who was first one then the other, was her husband's greatest asset, compensating for his meanness, rudeness, and unpopularity by giving the best parties in London at 94 Piccadilly (now the Naval and Military Club, known as 'The In and Out'). She wrote out all the invitations herself but, curiously enough, would tolerate gatecrashers if they were brazen enough. Some wives were liabilities: Melbourne's Lady Caroline Lamb, for instance, known as 'Bat'; Disraeli's wife who, as he said, 'was never quite sure which came first, the Greeks or the Romans', was thought embarrassing by his colleagues, but not by Disraeli himself; he resented and punished any slights. But he told her little. She said to Queen Victoria that she neither knew nor cared to know any cabinet secrets. By contrast, Palmerston used his wife to copy his most secret letters; and Gladstone said of his: 'My wife has known every political secret I have ever had, and has never betrayed my confidence.' He rightly remarked that a minister should tell his wife everything or nothing—an occasional confidence was fatal. Sometimes wives have played a decisive role. Thus, in September 1905, when Asquith, Grey, and Haldane combined in the 'Relugas Compact' to persuade their leader, Campbell-Bannerman, to retreat into the impotence of the House of Lords, it was Lady Campbell-Bannerman who got him to put down the conspiracy. Mrs Baldwin, another formidable lady, was instrumental in stiffening her husband's resolve to fight the Press Lords, Beaverbrook and Rothermere, in 1930. Clementine Churchill was also, on occasion, decisive in changing her partner's mood, though in her case it was to curb a naturally aggressive spirit.

In modern times, and with the outstanding exception of Lloyd George, British Prime Ministers, at least, have tended to be faithful to their wives. In fact, more political anecdotes revolve around drink than sex. It is now rare for a minister to make a speech or statement when drunk. But both Pitt the Younger and Asquith did so, and Pitt, a port-drinker, used to go behind the Speaker's Chair to vomit before making an important intervention in debate. Politicians have taken a wide variety of stimulants. Liverpool favoured a whiff of ether, Canning a dose of laudanum. Chancellors of the Exchequer, when making their annual budget statements, are traditionally allowed a restorative mixture. It was Gladstone who started this practice, sipping, at intervals in his speeches, which sometimes lasted four hours, a mixture of raw eggs and sherry prepared by his wife.

Drink, of course, was at the bottom of most parliamentary violence, especially when combined with discussion of the Irish Question. Between 1750 and early Victorian times duels, or threats of duels, between politicians were comparatively frequent. Shelburne fought one with a Scottish MP, Colonel William Fullerton, who accused him of treachery with the enemy. It took place in Hyde Park and Shelburne was wounded in the groin. He wrote to a friend: 'I don't think Lady Shelburne will be any the worse for it.' Pitt the Younger fought a duel with George Tierney MP on Putney Heath, both men firing into the air. Wellington fought duels; Palmerston, curiously enough, did not, though he had a furious fist-fight with another future Prime Minister, Aberdeen, at Harrow. Disraeli made a great song and dance over his proposed duel with Daniel O'Connell, but nothing came of it. The most famous act of violence in modern times was the kicking of Aneurin Bevan down the steps of White's by an angry but obscure member called Fox-Strangeways, a distant connection of Charles James Fox. But Michael Foot scarcely mentions the episode in his official biography of Bevan, and when I taxed Bevan himself on the subject he refused to discuss it. The details are in dispute.

There are, needless to say, many disputed anecdotes. To Lloyd George is attributed the saying, of the cold-hearted Sir John Simon: 'His smile was like the glitter of the brass plate on a coffin.' An alternative version has Daniel O'Connell saying it of Sir Robert Peel. In fact, it was coined by another Irishman, John Philpot Curran, and when O'Connell purloined it his victim was not Peel but Lord Stanley, later 14th Earl of Derby. Lloyd George's authentic remark of Simon was 'Men shuddered when he took their arm.' Again, there is the famous Ernest Bevin story. When Attlee remarked that Herbert Morrison was his own worst enemy, Bevin growled 'Not while I'm alive he ain't.' But Bevin is reputed to have said this of Dalton, Cripps, Bevan, and even R. H. S. Crossman, and the remark is attributed to other political bruisers.

Certainly every effort should be made to get the details of an anecdote correct, particularly in the modern period, where verification is usually possible. A famous story concerns F. E. Smith's characteristically contemptuous habit of using the gents of a famous club, to which he did not belong, on the way to his office. Members noticed, and eventually persuaded a frightened Club Secretary to tackle the Lord Chancellor the next time he did it. The Secretary complied, whereupon F. E. said, with well-simulated astonishment, 'Oh, this is a club, is it? I always thought it was a public lavatory.' Yes: but which club? I had been told it was the Royal Automobile Club in Pall Mall, which has a gents immediately opposite the entrance (I have used it myself on occasion). But Smith's latest and most thorough biographer, John Campbell, by using street plans and deducing the likely route he took, has 'proved' that it is the National Liberal Club. In my view, the location of this gents, right across the inner hall and down steps, makes it an unlikely contender, so I believe the issue is still open.

The trouble with checking the details is that they sometimes demolish the story. For instance, the late Sir Harold Nicolson was the greatest repository of political, diplomatic, and society anecdotes in London, and told them with great skill. They were usually accurate, but not always. He told me this tale of Churchill:

Sir Basil Thomson was a famous spycatcher, the head of the Special Branch at Scotland Yard. He finished Sir Roger Casement, among others, and later wrote an unreliable book about his cases, called *Queer People*. But he was a rather queer person himself. His services to the state were considered so valuable that he was kept on long after the official retirement age, in an advisory capacity, and was over seventy when he finally was put out to grass. That was on the 31 December 1926. On the evening of the next day, he was arrested for indecent exposure in Hyde Park. Churchill, who had worked closely with Thomson during the war, and was now Chancellor of the Exchequer, was asked to intervene, and get the charge quashed. He demanded of Thomson's friends the precise circumstances—date, place, time of day, even the approximate temperature. After many questions and answers, he spoke as follows: 'Sir Basil Thomson, a distinguished servant of the public, seventy years of age, verging on seventy-one, exposing himself, in Hyde Park, at nine in the evening on the First of January, in a temperature of two degrees of frost—*makes yer proud to be an Englishman*!' It was his way of saying there was nothing he could do. Thomson was duly convicted and fined £5.

Alas, Sir Basil Thomson resigned in 1921, when he was only sixty, and before Churchill went to the Treasury: there may be some element of truth in Nicolson's story, but its essence cannot be authentic.

We are fortunate to have lived in an age of such great political personalities. Churchill, indeed, must have given rise to more anecdotes than any politician in our history, except possibly for Gladstone and Disraeli. But many of his supposed sayings were fathered on him. Attlee, by contrast, was celebrated for what he did not say. No public man has ever doled out his words more sparingly, perhaps because he had a sharp, talkative, and overbearing wife, of whom he stood in awe, and who was reputed (among other things) to be the worst driver in the Home Counties. Douglas Jay, when President of the Board of Trade, inherited Attlee's official chauffeur, George, and he related to me a story George told with relish:

Mr Attlee, as he then was, never addressed a word to me, except that, when he first got in the car he would say 'Good morning, George', and when I finally dropped him each evening, he would say 'Good night, George'. Otherwise, not a word. The only time he ever spoke to me was once, when we were driving to Chequers for the weekend, a car overtook us and nearly sent us into the ditch. Mr Attlee said furiously 'Who's that bloody fool? I said: 'That was Mrs Attlee, Sir.' 'Best say no more about it.'

When Attlee was old and an earl, he delivered a series of lectures in America which he subsequently published in a slim volume called *From Empire to Commonwealth*. When the book appeared, I interviewed him about it on television, and knowing his habit of answering in monosyllables, I had prepared no less than forty questions for a short interview. We got through more than thirty, for he had a disconcerting habit of saying, in answer to one question 'What's your next question?' Afterwards, in the studio hospitality room, I asked him to autograph my copy of the book, and he took it off into a corner, spent a long time writing in it, and then handed it back, shut. What on earth had he been writing? There were others milling about, and I did not like to look until afterwards. Then I found, as I might have expected, he had written, in a quavering hand, 'Attlee'. Curiously enough, he became quite talkative when I gave him a lift back to London in the limousine the studio had provided for me (he, with his usual self-effacement, had not even asked for one). He told me that, in the old days, politicians often had sing-songs together, as indeed we know from tales Beaverbrook told about Lloyd George and his cabinet cronies. And Attlee sang for me some of these ditties, including old Boer War songs, in a weak but tuneful voice. I asked him where he wished to be dropped. 'Army & Navy Stores. Off to India tomorrow. Must get kitted up.' He disappeared through its swing doors, the last I saw of him.

Of course I cannot reproduce on the page the clipped tone, so evocative of pre-1914 Haileybury, with which Attlee enunciated his rare words. Nor can I convey the extraordinary vocal range, from melodious, lilting tenor to indignant squeak, which gave Aneurin Bevan's voice its power, and imitation of which—however inadequate—is essential to the telling of any Bevan anecdote. No man in our political history needed so much to be heard, and indeed seen. The cold words alone cannot conjure up his magic and his majesty. He was the first great man I knew at all well, and I cannot forget the first time I sat next to him, at the lavish annual *Tribune* lunch provided by its then proprietor, the millionaire Howard Samuel. Beside each plate was a splendid Monte Cristo cigar in its aluminium tube. At the end of the meal, Bevan took out, lit and puffed his with profound enjoyment. Then he noticed mine was untouched and asked why. I had only just become a Socialist, and I explained that I did not think it right that Socialists should enjoy such luxuries. 'Oooooh, you are one of *those*, are you?' asked Bevan with Olympian contempt. 'Well, give it here, boy', and he took my cigar and tucked it safely into his top pocket for future consumption.

That high Welsh tenor is gone for ever, as is the faint Worcestershire burr of Baldwin, or Curzon's short Derbyshire 'a's, the Liverpudlian glottal which underlay the acquired Oxford tones of F. E. Smith, and much more distant accents—Sir Walter Ralegh's 'broad Devonshire' and the long, drawling vowels of his mistress, Queen Elizabeth I. Our children will never experience the skill and relish with which Ernie Bevin mangled English syntax, just as we cannot quail before the fierce glance of Gladstone's eagle eye—so mesmeric that men were known to lose the power of speech when he transfixed them—or marvel at the exquisite courtesy of Chatham, 'who bowed so low that the tip of his nose was visible between his legs'. The magnetic tape will make things different for our progeny. In the meantime, we must be content with print, and in the pages which follow I have reproduced the bare bones of many stories, as recorded by contemporaries or tradition. The voices, the expressions, the gestures must be supplied by the reader's imagination.

PAUL JOHNSON

Iver, 1985

I

Richard Crookback

RICHARD, the third son, of whom we now entreat, was in wit and
courage equal with either of them [his elder brothers]; in body and
prowess, far under them both; little of stature, ill-featured of limbs,
crook-backed, his left shoulder much higher than his right, hard
favoured of visage, and such as in states called warly, in other men
otherwise; he was malicious, wrathful, envious and from his birth ever
froward. It is for truth reported, that the duchess, his mother, had so
much ado in her travail, that she could not be delivered of him uncut;
and that he came into the world with the feet forward, as men be born
outward, and (as the fame runneth) also not untoothed.

Sir Thomas More, Richard III, 1515–16; first pub. 1557

2

Off With His Head!

*On 13 June 1483, as part of his campaign to seize the crown, Richard Duke
of Gloucester, now Protector, appeared before the Council in the Tower and
accused the Queen (Elizabeth Woodville) and the late King's mistress, Jane
Shore, of attempting to murder him by witchcraft, and Shore's protector, the
Lord Chamberlain Hastings, of abetting them in treason.*

THEN, said the Protector, 'ye shall see in what wise that sorceress, and
that other witch of her counsel, Shore's wife, with their affinity, have
by their sorcery and witchcraft wasted my body'. And therewith he
plucked up his doublet-sleeve to his elbow, upon his left arm, where he
shewed a werish withered arm and small, as it was never other. And
thereupon every man's mind sore misgave him, well perceiving that this
matter was but a quarrel. For well they wist, that the Queen was
too wise to go about any such folly. And also, if she would, yet would
she of all folk least make Shore's wife of [her] counsel, whom of all
women she most hated, as that concubine whom the King her husband

had most loved. And also no man was there present but well knew, that his arm was ever such since his birth.

Nevertheless, the Lord Chamberlain (who from the death of King Edward kept Shore's wife, on whom he somewhat doted in the King's life, saving, as it is said, he that while forebare her of reverence towards his King, or else of a certain kind of fidelity towards his friend) answered and said: 'Certainly, my Lord, if they have so heinously done, they be worthy heinous punishment.'

'What,' quoth the Protector, 'thou servest me I ween with ifs and ands; I tell thee they have so done, and that I will make good on thy body, traitor.' And therewith, as in a great anger, he clapped his fist upon the board a great rap; at which token given, one cried 'Treason!' without the chamber. Therewith a door clapped, and in came there rushing men in harness as many as the chamber might hold. And anon the Protector said to the Lord Hastings: 'I arrest thee traitor.' 'What, me my Lord?' quoth he. 'Yea, thee traitor', quoth the Protector. And another let fly at the Lord Stanley, who shrunk at the stroke and fell under the table, or else his head had been cleft to the teeth; for, as shortly as he shrank, yet ran the blood about his ears.

Then were they all quickly bestowed in divers chambers; except the Lord Chamberlain, who the Protector bad speed and shrive him apace 'For by St Paul', quoth he, 'I will not to dinner before I see thy head off.' It booted him not to ask 'Why'; but heavily he took a priest at adventure, and made a short shrift; for a longer would not be suffered, the Protector made so much haste to dinner, which he might not go to till this were done, for saving of his oath. So was he brought forth into the Green, beside the chapel within the Tower, and his head laid down upon a long log of timber, and there stricken off.

Ibid.

3

Atoning for a Political Scandal

After the judicial murder of Lord Hastings, Richard took revenge on his brother's mistress, Jane Shore.

HE caused the Bishop of London to put her to open penance, going before the cross in procession upon a Sunday, with a taper in her hand.

In which she went in countenance and pace demure so womanly, and albeit she were out of all array save her kirtle [skirt] only, yet went she so fair and lovely, namely while the wondering of the people cast a comely run in her cheeks (of which she before had most miss), that her great shame won her much praise, among those who were more amorous of her body than curious of her soul. . . . This woman was born in London worshipfully friended, honestly brought up, and very well married, saving somewhat too soon; her husband an honest citizen, young and goodly and of good substance. But, foreasmuch as they were coupled ere she was ripe, she not very fervently loved for whom she never longed. Which was haply the thing that more easily made her incline unto the King's appetite, when he required her. Howbeit the respect of his royalty, the hope of gay apparel, ease, pleasure and other wanton wealth, were soon able to pierce a soft, tender heart. But when the King had abused her, anon her husband, as he was an honest man, and one who would his good, not presuming to touch a King's concubine, left her up to him altogether. When the King died, the Lord Chamberlain took her. . . . Proper she was and fair; nothing in her body that you would have changed, but if you would have wished her somewhat higher. Thus say they who knew her in her youth; albeit some who now see her (for yet she liveth) deem her never to have been well visaged. Whose judgement seemeth me somewhat like, as though men should guess the beauty of one long before departed, by her scalp taken out of the charnel house. For now is she old, lean, withered and dried up, nothing left but shrivelled skin and hard bone. And yet, being even such, whoso well advise her visage, might guess and devise which parts, how filled, would make it a fair face.

Ibid.

4

The Babes in the Tower

FOR Sir James Tyrel devised, that they should be murdered in their beds. To the execution whereof, he appointed Miles Forest, one of the four who kept them, a fellow fleshed in murder beforetime. To him he joined one John Dighton, his own horse-keeper, a big, broad, square, strong knave. Then, all the others being removed from them, this Miles Forest and John Dighton about midnight, the silly children lying in their beds, came into the chamber, and suddenly lapped them up among the clothes, so bewrapped them and entangled them, keeping down by force the feather-bed and pillows hard into their mouths, that within a while, smothered and stifled, their breath failing, they gave up to God their innocent souls unto the joys of heaven, leaving to their tormentors their bodies dead in the bed.

Whom after that the wretches perceived, first by the struggling with the pains of death, and after long lying still, to be thoroughly dead, they laid their bodies naked out upon the bed, and fetched Sir James to see them. Who, upon the sights of them, caused those murderers to bury them at the stair foot, meetly deep into the ground, under a great heap of stone.

Then rode Sir James in great haste to King Richard, and shewed him all the manner of the murder; who gave him great thanks, and as some say there made him knight. But he allowed not, as I have heard, that burying in so vile a corner, saying that he would have them buried in a better place, because they were king's sons—lo, the honourable courage of a king! Whereupon, they say, that a priest of Sir Robert Brakenbery took up the bodies again, and secretly interred them in place as, by the occasion of his death who only knew it, could never since come to light. Very truth it is, and well known, that at such time as Sir James Tyrel was in the Tower for treason committed against the most famous prince King Henry VII, both Dighton and he were examined, and confessed the murder in manner above written. But whither the bodies were removed they could nothing tell . . .

For first, to begin with the ministers, Miles Forest, at St Martins, piecemeal rotted away. Dighton indeed yet walketh on alive, in good possibility to be hanged ere he die. But Sir James Tyrel died at Tower Hill, beheaded for treason. King Richard himself, as ye shall hereafter hear, slain in the field, hacked and hewed of his enemies' hands, harried on horseback dead, his hair in despite torn and tugged like a cur dog. And the mischief that he took, within less than three years of the mischief that he did; and yet all the meantime spent in much pain and trouble outward, much fear, anguish and sorrow within. For I have heard by credible report of such as were secret with chamberers, that after this abominable deed done, he never had quiet in his mind, he never thought himself sure. Where he went abroad, his eyes whirled about, his body privily fenced, his hands ever on his dagger, his countenance and manner like one always ready to strike again. He took ill rest at nights, lay long waking and musing, sore wearied with care and watch, he rather slumbered than slept. Troubled with fearful dreams, suddenly sometime started he up, leapt out of his bed and ran about the chamber.

Ibid.

5

An Ungrateful Ruler

Henry VII forbade his nobles to keep their retainers in livery, and spared none of them when detected.

THERE remaineth to this day a report, that the King was on a time entertained by the Earl of Oxford (that was his principal servant both for war and peace), noble and sumptuously, at his castle at Henningham. And at the King's going away, the Earl's servants stood in a seemly manner in their livery coats with cognizances ranged on both sides, and made the King a lane. The King called the Earl to him and said, 'My Lord, I have heard much of your hospitality, but I see it is greater than the speech. These handsome gentlemen and yeomen which I see on both sides of me are (sure) your menial servants.' The Earl smiled and said, 'It may please your Grace, it were not for mine ease. They are most of them my retainers, that are comen to do me service at such a time as this, and chiefly to see your Grace.' The King started a little and said, 'By my faith, (my Lord) I thank you for your good cheer, but I may not endure to have my laws broken in my sight. My attorney must speak with you.' And it is part of the report, that the Earl compounded for no less than fifteen thousand marks. And to show further the King's extreme diligence, I do remember to have seen long since a book of accompt of Empson's, that had the King's hand almost to every leaf by way of signing, and was in some places postilled in the margent with the King's hand likewise, where was this remembrance: 'Item, received, of such a one, five marks, for a pardon to be procured, and if the pardon do not pass, the money to be repaid; except the party in some other ways satisfied.' And over against this memorandum, of the King's own hand: 'Otherwise satisfied.' Which I do the rather mention because it shews in the King a nearness, but yet with a kind of justness.

Francis Bacon, The Historie of the Raigne of King Henry the Seventh, 1622

6

Sir Thomas More

With the accession of Henry VIII, Sir Thomas More was rapidly promoted becoming Master of Requests (1514), Treasurer of the Exchequer (1521), and Chancellor of the Duchy of Lancaster (1525). His son-in-law adds:

AND from the pleasyre he took in his company, would his Grace sometimes come home to his house at Chelsea to be merry with him, whither on a time unlooked for he came to dinner, and after dinner in a fair garden of his walked with him by the space of an hour holding his arm about his neck. As soon as his Grace was gone, I rejoicing, told Sir Thomas More how happy he was, whom the King had so familiarly entertained, as I had never seen him do to any before, except Cardinal Wolsey, whom I saw his Grace once walk with arm in arm. 'I thank our Lord, son', quoth he, 'I find his Grace my very good lord indeed, and I do believe he doth as singularly favour me as any subject within this Realm. Howbeit (son Roper) I may tell thee, I have no cause to be proud thereof. For if my head would win him a castle in France, it should not fail to go'.

William Roper, *The Life of Sir Thomas More*, first. pub. 1626

7

The Solomon Touch

WHILE [Sir Thomas More] was sitting in his hall one day, a beggar come to him to complain that Lady More detained a little dog which belonged to her. The Chancellor sent for his lady and ordered her to bring the dog with her. He took it into his hands, and placing Lady More at the upper end of the hall, desired the beggar to stand at the lower end. 'I sit here', he said, 'to do every one justice', and he desired each of them to call the dog. The little favourite immediately forsook his new mistress and ran to the beggar; upon which Lady More was compelled to indulge her partiality by purchasing the animal.

Arthur Cayley, *Memoirs of Sir Thomas More*, 1808

8

THIS Duke [of Norfolk] coming on a time to Chelsea to dine with him, fortuned to find him at church singing in the choir with a surplice on his back; to whom, after service, as they went home together arm in arm, the Duke said, 'God body, God body (my Lord Chancellor) a parish clerk, a parish clerk, you dishonour the King and his office.' 'Nay', quoth Sir Thomas More, smiling upon the Duke, 'your Grace may not think that the King, your master and mine, will with me for serving God his master be offended, or thereby count his office dishonoured'.

Roper, *Life of More*

9

[When he resigned as Lord Chancellor, Lady More exclaimed:] 'Tilly valley, tilly valley, what will you do, Mr More? Will you sit and make goslings in the ashes? It is better to rule than be ruled.'

Ibid.

IO

NOW upon this resignment of his office came Sir Thomas Cromwell (then in the King's high favour) to Chelsea to him on a message from the King, wherein when they had thoroughly communed together. 'Mr Cromwell', quoth he, 'you are now entered into the service of a most noble, wise and liberal prince; if you will follow my poor advice, you shall, in giving counsel unto his Grace, ever tell him what he ought to do, but never tell him what he is able to do, so shall you show yourself a true faithful servant, and a right worthy Councillor. For if the lion knew his own strength, hard were it for any man to rule him.'

Ibid.

I I

WHEN Sir Thomas More had continued a good while in the Tower, my lady his wife obtained licence to see him, who at her first coming like a simple woman, and somewhat worldly too, with this manner of salutations bluntly saluted him, 'What the good year, Mr More,' quoth she, 'I marvel that you, that have been always hitherunto taken for so wise a man, will now play the fool to lie in this close filthy prison, and be content to be shut up among mice and rats, when you might be abroad at your liberty, and with the favour and good will both of the King and his Council, if you would but do as all the bishops and best learned of this Realm have done. And seeing you have at Chelsea a right fair house, your library, your books, your gallery, your garden, your orchards, and all other necessaries so handsomely about you, where you might, in the company of me your wife, your children, and household be merry, I muse what a God's name you mean here thus fondly to tarry.' After he had a while quietly heard her, with a cheerful countenance he said unto her, 'I pray thee good Mrs Alice, tell me, tell me one thing.' 'What is that?' quoth she. 'Is not this house as nigh heaven as mine own?' To whom she, after her accustomed fashion, not liking such talk, answered, 'Tilly valley, tilly valley.' 'How say you Mrs Alice, is it not so?' quoth he. 'Bone Deus, Bone Deus, man, will this gear never be left?' quoth she. 'Well then, Mrs Alice, if it be so, it is very well. For I see no great cause why I should much joy of my gay house, or of anything belonging thereunto, when if I should but seven years lie buried under the ground, and then arise and come hither again, I should not fail to find some therein that would bid me get out of the doors and tell me that were none of mine. What cause have I then to like such an house as would so soon forget his master?'

Ibid.

12

On the Scaffold

ON ascending this structure, he found it so weak that it was ready to fall. Upon which he said to the Lieutenant, 'I pray thee see me up safe, and for my coming down let me shift for myself.' As Henry had so prudently imposed silence upon him at this time, More only desired of the spectators that they would pray for him, and bear witness that he there suffered death in and for the faith of the catholic church. This said, he knelt, and repeated a psalm with great deliberation; perhaps the 51st,

the 56th or the 57th. He then rose cheerfully and the executioner asking his forgiveness, More kissed him and said, 'Thou wilt do me this
day a greater benefit than ever any mortal man can be able to give me.
Pluck up thy spirit, man, and be not afraid to do thy office. My neck is
very short: take heed therefore that thou strike not awry, for saving thy
honesty.' When he laid his head upon the block, he desired the
executioner to wait till he had removed his beard, 'For that had never
committed treason.' 'So with great alacrity and spiritual joy', adds his
great-grandson, 'he received the fatal blow of the axe' . . . His head
remained for some time fixed upon a pole on London Bridge, until the
piety of his daughter Margaret found an opportunity of purchasing it.
She is said to have preserved it in a leaden box, and to have ordered its
interment with her own body in the Roper vault, under a chapel
adjoining St Dunstan's, Canterbury.

Cayley, *Memoirs of More*

13

Queen Elizabeth

BOWYER, a Gentleman of the Black Rod, being charged by her
expresse command to look precisely to all admissions into the Privy-
Chamber, one day stayed a very gay Captain and a follower of my Lord
of *Leicesters*, from entrance; For that he was neither well known, nor a
sworn servant to the Queen: at which repulse, the Gentleman bearing
high on my Lords favour, told him, he might perchance procure him a
discharge: Leicester coming into the contestation, said publickely
(which was none of his wont) that he was Knave, and should not continue long in his office; and so turning about to go in to the Queen,
Bowyer (who was a bold Gentleman and well beloved) stept before him,
and fell at her Majesties feet, related the story and humbly craves her
Graces pleasure; and whether my Lord of *Leicester* was King or her
Majesty Queen? Whereunto she replied with her wonted oath (Gods
death) my Lord, I have wisht you well, but my favour is not so lockt up
for you, that others shall not partake thereof; for I have many servants,
unto whom I have, and will at my pleasure bequeath my favour, and
likewise resume the same; and if you think to rule here, I will take a
course to see you forth-coming: I will have here but one Mistress, and

no Master, and look that no ill happen to him, lest it be severely required at your hands. Which so quelled my Lord of *Leicester*, that his fained humility was long after one of his best virtues.

Sir Robert Naunton, Fragmenta Regalia, 1641

14

THAT same day, after dinner, my Lord of Hunsdon drew me up to a quiet gallery that I might hear some music; but he said he durst not avow it, where I might hear the Queen play upon the virginals. After I had hearkened awhile, I took by the tapestry that hung before the door of the chamber, and seeing her back was towards the door, I ventured within the chamber, and stood a pretty space hearing her play excellent well; but she left off immediately so soon as she turned about and saw me. She appeared to be surprised to see me, and came forward seeming to strike me with her hand; alleging that she used not to play before men, but when she was solitary, to shun melancholy.

Sir James Melville, Memoirs of His Own Life, 1549–93

15

THE remove of the Court from Windsor is still constantly put off. The carter that three times came to Windsor with his cart to carry away some of the stuff of the Queen's wardrobe, when he repared there for the third time and was told by those of the wardrobe that the remove held not, clapping his hand on his thigh cried out, 'Now I see that the Queen is a woman as well as my wife.' These words being overheard by her Majesty, who then stood at the window, she said 'What a villain is this!' and so sends him three angels* to stop his mouth.

Thomas Birch, Memoirs of the Reign of Queen Elizabeth, 1754

16

NOW though this Archbishop [Parker] dissembled not his Marriage, yet Queen *Elizabeth* would not dissemble her dislike of it. For whereas it pleased her often to come to his house, in respect of her favour to him (that had been her Mothers Chaplain) being once above the rest

---

* An angel was ten shillings.

greatly seated; at her parting from thence, the Archbishop and his Wife being together, she gave him very special thanks, with gratious and honourable terms, and then looking on his Wife, and you (saith she) Madame I may not call you, and Mistress I am ashamed to call you, so I know not what to call you, but yet I do thank you.

Sir John Harington, Nugae Antiquae, 1769

17

THE Queen, seeing Sir Edward Dyer in her garden, looked out at her window and asked him in Italian, 'What does a man think of when he thinks of nothing?' Sir Edward (who had not had the effect of some of the Queen's grants so soon as he had hoped and desired) paused a little, and then made answer, 'Madam, he thinks of a woman's promise.' The Queen shrunk in her head, but was heard to say, 'Well, Sir Edward, I must not confute you. Anger makes dull men witty, but it keeps them poor.'

Francis Bacon, Apophthegms, 1624

18

THIS Earle of Oxford [Edward de Vere, 17th earl, 1550–1604], making his low obeisance to Queen Elizabeth, happened to let a Fart, at which he was so abashed and ashamed that he went to Travell, 7 yeares. On his returne, the Queen welcomed him home, and sayd, My Lord, I had forgott the Fart.

John Aubrey, Brief Lives, 1669–96; first pub. 1813

19

The Parliament of 1581

MR Popham, when he was Speaker, and the Lower House had sat long, and done in effect nothing, coming one day to Queen Elizabeth, she said to him: 'Now, Mr Speaker, what hath passed in the Lower House?' He answered: 'If it please Your Majesty, seven weeks.'

Bacon, Apophthegms

20

Queen Elizabeth and Richard II

THE book of the depositing Richard II, and the coming in of Henry
IV, supposed to be written by Dr Hayward, who was committed to the
Tower for it, has much incensed Queen Elizabeth. And she asked Mr
Bacon, being then of her learned council, 'Whether there were no
treason contained in it?' Mr Bacon, intending to do him a pleasure, and
to take off the Queen's bitterness with a jest, answered: 'No madam,
for treason I cannot deliver opinion that there is any, but very much
felony.' The Queen, apprehending it gladly, asked 'How, and wherein?'
Mr Bacon answered: 'Because he had stolen many of his sentences
and conceits out of Cornelius Tacitus.'

Ibid.

21

Cecil v. Essex

SIR Robert Cecil is reported to be very busy coming and going very
often between London and the Queen, so that he appeareth with his
hands full of papers and his head full of matter, and so occupied pas-
seth through the Presence Chamber like a blind man, not looking upon
any.

N. E. McClure, *The Letters of John Chamberlain*, 1939

22

*In July 1592 the Earl of Essex tried, and failed, to persuade Queen Elizabeth
to make him Chancellor of Oxford University. He blamed Cecil and wrote to
him:*

SIR R.—I have been with the Queen and have had my answer. How it
agrees with your letter you can judge, after you have spoken with the
Queen. Whether you have mistaken the Queen, or used cunning with
me, I know not. I will not condemn you, but leave you to think if it were

your own case, whether you would not be jealous. Your friend, if I have
cause, R. Essex.

> *Collection of State Papers . . . left by Wm Cecil, Lord Burghley* eds. Samuel
> Haynes and William Murdin, 1740–59

23

*In February 1593 Essex sought to make his follower Sir Francis Bacon
Attorney-General. He and Cecil discussed the appointment after examining a
prisoner in the Tower. Anthony Standen writes to Bacon:*

THESE two returning back in a coach together, Sir Robert began of
himself, saying: 'My Lord, the Queen has resolved, e'er five days pass,
without any farther delay, to make an attorney-general. I pray your
lordship to let me known whom you will favour.' The earl answered,
that he wondered, that Sir Robert should ask him that question, seeing
it could not be unknown to him, that resolutely against all whosoever
he stood for Francis Bacon. 'Good Lord!' replied Sir Robert, 'I
wonder your lordship should go about to spend your strength in so
unlikely or impossible a matter', desiring his lordship to allege to him
but one only precedent for so raw a youth to that place of such
moment. The earl very cunningly working upon him said, that for the
attorneyship, which was but an ordinary office other than the prince's
favour, he could produce no pattern, because he had not made any
search for that purpose; but that a younger than Francis Bacon, of less
learning, and of no greater experience, was suing and shoving with all
for an office of far greater importance, greater charge and greater
weight, than the attorneyship. Such a one, the earl said, he could name
to him. Sir Robert's answer was, that he well knew, that his lordship
meant him; and that admitting that both his years and experience were
small, yet weighing the school which he studied in and the great wisdom and learning of his schoolmaster and the pains and observations
he daily passed in that school, he thought his forces and wisdom to be
sufficient to sway that machine; alleging with all his father's deserts in
these his long and painful travails of so long an administration to merit
a mark of gratitude from Her Majesty in the person of the son. And
with regard to the affair of Mr Francis Bacon, he desired his lordship
to consider of it. 'If at least', said he, 'your lordship has spoken on the
solicitorship, that might be easier digestion to Her Majesty.' The earl

upon this answered: 'Digest me no digestions. For the attorneyship for Francis is that I must have; and in that will I spend all my power, might, authority and amity, and with tooth and nail defend and procure the fame for him against whomsoever; and that whoever getteth this office out of my hands for any other before he have it, it shall cost him the coming by. And this be you assured of, Sir Robert; for now do I fully declare myself.'

Birch, Memoirs of the Reign of Queen Elizabeth

24

Bacon did not get the job. The prelude to Essex's fall was his disastrous expedition to Ireland and his sudden return to Court without permission, on 28 September 1599.

THIS morning, about 10 o'clock, he lighted at the court gate at Non-such in post and made all haste up to the Presence and so to the Privy Chamber, and stayed not till he came to the Queen's bedchamber, where he found the Queen newly up, her hair about her face. He kneeled unto her, kissed her hands and her neck and had some private speech with her, which seemed to give him great contentment, for coming from Her Majesty for to shift himself in his chamber, he was very pleasant and thanked God that though he had suffered much trouble and storms abroad he found a sweet calm at home. Tis much wondered at that he went so boldly to Her Majesty's presence, she not being ready, and he so full of dirt and mire that his very face was full of it. About 11 he was ready and went up again to the Queen and conferred with her till half an hour after 12. He went to dinner and during all that time discoursed merely of his travels and journeys in Ireland. . . . He was visited frankly by all sorts, of lords, ladies and gentlemen; only a strangeness was observed between him and Mr Secretary and that party. Then he went up to the Queen but found her much changed in that small time, for she began to call him to question for his return and was not satisfied in the manner of his coming away, and leaving all things at so great hazard . . .

29 September: Late last night, between 10 and 11 o'clock, a commandment came from the Queen to my Lord of Essex that he should keep his chamber. . . . Afterwards my Lord of Essex was commanded

from Court and committed to my Lord Keeper's; he is now come to London to York House in my Lord of Worcester's coach. At his going from Court few or none of his friends accompanied him.

Sidney Papers, ed. Arthur Collins, 1746

25

Early in 1601 the disgraced Essex, at liberty but stripped of favour, began to fortify his London house on the Thames; on 7 February, some of his men sought Shakespeare's inspiration for their intended treason.

YESTERDAY Sir Charles Percy, Sir Joscelyn Percy, the Lord Mounteagle and some others of my Lord of Essex's followers came to some of the Lord Chamberlain's players and would have them play that play of the deposing and killing of King Richard II, promising to give them 40s. more than their ordinary to play it. The players answered that the play of King Richard was so old and so long out of use that they should have little or no company at it. Nevertheless at their request and in consideration of 40s., they played it this afternoon at the Globe, when many of my Lord of Essex's followers were present.

State Papers, Domestic

26

Early the following day the Queen took action to quell the intended revolt:

THE Lord Mayor at this time received orders from the Queen to see that the citizens were all in their houses ready to obey orders; and Her Majesty sent to the Earl of Essex the Lord Keeper Egerton, Sir William Knollys the Comptroller, and Popham, Lord Chief Justice of the King's Bench, to know the reasons of this concourse at his house. But they were with difficulty admitted through a wicket, all their servants being shut out except the purse-bearer. In the courtyard they saw a confused multitude, and in the midst of them the Earl himself with the Earls of Rutland and Southampton and many others, who immediately surrounded them. The Lord Keeper then turning to his lordship signified to him, that himself and the others were sent by the Queen to know the cause of such a concourse, promising that if his lordship had been injured by any he should have right done to him. The Earl answered aloud that he knew that a design was concerted against his life and persons hired to kill him in his bed; that he had been perfidiously used; that letters had been counterfeited in his name; that they were met to defend themselves, and preserve their lives, since neither his patience nor misery could soften the malice of his enemies, who would not be satisfied without his blood . . .

The Lord Keeper pressing the Earl of Essex again to discover to them privately if not publicly his grievances, he was interrupted by a cry of the multitude: 'Away, my lord. They abuse your lordship's patience. They betray you. They undo you. You lose time.' The Lord Keeper then turning to them commanded them, upon their allegiance, to lay down their arms and then with the others followed the Earl, who was in this interval retired into the house, with a design to discourse with him privately. As they were going they heard a cry from some: 'Kill them: away with the Great Seal; keep them in custody.' When they were in the house the Earl ordered them to be locked in and told them that he desired that they would have patience for a little while: that he must now go into the City to take measures with the Lord Mayor and sheriffs and would soon return . . .

The Earl, having committed the defence of his house to Sir Gilly Mericke, went out immediately after with a company of about 200 men, but not properly armed, most of them having only swords with their cloaks on their shoulders. They were joined by the Earl of Bedford, the Lord Cromwell and others on their way into the City, in the entrance into which the Earl cried out 'For the Queen, for the Queen! A plot is laid for my life', and then proceeded directly to Mr Smith's the sheriff's house near Fenchurch. As he went thither he desired the citizens who came out to see him pass to arm themselves, since otherwise they would be of no service to him; but not one of the whole City, tho' well exercised in arms, and very full and greatly devoted to him, appeared in his favour. When he arrived at the sheriff's house he was in such an agitation of body and sweat so profusely that he was obliged to shift himself.

The Sheriff, upon whom he had from his own credulity and the report of others rashly depended, presently retired by a back door to the Lord Mayor. In the meantime, the Secretary's elder brother, Thomas, Lord Burghley, and Dethick, Garter-King-at-Arms, came into the City and proclaimed the Earl and his adherents traitors, though some endeavoured to oppose and prevent it; and the same proclamation was made by the Earl of Cumberland and Sir Thomas Gerard,

Knight Marshal, in other parts of the City. The Earl, hearing of this, rushed out of the Sheriff's house with great perplexity and confusion in his countenance crying out in the streets that England was going to be given up to the Infanta of Spain and endeavouring in vain to excite the citizens to arms. Seeing his ill-success in this and that his own people were secretly withdrawing from him, and being informed that the Lord Admiral was coming with a body of troops, he began to lose all hopes and resolved to return home and endeavour to procure favour with the Queen by means of the Lord Keeper and the other councillors whom he had left confined at his house. But Sir Ferdinando Gorges . . . persuaded the Earl to depute him to set the councillors at liberty and to intercede with them for Her Majesty's pardon, while there was hopes of it, no blood being yet shed, the Queen doubtful of the event and the minds of the citizens uncertain. His Lordship consented that the Chief Justice should be discharged but he refusing his liberty without that of the Lord Keeper, Sir Ferdinando set them all free, and went by water with them to the Queen.

In the meanwhile, the Earl finding himself stopped by the soldiers posted near the westgate of St Paul's by order of the Bishop of London . . . [and] being repulsed and shot through his hat, and finding that many of his companions had slipped away, with the few who still remained retreated to Queenhithe, where he procured boats and returned to Essex House. The discharge of the councillors was a great disappointment and vexation to them. But having burnt such papers as might make a discovery, he proceeded to the fortifying of his house, from a sanguine expectation of assistance from the City. But it was soon invested by the Lord Admiral, who posted the Earls of Cumberland and Lincoln, the Lords Thomas Howard, Grey, Burghley and Compton, and others, and a body of horse and foot on the land; while the Lord Admiral himself with his son the Lord Effingham, the Lord Cobham, Sir John Stanhope, Sir Robert Sidney and Mr Fulke Greville besieged the house towards the garden and river. Everything being now ready for storming the house, the Lord Admiral ordered Sir Robert Sidney to summon the besieged to yield. The Earl of Southampton answered: to whom? To their enemies? That this would be throwing themselves into destruction. To the Queen? That this would be confessing themselves guilty. But that if the Lord Admiral would give hostages for their security they would present themselves to Her Majesty; otherwise they were unanimously resolved to die defending themselves. The Lord Admiral returned an answer by Sir Robert

Sidney that no terms were to be proposed by rebels, nor hostages to be given to them: but he intimated to the Earl that, out of regard for the ladies, he would permit his Countess and his sister Rich and their women to depart. His Lordship received this as a favour and desired an hour or two to be allowed him for fortifying again the place where they should go out; which was granted. Before the expiration of the hour, the Earl in despair determined to force his way through, in which he was encouraged by the Lord Sandys, who was more advanced in age than the rest and declared that the boldest councils were the safest, and that it was more honourable for men of quality to die sword in hand than by the executioner. But the Earl soon changing his mind began to think of a surrender and signified he would submit on certain conditions. And upon the Lord Admiral refusing to grant any, he intimated that he did not insist upon prescribing terms but was willing to receive them, and only requested these three, that they should be civilly treated, which the Lord Admiral promised, that their cause should be justly and lawfully heard, of which the Lord Admiral said that there was no doubt to be made, and that Mr Ashton, the Minister, might attend him in prison for the comfort of his soul: for which, with his other requests, the Lord Admiral engaged to intercede with the Queen. Immediately after this the lords and gentlemen fell on their knees and delivered up their swords to the Lord Admiral, about ten at night. The Earls of Essex and Southampton were at first conveyed by the Lord Admiral to the Archbishop's palace at Lambeth and not to the Tower, because the night was dark and stormy and the passage through the river impracticable; but they were soon after by the Queen's order carried thither in a barge.

William Camden, *Elizabeth*, 1688

27

Queen Elizabeth was still brooding on the business six months later.

MR WILLIAM LAMBARDE, that in January last was charged with care of the records that be reposed in the Tower of London, today presented her Majesty with his *pandecta* or digest thereof. He had intended to present the book by the hands of the Countess of Warwick, but the Queen would not, 'for', quoth she, 'if any subject of mine do me a service, I will thankfully accept it from his own hands.' Then opening the book she said: 'You shall see that I can read', and so with an audible voice read over the epistle and the title. He severally expounded the meanings, whereat the Queen, seeming well satisfied, said that she would be a scholar in her age and thought it no scorn to learn during her life, being of the mind of that philosopher who in his last years began with the Greek alphabet. At length she fell upon the reign of King Richard the Second, saying: 'I am Richard the Second, know ye not that?' To which Mr Lambarde answered: 'Such a wicked imagination was determined and attempted by a most unkind gentleman, the most adorned creature that ever your Majesty made.' The Queen answered: 'He that will forget God will also forget his benefactors; this tragedy was played forty times in open streets and houses.' She asked him whether he had seen any true picture or lively representation of the countenance of King Richard. To which Mr Lambarde answered that he had seen none but such as be in common hands. The Queen replied: 'The Lord Lumley, a lover of antiquities, discovered it fastened on the backside of a door in a base room, which he presented unto me, praying, with my good leave, that I might put it in order with the rest of the ancestors and successors. I will command Thomas Kniyvett, keeper of my house and gallery at Westminster, to show it unto thee.' Then she proceeded to the Rolls. At length she commended the work, not only for the pains thereof but also for that she had not received since her first coming to the crown any one thing that brought therewith so much delectation unto her; and so being called away to prayer, she put the book in her bosom, having from first to last forbidden Mr Lambarde to fall upon his knee before her, concluding 'Farewell, good and honest Lambarde.'

Printed in John Nichols, *Progresses of Queen Elizabeth*, 1788–1821

28

The Old Queen

QUEEN ELIZABETH never saw her self after she became old in a true Glass. They painted her & sometimes would vermilion her nose. She had allwayes about Christmas evens set dice, that threw sixes and fives, and she knew not they were other, to make her win and esteame her self fortunate. That she had a membrane on her which made her incapable of man, though for her delight she tryed many; at the coming

over of Monsieur ther was a French Chirurgion who took in hand to
cut it, yett fear stayed her & his death.

William Drummond of Hawthornden, *Notes of Conversations with Ben
Jonson 1619*, 1842

29

[October 1601] She was quite disfavoured and unattained, and these
troubles waste her much. She disregardeth every costly cover that
cometh to the table, and taketh little but manchet and succory pottage.
Every new message from the City doth disturb her, and she frowns on
all the ladies . . . the many evil plots and designs hath overcome all her
Highness's sweet temper. She walks much in her Privy Chamber, and
stamps with her feet at ill news, and thrusts her rusty sword at times
into the arras in great rage.

Harington, *Nugae Antiquae*

30

Sir Walter Ralegh

CAPTAIN RALEIGH coming out of *Ireland* to the *English Court* in
good habit (his Cloaths being then a considerable part of his estate)
found the Queen walking, till meeting with a *Plashy place*, she seemed
to scruple going thereon. Presently *Raleigh* cast and spred his new
Plush Cloak on the ground, whereon the Queen trod gently, rewarding
him afterwards with many *Suits*, for his so free and seasonable tender
of so fair *a foot Cloath*.

Thomas Fuller, *The History of the Worthies of England*, 1662

31

HE had in the outward man, a good presence, in a handsome and well-
compacted person, a strong naturall wit, and a better judgement, with a
bold and plausible tongue, whereby he could set out his parts to the
best advantage; and to these he had the adjuncts of some generall
Learning, which by diligence he forced to a great augmentation, and
perfection; for he was an indefatigable Reader, whether by Sea or

Land, and none of the least observers both of men and the times; and I am confident that among the second causes of his growth, that variance between him and my Lord *Grey* in his descent into Ireland, was a principall: for it drew them both over the Councell Table, there to plead their cause, where (what advantage he had in the cause I know not) but he had much better in the telling of his tale; and so much that the Queen and the Lords took no slight mark of the man and his parts; for from thence he came to be known, and to have accesse to the Queen and the Lords; and then we are not to doubt how such a man would comply, and learn the way of progression. And whether *Leicester* had then cast in a good word for him to the Queen, which would have done him no harm, I doe not determine: But true it is, He had gotten the Queens eare at a trice, and she began to be taken with his elocution, and loved to hear his reasons to her demands: and the truth is, she took him for a kind of Oracle, which nettled them all.

Naunton, Fragmenta Regalia

32

THERE was a lady of the West Country, that gave great entertainment at her house to most of the gallant gentlemen thereabout; and amongst others Sir Walter Ralegh was one. This lady, though otherwise a stately dame, was a notable good housewife; and in the morning betimes she called to one of her maids that looked to the swine, and asked: 'Is the piggy served?' Sir Walter Ralegh's chamber was fast by the lady's, so as he heard her. A little before dinner, the lady came down in great state into the great chamber, which was full of gentlemen. And as soon as Sir Walter Ralegh set eye upon her, 'Madam,' saith he, 'is the piggy served?' The lady answered: 'You know best whether you have had your breakfast.'

Bacon, Apophthegms

33

Ralegh and Son

MY old friend James Harington Esq., was well acquainted with Sir Benjamin Ruddyer, who was an acquaintance of Sir Walter Ralegh's.

He told Mr J. H. that Sir Walter Ralegh, being invited to dinner with some great person, where his son was to goe with him: He sayd to his Son, Thou are such a quarrelsome, affronting creature that I am ashamed to have such a Beare in my Company. Mr Walt humbled himselfe to his Father, and promised he would behave himselfe mightily mannerly. So away they went, and Sir Benjamin, I think, with them. He sate next to his Father and was very demure at leaste halfe dinner time. Then sayd he, I this morning, not having the feare of God before my eies, but by the instigation of the devill, went to a Whore. I was very eager of her, kissed and embraced her, and went to enjoy her, but she thrust me from her, and vowed I should not, *For your father lay with me but an hower ago.* Sir Walt, being so strangely surprized and putt out of his countenance at so great a Table, gives his son a damned blow over the face; his son, as rude as he was, would not strike his father, but strikes over the face of the Gentleman that sate next to him, and sayed, *Box about, 'twill come to my Father anon.*

Aubrey, *Brief Lives*

34

James I

HE was of a middle stature, more corpulent through his cloathes then in his body, yet fat enough, his cloathes ever being made large and easie, the doublets quilted for steletto proofe, his breeches in great pleits and full stuffed: he was naturally of a timorous disposition, which was the reason of his quilted doublets; his eyes large, ever rowling after any stranger that came in his presence, insomuch as many for shame have left the roome, as being out of countenance; his beard was very thin: his tongue too large for his mouth, which ever made him speak full in the mouth, and made his drink very uncomely, as if eating his drink, which came out into the cup of each side of his mouth; his skin was soft as taffeta sarsnet, which felt so, because hee never washt his hands, onely rubb'd his fingers ends slightly with the wet end of a napkin; his legs were very weake, having had (as was thought) some foul play in his youth, or rather before he was born, that he was not able to stand at seven years of age, that weakness made him ever leaning on other men's shoulders; his walke was ever circular, his fingers ever in that walke fidling about his cod-piece; he was very temperate in his exercises and in his dyet, and not intemperate in his drinking; however, in his old age, Buckingham's joviall suppers, when he had any turne to doe with him, made him sometimes overtake, which he would the very next day remember and repent with tears; it is true he drank very often, which was rather out of a custom than any delight, and his drinks were of that kind for strength, as frontiniack, canary, high country wine, tent wine and Scottish ale, that, had he not had a very strong brain, might have daily been overtaken, although he seldom drank at any one time above four spoonfulls, many times not above one or two . . . He was very witty, and had as many ready witty jests as any man living, at which he would not smile himself, but deliver them in a grave and serious manner.

Sir Anthony Weldon, 'Court and Character of King James' (1650) in
Secret History of the Court of King James the First, ed. Sir Walter Scott, 1811

35

THE King with the Prince and Sir George Villiers (later Duke of Buckingham), being in the Garden at Greenwich at the fountaine, wherein the Statue of Bacchus is placed, which with a device therein, by the turning of a pin, doth Cast out water. The Prince being merrily disposed, observing Sir George Villiers to stand opposite to the Picture, turned the pinn, and the water spouted in Sir George Villiers his face, whereat he was very much offended; the King observing his discontentment was so exceedingly moved against the Prince for doing it, as besides the hard words he gave him, which was that he had a malicious and dogged disposicion, gave his Highnes 2 boxes in the eare.

Letter from Edward Sherburn to Sir Dudley Carleton, 31 May 1616.
State Papers, Domestic

36

James's Favourites

NOW, as no other reason appeared in favour of their choyce but handsomnesse, so the love the King shewed was as amorously convayed, as if he had mistaken their sex, and thought them ladies; which I have seene Sommerset and Buckingham labour to resemble, in the effeminateness of their dressings; though in whoreson lookes and wanton gestures

they exceeded any part of woman kind my conversation did ever cope
withall. Nor was his love, or what else posterity will please to call it,
(who must be the judges of all that history shall informe) carried on
with a discretion sufficient to cover a lesse scandalous behaviour; for
the kings kissing them after so lascivious a mode in publick, and upon
the theatre as it were of the world, prompted many to imagine some
things done in the tyring-house, that exceed my expressions no lesse
than they do my experience. And therefore left floating upon the waves
of conjecture, which hath in my hearing tossed them from one side to
another. I have heard that Sir Henry Rich, since Earle of Holland, and
some others, refused his majesties favour upon those conditions they
subscribed to, who filled that place in his affection, Rich losing that
opportunity his curious face and complection affording him, by turning
aside and spitting after the King had slabbered his mouth.

Francis Osborne, 'Traditionall Memoyres on the Raigne of King James
the First' in Secret History, ed. Scott

37

Court Debauchery

*The state visit of James I's father-in-law, the King of Denmark, was
described in a letter from Sir John Harington, August 1606:*

I THINK the Dane hath strangely wrought on our good English
nobles; for those whom I never could get to taste good liquor, now follow the fashion and wallow in beastly delights. The ladies abandon
their sobriety and are seen to roll about in intoxication. In good sooth,
the parliament did kindly to provide his Majestie so seasonably with
money, for there hath been no lack of good livinge; shews, sights and
banquetings, from morn to eve. One day a great feast was held, and
after dinner the representation of Solomon his Temple and the coming of the Queen of Sheba was made, or (as I may better say) was
meant to have been made, before their Majesties, by device of the Earl
of Salisbury and others. But alas! as all earthly thinges do fail to poor
mortals in enjoyment, so did prove our resentment hereof. The Lady
who did play the Queens part, did carry both precious gifts to both
their Majesties; but, forgetting the steppes arising to the canopy, over-
set her caskets into his Danish Majesties lap, and fell at his feet, tho I

rather think it was in his face. Much was the hurry and confusion; cloths and napkins were at hand to make all clean. His Majesty then got up and would dance with the Queen of Sheba; but he fell down and humbled himself before her, and was carried to an inner chamber and laid on a bed of state; which was not a little defiled with the presents of the Queen which had been bestowed on his garments; such as wine, cream, jelly, beverage, cakes, spices and other good matters. The entertainment or shew went forward, and most of the entertainers went backward, or fell down; wine did so occupy their upper chambers. Now did appear, in rich dress, Hope, Faith and Charity. Hope did assay to speak, but wine rendered her endeavours so feeble that she withdrew and hoped the King would excuse her brevity: Faith was then all alone, for I am certain she was not joyned with good works, and left the court in a staggering condition: Charity came to the King's feet, and seemed to cover the multitude of sins her sisters had committed; in some sorte she made obeysance and brought giftes, but said she would return home again, as there was no gift which heaven had not already given his Majesty. She then returned to Hope and Faith, who were both sick and spewing in the lower hall. Next came Victory, in bright armour, and presented a rich sword to the King, who did not accept it, but put it by with his hand; and, by a strange medley of versification, did endeavour to make suit to the King. But Victory did not tryumph long; for, after much lamentable utterance, she was led away like a silly captive and laid to sleep in the outer steps of the antechamber. Now did Peace make entry, and strive to get foremost to the King; but I grieve to tell how great wrath she did discover unto those of her attendants; and, much contrary to her semblance, most rudely made war with her olive branch, and laid on the pates of those who did oppose her coming. . . . I do often say (but not aloud) that the Danes have again conquered the Britains, for I see no man, or woman either, that can now command himself or herself. I wish I was at home.

Harington, *Nugae Antiquae*

38

Hampton Court Conference

In 1604 James I presided over an abortive attempt to reconcile the Anglican establishment with the Nonconformists. On the second day of the conference, which took place at Hampton Court, the Puritan leader, Dr Reynolds, President of Corpus Christi College, Oxford, attacked the powers of the bishops.

AT which speech his Majestie was somewhat stirred; yet, which is admirable in him, without passion or shew thereof: thinking, that they aymed at a *Scottish* Presbytery, 'which', saith he, 'as wel agreeth with a Monarchy, as God and the Devill. Then *Jack & Tom, & Will & Dick*, shall meete, and at their pleasures censure me and my Councell and all our proceedinges: Then *Will* shall stand up and say, it must be thus; then *Dick* shall reply and say, nay, marry, but wee will have it thus. And therefore, here I must once reiterate my former speech, Le Roy S'amusera: Stay, I pray you, for one seven years, before you demaunde that of mee, and if then you finde me purseye and fat, and my winde-pipes stuffed, I will perhaps hearken to you: for let that *governement* bee once up, I am sure, I shall bee kept in breath; then shall we all of us have work enough both our hands ful. But, Doctor *Reynalds*, till you finde that I grow lazy, let that alone.' And here because Doctor *Reynalds* had twice before obtruded the *Kings Supremacy*. . . . his Majestie at those times said nothing; but now growing to an end, he sayde, 'I shal speak of one matter more; yet, somewhat out of order, but it skilleth not. Doctor Reynalds', quoth the King, 'you have often spoken of my *Supremacy*, and it is well: but know you any here, or any else where who like of the present *Governement Ecclesiasticall*, that finde fault, or dislike my *Supremacy*?' Dr Reynolds saide: 'no'. 'Why then', saith his Majesty, 'I will tell you a tale. After that the Religion restored by King Edward the 6 was soone overthrown by the succession of Queene Mary, here in *England*, we in *Scotland* felt the effect of it. Whereupon Master Knox writes to the Queene *Regent* . . . telling her that she was *Supreme head* of the church, and charged her, as she would aunswere it before Gods Tribunall, to take care of *Christ his Evangil*, and of suppressing the Popish Prelates who withstoode the *same*. But how long, trow yee, did this continue? Even so long, till by her authority the popish Bishops were repressed, hee himselfe and his adherentes were brought in and wel setled, and by these means made strong enough to undertake the matters of *Reformation* themselves. Then, loe!, they began to make smal account of her *Supremacy*, nor would longer rest upon her authority, but tooke the cause into their own hand. . . . And how they dealt with me, in my *Minority*, you all know; it was not done secretly, and though I would, I cannot conceale it. I will apply it thus.' And then putting his hand to his hat, his Majestie saide: 'My lords the Bishops, I may thanke you, that these men doe thus plead for my *Supremacy*; they think they cannot make their party good against you, but by appealing unto it, as if you, or some that adhere unto you, were not well affected towardes it. But if once you were out, and they in place, I know what would become of Supremacy. *No Bishop, No King* . . . and rising from his Chaire, as hee was going to his inner Chamber, 'If this be al', quoth he, 'that they have to say, I shall make them conforme themselves, or I wil harrie them out of the land, or else doe worse.'

William Barlow, 'The summe and substance of the conference . . . at
Hampton Court,' reprinted in E. Cardwell, A History of Conferences, 1849

39

James and Ralegh

AT a consultation at Whitehall after Queen Elizabeth's death, how matters were to be ordered and what ought to be done, Sir Walter Ralegh declared his opinion 'twas the wisest way for them to keepe the Government in their owne hands and sett up a Commonwealth, and not to be subject to a needy, beggarly nation. It seems there were some of this caball who kept this not so secret but that it came to King James' eare, who, where the English Noblesse mett and received him, being told upon presentment to his Majesty their names, when Sir Walter Ralegh's name was told, Ralegh, said the King, O my soule, mon, I have heard rawly of thee.

Aubrey, Brief Lives

40

Ralegh was executed by James I in Old Palace Yard, Westminster, 29 October 1618.

PUTTING off his doublet and gowne, he desired the headsman to shew him the Axe, which not being suddenly granted unto him, he said I prithee, let me see it, dost thou thinke I am afraid of it, so it being given unto him, he felt along the edge of it, and smiling spake unto Mr Sheriffe saying, this is a sharpe medicine, but it is a physician that will cure all diseases.

> Sir Thomas Overbury, *The Arraignment and Conviction of Sr. Walter Rawleigh*, 1648

41

Grand Remonstrance

The parliamentary campaign against the monarchy of Charles I culminated in a huge compilation of grievances termed the Grand Remonstrance. It was pushed through only with great difficulty, as Lord Falkland had warned Oliver Cromwell, and the fierce debate foreshadowed the deep division in the country which produced civil war. Edward Hyde, later Earl of Clarendon, described the moment when the moderate reformers, such as himself, split off from the extremists.

November 1641 . . . the next morning, the debate being entered upon about nine of the clock in the morning, it continued all that day; and candles being called for when it grew dark (neither side being very desirous to adjourn it till the next day; though it was evident, very many withdrew themselves out of pure faintness and disability to attend the conclusion), the debate continued, till after it was twelve of the clock, with much passion; and the House being then divided, upon the passing or not passing it, it was carried for the affirmative by nine voices, no more; and as soon as it was declared, Mr Hampden moved, 'that there might be an order for the present printing it'; which produced a sharper debate than the former. It appeared then, that they did not intend to send it up to the House of Peers for their concurrence; but that it was upon the matter an appeal to the people; and to infuse jealousies into their minds. It had never been the custom to publish any

debates, or determinations of the House, which were not regularly first
transmitted to the House of Peers; nor was it thought, in truth, that the
House had authority to give warrant for the printing of any thing; all
which was offered by Mr Hyde, with some warmth, as soon as the
motion was made for the printing it; and he said, 'he did believe the
printing it in that manner was not lawful; and he feared it would produce mischievous effects; and therefore desired the leave of the
House, that if the question should be put, and carried in the affirmative, that he might have liberty to enter his protestation . . . When
immediately together many afterwards, without distinction, and in
some disorder, cried out, 'They did protest'; so that there was scarce
any quiet and regular debate. But the House by degrees being quieted,
they all consented, about two of the clock in the morning, to adjourn
till two of the clock the next afternoon. And as they went out of the
House, the Lord Falkland asked Oliver Cromwell, 'Whether there had
been a debate?' to which he answered, 'that he would take his word
another time'; and whispered him in the ear, with some asservation,
'that if the Remonstrance had been rejected, he would have sold all he
had the next morning, and never had seen England more; and he knew
there were many other honest men of the same resolution'. So near
was the poor kingdom at that time to its deliverance.

Selections from Clarendon, ed. G. Huehns, 1955

42

Portrait of Prynne

*William Prynne MP began public life as a critic of Archbishop Laud, for
which he had his ears cut off and was put in the pillory; later he became a
royalist and after the Restoration Keeper of the Records.*

His Eares were not quite cutt off, only the upper part, his tippes were
visible. . . . His manner of Studie was thus: he wore a long quilt cap,
which came 2 or 3, at least, inches over his eies, which served him as
an Umbrella to defend his Eies from the light. About every three
houres his man was to bring him a roll and a pott of Ale to refocillate his
wasted spirits; so he studied and dranke, and munched some bread;
and this maintained him till night, and then he made a good supper. . . . He endured severall Imprisonments for the King's cause, and
was (really) very instrumental in his restauracion. Upon the opening of

the Parliament, viz. letting in the Secluded Members, he girt on his old
long rustie Sword (longer than ordinary). Sir William Waller marching
behind him (as he went to the Howse), W. Prynne's long sword ranne
between Sir William's short legges, and threw him downe, which
caused laughter.

Aubrey, Brief Lives

43

Outrage of the Commons

*At the beginning of 1642, an exasperated Charles I issued writs of high
treason against John Pym and four other members of the Commons; and on
the afternoon of 4 January rumours circulated in Westminster that he was
coming to the House to arrest them attended by troops.*

THE House required the five Members to depart the House forthwith,
to the end to avoid Combustion in the House, if the said Soldiers
should use Violence to pull any of them out. To which Command of
the House, four of the said Members yielded ready Obedience, but Mr
Stroud was obstinate, till *Sir Walter Earle* (his ancient acquaintance)
pulled him out by force, the King being at that time entering into the
New Palace Yard in *Westminster*. And as his Majesty came through
Westminster Hall, the Commanders, Reformadoes, etc that attended
him made a lane on both sides of the Hall (through which his Majesty
passed and came up the stairs to the House of Commons) and stood
before the Guard of Pensioners and Halbardiers (who also attended
the King's person), and the door of the House of Commons being
thrown open, his Majesty entered *the House*, and as he passed up
towards *the Chair*, he cast his eye on the Right-hand near the Bar of
the House, where Mr Pym used to sit. But his Majesty not seeing him
there (knowing him well) went up to the chair, and said, *By your leave
(Mr Speaker) I must borrow your Chair a little*, whereupon the Speaker
came out of the Chair, and his Majesty stepped up into it. After he had
stood in the Chair a while, casting his Eye upon the Members as they
stood up *uncovered*, but could not discern any of the five Members to be
there, nor indeed were they easy to be discovered (had they been
there) among so many bare faces standing up together.

Then his Majesty made this Speech: *Gentlemen, I am sorry for this
occasion of coming unto you. Yesterday I sent a Serjeant-at-Arms upon a*

very Important occasion to apprehend some that by my Command were
accused of High Treason, whereunto I did expect Obedience and not a Mess-
age. And I must declare unto you here, that albeit no King that ever was in
England shall be more careful of your Privileges to maintain them to the
uttermost of his power than I shall be, yet you must know that in cases of
Treason, no person hath a privilege. And therefore I am come to know if any
of these persons that were accused are here. For I must tell you Gentlemen,
that so long as these persons that I have accused (for no slight Crime but for
Treason) are here, I cannot expect that this House will be in the Right way
that I do heartily wish it. Therefore I am come to tell you that I must have
them wheresoever I find them. Well, since I see all the Birds are Flown, I do
expect from you, that you shall send them unto me as soon as they return
hither. But I assure you in the word of a King, I never did intend any Force
but shall proceed against them in a legal and fair way, for I never meant any
other . . .

When the King was looking about the House, the Speaker standing
below by the Chair, his Majesty ask'd him, whether any of these persons were in the House: Whether he saw any of them? and where they
were? To which the Speaker falling on his Knee, thus Answered: *May*
it please your Majesty, I have neither Eyes to see, nor Tongue to speak, in this
place, but as the House is pleased to direct me, whose Servant I am here, and
humbly beg your Majesty's Pardon, that I cannot give any other Answer than
this, to what your Majesty is pleased to demand of me.

The King then having Concluded his Speech, went out of the
House again, which was in great disorder and many Members cryed
out aloud so he might hear them *Privilege! Privilege!* and forthwith
Adjourned until the next day at One of the Clock.

The same evening his Majesty sent James Maxwell, Usher of the
House of Peers, to the House of Commons to require Mr Rushworth
the Clerk Assistant, whom his Majesty had observed to take his
Speech in Characters at the Table of the House, to come to his Majesty. And when Maxwell brought him to the King, his Majesty commanded him to give him a *Copy of his Speech* in the House. Mr
Rushworth humbly besought his Majesty (hoping for an excuse) to call
in mind how *Mr Francis Nevil*, a Yorkshire Member of the House of
Commons, was committed to the Tower but for telling his Majesty
what words were spoke in the House by Mr Henry Bellasis said to the
Lord Faulconbridge, to which his Majesty smartly replied 'I do not ask
you to tell me what was said by any Member of the House but what I
said myself': whereupon he readily gave Obedience to his Majesty's

Command, and in his Majesty's presence in the Room, called the *Jewel House*, he Transcribed his Majesty's speech out of his Characters, his Majesty staying in the room all the while, And then and there presented the same to the King, which his Majesty was pleased to command to be sent speedily to the Press, and the next Morning it came forth in print.

John Rushworth, Historical Collections, 1691

44

Royalist Manners

King Charles I made Oxford his headquarters, a compliment the Fellows, though favouring his cause, could have dispensed with.

To give a further character of the court, though they were neat and gay in their apparell, yet they were very nasty and beastly, leaving at their departure their excrements in every corner, in chimneys, studies, cole-houses, cellars. Rude, rough, whoremongers; vaine, empty, careless.

Anthony Wood, Life and Times, first pub. 1891

45

Laud's Innovation

Archbishop Laud, executed in 1645, was detested by the parliament-men for his enforcing of Anglican worship; John Aubrey, a social conservative, had a quite different grievance:

W. LAUD, Archbishop of Cant., was a great lover of Catts. He was presented with some Cyprus catts, i.e. our Tabby-catts, which were sold, at first for 5 pounds a piece: this was about 1637 or 1638. I doe well remember that the common English Catt, was white with some blewish piednesse: sc. a gallipot blew. The race or breed of them are now almost lost.

Aubrey, Brief Lives

46

Cornet Joyce

2 June 1647. The same morning that Cromwell left London, Cornet
Joyce, who was one of the agitators in the army, a tailor, a fellow who
had two or three years before served in a very inferior employment in
Mr Hollis's house, came with a squadron of fifty horse to Holmby,
where the King was, about the break of day; and, without any interruption by the guard of horse or foot which waited there, came with two or
three more, and knocked at the King's chamber door and said 'he must
presently speak with the King'. His Majesty, surprised at the manner
of it, rose out of his bed; and half dressed, caused the door to be
opened, which he knew otherwise would be quickly broken open; they
who waited in the chamber being persons of whom he had little knowledge, and less confidence. As soon as the door was opened, Joyce and
two or three more came into the chamber, with their hats off and pistols in their hands. Joyce told the King 'that he must go with him'. His
Majesty asked, 'whither?' he answered 'to the army'. The King asked
him, 'where the army was?' he said 'they would carry him to the place
where it was'. His Majesty asked 'by what authority they came?' Joyce
answered 'by this'; and shewed him his pistol.

Clarendon

(*According to another account, the King then commented ironically; 'It is as
fair a commission and as well written as I have seen a commission written in
my life.'*)

47

The General's Lady

The trial of Charles I opened on 20 January 1649.

THERE was an accident happened that first day, which may be fit to be
remembered. When all those who were commissioners had taken their
places, and the King was brought in, the first ceremony was, to read
their commission; which was the ordinance of parliament for the trial;
and then the judges were all called, every man answering to his name

as he was called, and the president being first called and making answer, the next who was called being the general, Lord Fairfax, and no answer being made, the officer called him a second time, when there was a voice heard that said, 'he had more wit than to be there'; which put the court into some disorder, and somebody asking, who it was, there was no answer but a little murmuring. But presently, when the impeachment was read, and that expression used, of 'all the good people of England', the same voice in a louder tone answered, 'No, not the hundredth part of them'; upon which, one of the officers bid the soldiers give fire into that box whence those presumptuous words were uttered. But it was quickly discerned that it was the general's wife, the Lady Fairfax, who had uttered both those sharp sayings; who was presently persuaded or forced to leave the place, to prevent any new disorder.

Clarendon

48

Academic Witch-Hunting

The Oxford Fellows were purged first by the parliamentarians in 1648; then by the returning royalists in 1660. Anthony Wood (1632–95), Fellow of Merton, described both processes.

May 1648.   My name's Whitehall, God bless the poet
             If *I* submit, the King shall know it:

Quoth Robert Whitehall of Christ Church to the Visitors, anno 1648. The said Whitehall was turned out of his place; but, by cringing to the committee at London, became soone after fellow of Merton Coll. where, following the trade of drinking as he was wont, procured to himself a red face. . . . Friday 12 May: the members of Merton College appear'd, and when Anthony Wood was called in (for the members were called in one by one) he was asked this question by one of the Visitors: 'Will you submit to the authority of parliament in this visitation?' To which he gave this answer, and wrote it downe on a paper lying on the table as he was directed: 'I do not understand the business and therefore I am not able to give a direct answer.' Afterwards his mother and brother Edward, who advised him to submit in plaine terms, were exceedingly angry with him and told him he had ruined

himself and must therefore go a-begging. At length, by the inter-
cession of his mother made to Sir Nathaniel Brent (who usually call'd
her his little daughter, for he knew her, and us'd to set her on his
knee . . .), he was conniv'd at and kept in his place, otherwise he had
infallibly gone to the pot.

January 1661. [The royalists began by restoring surplices; the Puritans
retaliated.] Nay, some varlets of Christ Church were so impudent
(whether set on by the Presbyterians or no, I know not) to goe on the
21 January this yeare about 11 or 12 of the clock at night to a chamber
under the common hall (where the choiresters learne their grammar)
and thence to take away all such surplices that they could find: and
being so done, to throw them in a common privy house belonging to
Peckwater Quadrangle, and there with long sticks to thrust them
downe into the excrements. The next day being discovered, they were
taken up and washed; but so enraged were the deane and canons, that
they publickly protested, if they knew the person or persons that had
committed that act, they should not onlie loose their places and be
expelled the Universitie but also have their eares cut off in the market
place. The Presbyterians were wonderfully pleased at this action,
laughed hartily among themselves, and some in my hearing have protested that if they knew the person that did this heroick act they would
convey to him an encouraging gratuity.

Wood, *Life and Times*

49

Civil War Philosophies

*Three conflicting political philosophies emerged during the angry arguments
that followed the Civil War: the democratic was put by Colonel Rainborough,
and the bourgeois by General Cromwell, during the Putney Debates in 1647;
Charles I put the monarchical on the scaffold two years later.*

Colonel Rainborough: For really I think that the poorest he that is in
England hath a life to live, as the greatest he; and therefore truly, Sir, I
think it's clear, that every man that is to live under a government ought
first by his own consent to put himself under that government; and I do
think that the poorest man in England is not at all bound in a strict
sense to that government that he hath not had a voice to put himself
under; and I am confident that, when I have heard the reasons against

it, something will be said to answer those reasons, insomuch that I should doubt whether he was an Englishman or no, that should doubt of these things.

Oliver Cromwell: For you to make this the rule, I think you must fly for refuge to an absolute Natural Right, and you must deny all Civil Right . . . For my part I think that [the notion of Natural Rights] no right at all. I think that no person hath a right to an interest or share in the disposing or determining of the King, and in choosing those that shall determine what laws we shall be ruled by here—no person hath a right to this—that hath not a permanent, fixed interest in this King-dom . . . But that by a man's being born here he shall have a share in that power that shall dispose of the lands here, and of all things here, I do not think it a sufficient ground.

'The Putney Debates', printed in *Puritanism and Liberty*, ed. A. S. P. Woodhouse, 1974

King Charles I: I must tell you that [the] liberty and freedom [of the people] consists in having a government, those laws by which their life and their goods may be most their own. It is not for having a share in government, Sir, that is nothing pertaining to them. A subject and a Sovereign are clear different things. . . . Sir, it was for this that now I am come here. If I would have given way to an arbitrary way, to have all changed according to the power of the sword, I need not have come here; and therefore I tell you (and I pray God it be not laid to your charge) that I am the Martyr of the people.

Memoirs of Bishop Juxon, first printed 1869

50

Charles I's End

ON the day of his execution, he dressed with special care, telling his servant Herbert, in combing his hair: 'Prithee, though it be not too long to stand upon my shoulders, take the same pains with it as you were wont to do: I am to be a bridegroom today and must be trimmed.' He added: 'Let me have a shirt on more than ordinary, by reason the season is so sharp as probably may make me shake, which some observers may imagine proceeds from fear. I fear not death. It is not terrible to me. I bless my God I am prepared.' He was kept waiting four hours, between ten and two, before being taken to the scaffold.

There, he 'looked very earnestly upon the block and asked if it could be no higher'; but this was refused. After his last speech and his profession of faith, he handed his 'George' [garter] to Bishop Juxon to give to the Prince of Wales, with the word: 'Remember'. To Colonel Hacker, in charge of the guard, he said 'Take care that they do not put me in pain'. Then, to Juxon: 'I go from a corruptible to an incorruptible crown, where no disturbance can be, no disturbance at all.' Then, looking again at the block: 'Is is fast?' 'It is fast, Sir.' To the headsman, 'Young Gregory' Brandon, disguised with false hair and a beard: 'Strike when I put my arms out this way' (stretching them). Then 'immediately stooping down, he laid his head on the block'. But his hair came loose, and Brandon put it back again; the King, thinking he was going to strike, said 'Stay for the sign.' Brandon: 'Yes I will, an it please Your Majesty.' Then the King gave the sign. Philip Henry, a 17-year-old Christ Church student, testified: 'At the instant when the blow was given there was such a dismal groan among the thousands of people that were within sight of it (as it were with ONE CONSENT) as he had never *heard before*; and desired he might never hear the like again, noe see such a cause of it.' Then, 'immediately after the stroke was struck . . . according to order, one troop [began] marching from Charing Cross towards King Street, purposely to disperse and scatter the people'. Nevertheless, many crowded round the scaffold to 'dip their handkerchiefs' in the King's blood and were 'admitted for moneys'. The soldiers sold pieces of the blood-stained scaffold boarding, from a shilling to half a crown each, 'according to the quality of the persons that sought them'. Payment was also charged to see Charles in his coffin at St James's Palace, 'by which means the soldiers got store of moneys, insomuch as one was heard to say, "I would we could have two or three such majesties to behead, if we could but make such use of them" '.

S. R. Gardiner, *History of the Commonwealth and Protectorate*, 1903

51

Cromwell and the Rump

AT 11.15 am on 20 April 1653, Cromwell entered parliament to dissolve it. After listening to the debate for a time, then beginning to speak in calm tones, he changed to 'a furious manner', walking up and down the House, stamping the ground with his feet and shouting 'with so much passion and discomposure of mind as if he had been distracted'. He said: 'It is time for me to put an end to your sitting in this place, which you have dishonoured by your contempt of all virtue and defiled by your practice of every vice. Ye are a factious crew, and enemies to all good government. Ye are a pack of mercenary wretches and would like Esau sell your country for a mess of pottage.' He pointed to individuals, and called them 'whoremasters, drunkards, corrupt and unjust men' adding 'Ye have no more religion than my horse. Ye are grown intolerably odious to the whole nation . . . Perhaps ye think this is not parliamentary language. I confess it is not, neither are you to expect any such from me. . . . It is not fit that ye should sit as a parliament any longer. Ye have sat long enough unless you had done more good.' When Sir Peter Wentworth protested at such language from one they had 'so highly trusted and obliged', Cromwell retorted: 'Come, come, I will put an end to your prating. Ye are no parliament. I say ye are no parliament. I will put an end to your sitting.' He shouted to Thomas Harrison, 'Call them in', and the musketeers entered. He pointed to the Speaker: 'Fetch him down.' Harrison hesitated: 'The work is very great and dangerous', then obeyed. Sir Henry Vane protested: 'This is not honest, yea it is against morality and common honesty.' Cromwell: 'Oh Sir Henry Vane, Sir Henry Vane, the Lord deliver me from Sir Henry Vane.' Then, turning to the mace: 'What shall we do with this bauble? Here, take it away.' Then, to the Members: 'I command ye therefore, upon the peril of your lives, to depart immediately out of this place. Go, get ye out! Make haste! Ye venal slaves be gone! Take away that shining bauble and lock up the doors.' By 11.40 the House was cleared and locked. Someone put up a poster: 'This House is to be Lett; now unfurnished.'

Ibid.

52

Cromwell and Manchester

At a parliamentary Council-of-War, 10 November 1644:

Earl of Manchester: 'If we beat the King ninety-nine times, yet he is king still and so will his posterity be after him; but if the king beat us once we shall all be hanged, and our posterity be made slaves.'

Cromwell: 'My Lord, if this be so, why did we take arms at first? This is against fighting ever hereafter. If so, let us make peace, be it never so base.'

Calendar of State Papers, Domestic, 1644–5

53

Cromwell and Conscience

To the General Assembly of the Church of Scotland: 'I beseech you in the bowels of Christ, think it possible you may be mistaken.'

To the Catholic Governor of Ross in Ireland: 'For that which you mention concerning liberty of conscience, I meddle not with any man's conscience. But if by liberty of conscience you mean a liberty to exercise the mass, I judge it best to use plain dealing and to let you know, where the Parliament of England have power that will not be allowed of.'

W. E. Abbott, *Writings and Speeches of Oliver Cromwell*, 1937–47

54

Cromwell's Dilemma

[THE parliamentarians] overthrow all ecclesiastical and civil establishments before they are concerted how to frame any new; or as Mr Cromwell (who from a very mean figure of a man in the beginning of this parliament rose to that prodigious greatness before the end) said to Sir Thomas Chichele and myself once in the House in the matters concerning religion, 'I can tell you, sirs, what I would not have, though I cannot what I would.'

Sir Philip Warwick, *Memoirs*, 1813

55

The Christmas Terror

25 December 1657—I went with my Wife to London to celebrate Christmas Day. Mr Gunning preached in Exeter Chapel on *vii Micah* 2.

Sermon ended, as he was giving us the holy Sacrament, the Chapel was surrounded by Soldiers. All the Communicants and Assembly surpriz'd & kept Prisoners by them, some in the house, others carried away. It fell to my share to be confined to a room in the house, where yet were permitted to Dine with the master of it, the Countess of Dorset, Lady Hatton & some others of quality who invited me. In the afternoon came Colonel Whaley, Goffe & others from Whitehall to examine us one by one, and some they committed to the Marshalesea, some to prison, some Committed. When I came before them they took my name & abode, examined me, why contrary to an Ordinance made that none should any longer observe the superstitious time of the Nativity (so esteem'd by them) I durst offend, & particularly be at Common Prayers, which they told me was but the Mass in English, and particularly pray for Charles Stuart, for which we had no scripture. I told them we did not pray for Charles Stuart but for all Christian Kings, Princes etc Governors. They replied, in so doing we prayed for the King of Spain too, who was their Enemy and a Papist, with other frivolous and ensnaring questions, with much threatening, and finding no colour to detaine me longer, with much pitty of my Ignorance, they dismiss'd me. These were men of high flight, and above Ordinances: & spake spiteful things of our B. Lord's nativity: so I got home late the next day, blessed be God. These wretched miscreants held their muskets against us as we came up to receive the Sacred Elements, as if they would have shot us at the Altar, but yet suffering us to finish the Office of Communion, as perhaps not in their Instructions what they should do in case they found us in that Action.

John Evelyn, Diary

56

Marvell's Honesty

The poet Andrew Marvell (1621–78) was a Republican civil servant during the Civil War and Milton's assistant as Latin Secretary to the Council; between 1660 until his death he was MP for Hull, writing the Corporation over 300 newsletters about parliamentary doings. He was regarded as a politician of strong principle and incorruptible.

MR MARVELL, who then [c.1673–4] lodged up two Pair of Stairs in a little Court in the *Strand*, was writing when the Lord Treasurer [Earl of Danby] opened the Door abruptly on him. Surprized at the Sight of so unexpected a Visiter, he told him he believed he had mistook his Way. The Lord *Danby* replyed, not now I have found Mr *Marvell*, telling him that he came with a Message from his Majesty, which was to know what he could do to serve him. But coming to a serious Explanation of his Meaning, he told the Lord Treasurer he knew the Nature of Courts full well, he had been in many; that whoever is distinguished by a Prince's Favours is certainly expected to vote in his Interest. The Lord *Danby* told him, his Majesty had only a just Sense of his Merits, in Regard to which alone he desired to know whether there was any Place at Court he could be pleased with. These Offers had no Effect on him, tho urged with the greatest Earnestness. He told the Lord Treasurer he could not accept them with Honour, for he must be either ingrateful to the King in voting against him, or false to his Country in giving into the Measures of the Court; therefore the only Favour he begged of his Majesty was, that he would esteem him as dutyful a Subject as any he had, and more in his proper Interest in refusing his Offers, than if he had embraced them. The Lord *Danby*, finding no argument could prevail, told him the King his Master had ordered a thousand Pounds for him, which he hoped he would receive, till he could think what farther to ask of his Majesty. This last Offer was rejected with the same Stedfastness of Mind, as was the first; tho, as soon as the Lord Treasurer was gone, he was forced to send to a Friend to borrow a Guinea.

Works of Andrew Marvell, ed. Thomas Cooke, 1726

57

[MARVELL] was in his conversation very modest, and of very few words: and though he loved wine he would never drinke hard in company, and was wont to say that, he would not play the good fellow in any man's company in whose hands he would not trust his life. He had not a generall acquaintance. . . . His native towne of Hull loved him so well that they elected him for their representative in Parliament, and gave him an honourable pension to maintaine him. He kept bottles of wine at his lodgeing, and many times he would drinke liberally by himselfe to refreshe his spirits, and exalt his Muse. . . . Some suspect that he was poysoned by the Jesuites, but I cannot be positive.

Aubrey, *Brief Lives*

58

Royal Revenge

17 October 1660—This day were executed those murderous Traytors at Charing Cross, in sight of the place where they put to death their natural Prince, and in the presence of the King his sonn, whom they also sought to kill: taken in the trap they laid for others. The Traytors executed were Scot, Scroop, Cook, Jones. I saw not their execution but met their quarters mangled & cutt a reaking as they were brought from the Gallows in baskets on the hurdle: O miraculous providence of God!

Evelyn, *Diary*

59

13 October 1660—I went to Charing Cross, to see Major-General Harrison hanged, drawn, and quartered; which was done there, he looking as cheereful as any man could do in that condition. He was presently cut down, and his head and heart shown to the people, at which there was great shouts of joy. It is said, that he said that he was sure to come shortly at the right hand of Christ to judge them that now had judged him; and that his wife do expect his coming again. Thus it was my chance to see the King beheaded at White Hall, and to see the first blood shed in revenge for the King at Charing Cross. Setting up shelves in my study.

Samuel Pepys, *Diary*

60

In 1651 Thomas Hobbes (1588–1679) published England's greatest work of political philosophy, the Leviathan. *His Wiltshire neighbour John Aubrey described how it came to be written.*

WHEN the Parliament sate that began in April 1640 and was dissolved in May following, and in which many pointes of the Regall Power, which were necessary for the Peace of the Kingdome and Safety of his

Majesty's Person, were disputed and denyed, Mr Hobbes wrote a little
Treatise in English, wherein he did sett-forth and demonstrate, that
the sayd Powers and Rights were inseparably annexed to the Sovereignty, which sovereignty they did not then deny to be in the King; but
it seems understood not, or would not understand, that Inseparability.
Of this Treatise, though not printed, many Gentlemen had copies,
which occasioned much talke of the Author; and had not his Majestie
dissolved the Parliament, it had brought him in danger of his life.
Bishop Manwaring (of St David's) preached *his Doctrine*; for which,
among others, he was sent prisoner to the Tower. Then, thought Mr
Hobbes, tis time now for me to shift for my selfe, and so withdrew into
France, and resided at Paris. This little MS treatise grew to be his
Booke *De Cive*, and last grew there to be the so formidable LEVIATHAN,
the manner of writing of which booke (he told me) was thus. He sayd
that he sometimes would sett his thoughts upon researching and con-
templating, always with this Rule that he very much and deeply considered one thing at a time (*scilicet*, a week or sometimes a fortnight).
He walked much and contemplated, and he had in the head of his
Staffe a pen and inke-horne, carried always a note-book in his pocket,
and as soon as a notion darted, he presently entred it into his Booke, or
els he should perhaps have lost it. He had drawne the Designe of the
Booke into Chapters, etc, so he knew whereabout it would come in.
Thus that booke was made.

Aubrey, *Brief Lives*

61

*In 1673 England's other great political philosopher, John Locke
(1632–1704), was Secretary of Presentations while his patron, the Earl of
Shaftesbury, was Lord Chancellor. Hobbes always had difficulty in getting his
political works published, and on Shrove Tuesday Aubrey wrote to Locke
asking for his help.*

SIR, I was at your lodging twice to have kissed your hand before I came
out of town, to have recommended a MS or two (worthy of your peru-
sal) of my old friend Mr Thomas Hobbes. One is a treatise concerning
the law (*De Legibus*) which I importuned him to undertake about eight
years since, and then in order thereto presented him with my Lord

Bacon's *Elements of the Law*. All men will give the old gentleman that right as to acknowledge his great felicity in well defining—especially the common superstruction of their old fashioned axioms, right or wrong, for grand practisers have not the leisure to be analytics. Mr Hobbes seemed then something doubtful he should not have days enough left to get about such a work. In this treatise he is highly for the King's prerogative. Chief Justice Hale has read it and very much mislikes it; is his enemy and will not license it . . . Tis pity fire should consume it, or that it should miscarry, as I have known some excellent things. I never expected to see it printed, and intended to have a copy, which the bookseller will let me have for 50s and, God willing, will have one on my return. He writes short, and therefore the fitter for your reading, because so full of business. When you go by the Palsgrave Head Tavern, be pleased to call on Mr W. Crooke at the Green Dragon and remember me to him and he will show it to you. I have a conceit that if your Lord saw it, he would like it. You may see likewise [Hobbes's] *History of England from 1640 to 1660* about a quire of paper which the King has read and likes extremely, but tells me there is so much truth in it he dares not license for fear of displeasing the bishops. The old gentleman is still very strangely vigorous. If you see him (which he would take kindly) pray my service to him. Your most humble servant, Jo: Aubrey

Printed in Maurice Cranston, *John Locke*, 1959

62

The Merry Monarch

Advice of the Duke of Newcastle, Charles II's tutor: 'Above all, be civil to women.'

Charles II to Bishop Burnet: 'I am sure God will never damn a man for allowing himself a little pleasure.'

On German princesses: 'Odd's fish, they are all dull and foggy!'

Sticking up for a mistress: 'Whosoever I find to be my Lady Castlemaine's enemy in this matter, I do promise on my word to be his enemy as long as I live.'

On changing his mind about a woman: 'If you were as well acquainted with a little fantastical gentleman called Cupid as I am, you would neither wonder nor take ill any sudden changes which do happen in the affairs on his conducting.'

Rochester on Charles II's endowments:

> Nor are his high desires above his strength
> His sceptre and his prick are of a length

Charles, known as 'Old Rowley' after a famous stallion, overhearing a housemaid singing the scurrilous ballad, 'Old Rowley the King', knocked on the door. *Housemaid*: 'Who's there?' *Charles*: 'Old Rowley himself, Madam.'

Charles II was very dark; at the theatre, observing the swarthy appearance of the murderers in *Macbeth*, he asked: 'Pray, what is the meaning that we never see a Rogue in a Play but Odd's fish, they always clap him in a black Periwig? When it is well known that one of the greatest Rogues in England [Shaftesbury] always wears a fair one?'

To William of Orange on his wedding night: 'Now nephew, to your work! Hey! St George for England!'

To Sir Peter Lely, on studying his portrait: 'Odd's fish, I am an ugly fellow.'

A gentleman, bitten by one of Charles's spaniels: 'God bless your Majesty! And God damn your dogs!'

Sir Robert Viner, his host, drank too much and sought to prevent Charles from leaving: 'Sir, you stay and take the other bottle.' *Charles* (acquiescing reluctantly): 'He that's drunk is as great as a king.'

A friend, on Charles's health: 'He will keep well if he can be kept from fishing when a dog would not be abroad.'

Charles at toilet: 'As soon as he had put on his nightgown, he went to ease himself, and often more out of custom than necessity, by reason nobody would come in there but the gentleman and groom-in-waiting; and there he laughed and was most merry and diverting.'

William Penn, the Quaker: 'Friend Charles, why dost thou not keep on thy hat?' *Charles* (always polite): 'It is the custom of this place that only one man should remain uncovered at a time.'

Charles at Newmarket: 'He mixed himself amongst the crowd, allowed every man to speak to him that pleased; went a-Hawking in the morning, to cock matches or foot races in the afternoon (if there were no horse-races) and to plays in the evening acted by very ordinary Bartholomew Fair comedians.'

An attendant who slept in his bedroom: 'Several circumstances made the lodging very uneasy—the great grate filled with Scotch coal that burnt all night, a dozen dogs came to our bed, and several pendulums that struck at the half and quarter, and all not going alike, it was a continual chiming.'

To Shaftesbury, refusing to legitimize the Protestant bastard Monmouth: 'My Lord, let there be no self-delusion. I will never yield and will not let myself be intimidated. Men ordinarily become more timid as they grow old. As for me, I shall be on the contrary bolder and firmer and I will not stain my life and reputation in the little time that perhaps remains to me to live.'

On Presbyterianism: 'Not a religion for gentlemen.'

To the Whigs: 'I, who will never use arbitrary government myself, am resolved not to suffer it in others.'

To his attendant Thomas Bruce, on dissolving his last parliament: 'I am now a better man than you were a quarter of an hour since: you had better have one king than five hundred.'

On his brother: 'I am weary of travelling and am resolved to go abroad no more. But when I am dead and gone I know not what my brother will do: I am much afraid that when he comes to wear the crown he will be obliged to travel again.'

On his deathbed: 'I am sorry, gentlemen, for being such a (unconscionable) time a-dying.'*

Rochester's epitaph: Here lies our sovereign Lord the King
                       Whose word no man relies on.
                       Who never said a foolish thing
                       Nor ever did a wise one.

---

* 'Unconscionable' was added by Macaulay; the rest is authentic.

63

The Merry Monarch's End

6–8 February 1685. I am never to forget the unexpressible luxury and profanesse, gaming and all dissolution, and as it were total forgetful-ness of God (it being Sunday evening) which this day sennight I was witness of; the King, sitting and toying with his Concubines, Ports-mouth, Cleaveland & Mazarine, etc. A French singing boy singing love songs, in that glorious gallery, whilst about twenty of the great Cour-tiers and other dissolute persons were at Basset round a large table, a bank of at least 2,000 in Gold before them, upon which two Gents that were with me made reflections with astonishment, it being a scene of the utmost vanity; and sure as they thought would never have an End: six days after, all was in the dust.

Evelyn, *Diary*

64

The Odour of Justice

Sir Edmund Saunders (?1640–1683) was a penniless orphan errand-boy, who made his way to and in the Bar by prodigies of self-education, and who was promoted to Lord Chief Justice by Charles II as a supporter of royal pre-rogative. But he lived in a slum almost till the end of his life.

As to his person, he was very corpulent and beastly, a mere lump of morbid flesh. He used to say '*by his troggs* (such an humorous way of talking he affected) *none could say he wanted issue of his body, for he had nine in his back*'. He was a fetid mass that offended his neighbours at the bar in the sharpest degree. Those whose ill-fortune it was to stand near him were confessors, and in summer-time almost martyrs. This hateful decay of his carcase came upon him by continual sottishness; for, to say nothing of brandy, he was seldom without a pot of ale at his nose, or near him. That exercise was all he used; the rest of his life was sitting at his desk or piping at home; and that *home* was a tailor's house in Butcher Row, called his lodging, and the man's wife was his nurse or worse: but by virtue of his money, of which he made little account, though he got a great deal, he soon became master of the family; and

being no changeling, he never removed, but was true to his friends and
they to him to the last hour of his life. With all this, he had a goodness
of nature and disposition in so great a degree that he may be deser-
vedly styled a *philanthrope*. He was a very *Silenus* to the boys, as in this
place I may term the students of the law, to make them merry when
ever they had a mind to it. He had nothing of rigid or austere in him. If
any near him at the bar grumbled at his stench, he ever converted the
complaint into content and laughing with the abundance of his wit. As
to his ordinary dealing, he was as honest as the driven snow was white;
and why not, having no regard for money or desire to be rich? And for
good nature and condescension there was not his fellow. I have seen
him for hours and hours together before the court sat, stand at the bar,
with an audience of students over against him, putting of cases, and
debating so as suited their capacities and encouraged their industry.
And so in the Temple, he seldom moved without a parcel of youths
hanging about him, and he merry and jesting with them. Once, after he
was in the King's business, he dined with the Lord Keeper, and there
he showed another qualification he had acquired, and that was to play
jigs upon a harpsichord, having taught himself with the opportunity of
an old virginal of his landlady's; but in such a manner, not for defect
but figure, as to see him was a jest.

Roger North, *Lives of the Norths*, 1742–4

65

The Earthy Duchess

THE Earl of Clarendon, chief minister to Charles II, learnt to his consternation in 1660 that his daughter Anne had formed a liaison with the
Duke of York, the future James II. According to his account, he said
'he would turn her out of his house, as a strumpet, to shift for herself,
and would never see her again'. Told the pair were married, 'he fell
into new commotions' and said 'that he had much rather his daughter
should be the duke's whore than his wife: in the former case nobody
could blame him for the resolution he had taken, for he was not
obliged to keep a whore for the greatest prince alive; and the indignity
to himself he would submit to the good pleasure of God. But if there
were any reason to suspect the other, he was ready to give a positive
judgment, in which he hope their lordships would concur with him;

that the king should immediately cause the woman to be sent to the
Tower, and to be cast into a dungeon, under so strict a guard, that no
person living should be admitted to come to her; and then that an act
of parliament should be immediately passed for the cutting off her
head, to which he would not only give his consent, but would very willingly be the first man that should propose it.' The couple were married
nonetheless, and Anne gave birth to two queens-regnant, Mary II and
Queen Anne. The Duchess was chiefly notable for her drinking feats.
John Aubrey recorded: 'Colonel Popham's great tankard, the Duchess
of York dranke it (almost) off at a draught.' Anthony Wood was more
censorious, recording in 1671: 'March 31. Died Anne, Duchess of
York. She died with eating and drinking; died fast and fustie; sala-
cious; lecherous.'

66

Monmouth's End

*The Duke of Monmouth, illegitimate son of Charles II, led a Protestant rising
against James II but was defeated and taken at Sedgemoor in July 1685.*

15 July 1685—This day was Monmouth brought to London. Examin'd
before the King to whom he made great submission, acknowledges his
seduction by Fergusson the Scot, whom he named the bloudy Villain.
Thence sent to the Tower, has an interview with his late Dutchesse,
whom he received coldly, having lived dishonestly with the Lady Hen.
Wentworth for two years; from obstinately asserting his conversation
with that debauched woman to be no sin, seeing he could not be persuaded to his last breath, the Divines, who were sent to assist him,
thought not fit to administer the holy Communion to him. For the rest
of his faults he professed great sorrow, and so died without any apparent feare, would make use of no cap, or other circumstance, but lying
downe bid the fellow do his office better than to my late Lord Russell,
& gave him gold. But the wretch made five Chopps before he had his
head off, which so incens'd the people, that had he not been guarded
& got away they would have torne him in pieces. He made no Speech
on the Scaffold (which was on Tower hill) but gave a paper (containing
not above 5 or 6 lines) for the King, in which he disclaimes all Title to
the Crowne, acknowledges that the late King (his Father) had indeed
told him, he was but his base sonn, & so desired his Majestie to be

kind to his Wife & Children. This Relations I had from the Mouth of
Dr Tenison, Rector of St Martins, who with the Bishops of Ely &
Baths & Wells, was one of the Divines his Majestie sent to him, & were
at the Execution. Thus ended this quondam Duke, darling of his
Father, and the Ladies, being extraordinarily handsome and adroit; an
excellent souldier and dancer, a favourite of the people, of an Easy
nature, debauched by lust, seduced by crafty knaves who would have
set him up only to make a property; took this opportunity of his Majestie being of another Religion to gather up a party of discontented;
failed of it; and perished.

Evelyn, *Diary*

67

A Queenly Death

*At the end of 1694 there was an appalling epidemic of smallpox in England.
One of the victims was Queen Mary II.*

SHE received the intimation of her danger with true greatness of soul.
She gave orders that every lady of her bedchamber, every maid of
honour, nay every menial servant who had not had the smallpox should
instantly leave Kensington House. She locked herself up during a
short time in her closet, burned some papers, arranged others, and
calmly waited her fate . . . All this time, William remained night and
day by her bedside. The little couch on which he slept when he was in
camp was spread for him in the antechamber; but he scarcely laid
down upon it; the sight of his misery, the Dutch envoy wrote, was
enough to melt the hardest heart. Tenison, the Archbishop of Canterbury, undertook to tell her that she was dying. He was afraid that such
a communication abruptly made might agitate her violently, and began
with much management. But she soon caught his meaning, and with
that meek womanly courage which so often puts our bravery to shame,
submitted herself to the will of God. She called for a small cabinet in
which her most important papers were locked up, gave orders that as
soon as she was no more it should be delivered to the King, and then
dismissed worldly cares from her mind. She received the eucharist and
repeated her part of the office with unimpaired memory and intelligence, though in a feeble voice. She observed that Tenison had been
long standing at her bedside and with that sweet courtesy which was

habitual with her, faltered out her commands that he should sit down, and repeated them till he obeyed. After she had received the sacrament, she sank rapidly and uttered only a few broken words. Twice she tried to take a last farewell of him whom she had loved so truly and entirely; but she was unable to speak. He had a succession of fits so alarming that his privy councillors, who were assembled in a neighbouring room, were apprehensive for his reason and his life. A few minutes before the Queen expired, William was removed almost insensate from the sickroom.

Thomas Babington Macaulay, *History of England*, 1849–61

68

Queen Anne, Sarah, and Abigail

The relationship between Queen Anne, Sarah, Duchess of Marlborough and Abigail Masham (née Hill), the bedchamber-woman who replaced Sarah in Anne's affections, is one of the most curious stories in the history of British politics. Anne, younger daughter of James II, was ill-favoured by nature, her only gift being her voice. Lord Dartmouth recorded:

CHARLES II was so pleased with the natural sweetness of her voice that he ordered Mrs Barry, a famous actress, should teach her to speak, which she did with such success, that it was a real pleasure to hear her, though she had a bashfulness that made it very uneasy to herself to say much in public.

Burnet, *History of His Own Times*, 1724–34

69

This shyness arose in great part from Anne's appallingly poor sight; but, next to shyness, her most marked characteristic was obstinacy. Duchess Sarah later wrote:

HER positive sticking to any point which she had once affirm'd or desir'd to be believ'd was a peculiarity of Temper which had from Her infancy been observ'd in Her. I remember her Sister Queen Mary used to tell a story that shews it to have been one of Her favourite and deep-rooted perfections. When they were children, walking in the park together, a dispute was started between them, whether something they saw at a great distance were a Man or a Tree; her sister being of the former opinion & She of the latter. When they came so near that their Eyesight could convince them it was a Man, the Lady Mary said, Now sister, are you satisfied that It is a Man? But Lady Anne, after she saw what it was, turn'd a way, & persisting still in her own Side of the Question, cried out, No, Sister, It is a Tree.

Duchess of Marlborough, The Character of Princes, first pub. 1838

70

Anne's weaknesses made her a woman of free but passionate friendships, and for thirty years she and Duchess Sarah were intimates, Sarah being (to all appearances) the dominant partner. Anne called Sarah and her husband Marlborough 'Mr and Mrs Freeman'; she was 'Mrs Morley' or 'Morley'; and William III, whom Ann hated, was while he still lived 'Mr Caliban'. Princess Anne wrote to Sarah in 1697:

I WISH I could have a Mrs Freeman in every post in my family. I think it very hard that I who like to live well, should pay more and be worse served then any body upon earth, & therefore I will try if I can put things in a better method, tho it will be impossible for me to have every thing don to my mind unless I could meet with a Mrs Freeman in every post in my family, but her fellow I doe really believe is not to be found the world over, & I am sure I never can have any friend that will bee so deare to me as she is.

Blenheim MSS, quoted in Edward Gregg, Queen Anne, 1980

71

When Anne became Queen, the Marlboroughs were dominant at Court, the Queen writing to Sarah on 27 May 1703:

THE thoughts that both my dear Mrs Freeman & Mr Freeman seems to have of retyering gives me no small uneasyness & therefore I must say something on that Subject, it is no wonder at all people in your posts should be weary of ye world who are soe continually troubled with all ye hurry & impertinencys of it, byt give me leave to say, you should a little consider your faithful friends & poor Country, which must be ruined if ever you should putt your melencoly thoughts in execution, as for your poor unfortunat faithfull Morly she could not beare it, for if ever you should forsake me, I would have nothing more to do with the world, but make another abdycation, for what is a Crown, when ye support of it is gon, I never will forsake your dear self, Mr Freeman, nor Mr Montgomery [Godolphin], but allways be your constant faithfull servant, & we four must never part, till death mows us down with his impartiall hand.

Blenheim MSS. Ibid.

72

In April 1697 Sarah had been instrumental in obtaining for Abigail Hill, an impoverished cousin, the menial post of bedchamber-woman to Anne. Later, Abigail wrote a detailed description of her duties, emphasizing the class distinction between the women and the ladies of the bedchamber (of which Sarah, as Mistress of the Robes, was the head):

THE bedchamber-*woman* came in to waiting before the Queen's prayers, which was before Her Majesty was dressed. The Queen often shifted in a morning; if Her Majesty shifted at noon, the bedchamber-*lady* being by, the bedchamber-*woman* gave the shift to the *lady* without any ceremony, and the *lady* put it on. Sometimes, likewise, the bedchamber-*woman* gave the fan to the *lady* in the same manner; and this was all the bedchamber-*lady* did about the Queen at her dressing. When the Queen washed her hands, the page of the backstairs brought and set down upon a side-table the basin and ewer; then the bedchamber-*woman* set it before the Queen, and knelt on the other side of the table over against the Queen, the bedchamber-*lady* only looking on. The bedchamber-*woman* poured the water out of the ewer upon the Queen's hands. The bedchamber-*woman* pulled on the Queen's gloves, when she could not do it herself. The page of the backstairs was called on to put on the Queen's shoes. When the Queen dined in public, the page reached the glass to the bedchamber-*woman*, and she to the *lady* in waiting. The bedchamber-*woman* brought the chocolate, and gave it without kneeling.

Letters of Henrietta, Countess of Suffolk, 1824

73

Abigail, then, was a menial; and initially it was Anne who was jealous of her,
writing to Sarah in 1703:

I FANCY now you are in town you will be tempted to see the opera,
which I should not wonder at, for I should be so too, if I were able to
stir, but when that will be God knows, for my feavor is not quite gone,
and I am still so lame I cannot go without limping. I hope Mrs Freeman has no thoughts of going to the Opera with Mrs Hill, and will
have a care of engaging herself too much in her company for, if you
give way to that, it is a thing that will insensibly grow upon you. Therefore give me leave once more to beg for your own sake, as well as poor
Mrs Morley's, that you would have as little to do with that enchantress
as tis possible, and pray pardon me for saying this.

Blenheim MSS quoted in J. S. Reid, John and Sarah, 1914

74

It was, in fact, Sarah's neglect, absence from Court and preoccupation with
military and political affairs which fatally undermined her position in Anne's
heart, which was gradually taken over by Abigail. By the end of 1707 Sarah
grasped that she was in danger of being ousted. In her own words:

AFTER some time it was thought proper that [Abigail Hill] should
write to me and desire I would see her; to which I consented, and
appointed her a time. When she came I began to tell her that it was
very plain the Queen was much changed towards me, and that I could
not attribute this to anything but her secret management; that I knew
she had been very frequently with her Majesty in private, and that the
very attempt to conceal this, by artifice, from such a friend as I had
been to her was alone a very ill sign, and enough to prove a very bad
purpose at bottom. To this she very gravely answered that *she was sure*
the Queen, who had loved me extremely, would always be very kind to me. It
was some minutes before I could recover from the surprise with which
so extraordinary an answer struck me. To see a woman, whom I had
raised out of the dust, put on such a superior air, and to hear her
assure me by way of consolation, that the Queen would always be very

kind to me! At length I went on to reproach her with her ingratitude
and her secret management with the Queen to undermine those who
had so long and with so much honour served her Majesty.

Account of the Conduct of the Dowager Duchess of Marlborough, 1742

75

*By this point it was too late for Sarah to regain the Queen's affection, for the
rise of Abigail was inextricably mixed with the royal break with the Whig
ministers or 'junto', and the coming to power of Robert Harley, St John, and
the Tories. After bombarding Anne with angry and reproachful letters, Sarah
had her final interview with the monarch, on Maundy Thursday 6 April
1710. What follows is a digest of the many accounts Sarah subsequently gave
of their conversation.*

Queen: I was about to write to you.

Lady Marlborough: Began to open her case, when the Queen said,
'Whatever you have to say, you may put it in writing', she repeating this
interruption four or five times.

Lady Marlborough: There is a thousand lyes made of me which are so
rediculous that I should never have thought it necessary to goe about to
clear myself of what never entered into my head . . . & I doe assure
your Majesty that there is severall things which I have heard has been
told to your Majesty, that I have said of you, that I am no more capable
of, then I am of killing my children. [This referred to Anne's supposed
lesbian relationship with Abigail, and when Sarah repeated the story,
the Queen] 'turned her face from me, as if she fear'd blushing upon
something I might say to her'.

Queen: There is without doubt many lies told.

Lady Marlborough: Pray, Madam, tell me what you have heard of me
that I may not trouble you to repeat more disagreeable things than is
necessary.

Queen: You said you desired no answer, & shall give you none.

Lady Marlborough: My informant urged me to vindicate myself to your
Majesty, though I do not know who told lies of me. I never pressed her
to know, & much less should I ask of your Majesty who had said things

to my prejudice, I only beg to know what you have heard that I might be able to clear my self in any thing in which I was wronged.

Queen: You said you desired noe answer & I shall give you none.

Lady Marlborough then attacked the Duke and Duchess of Somerset, and I observed all the time I talked to the Queen upon that matter she had a more than ordinary attention but answered not one word.

Queen: I shall make you noe answer to any thing you say.

Lady Marlborough: Will your Majesty make me some answer att some other time, since you won't now.

Queen: I shall make you no answer.

Then my tears dropt again, which was strange, but I could not help it, & I suppose it must bee at such inhuman usage.

Lady Marlborough: You know, Madam, how much I have dispised interest in comparison of serving you, & of doing what was right, & you are sure I would not disown any thing that were true, & I asure your Majesty I have never don any thing that you have reason to bee displeased att, then I cryed again.

Queen: I shall make you noe answer to any thing you say, at which I made my chursey, saying I was confydent she would suffer in this world, or the next for so much inhumanity. [The Queen told her doctor, Sir David Hamilton] that when the Duchess left her, she said, that God would punish her either in this world or in the next for what she had done to her this day. The Queen said it was very hard passing a Sentence upon any body, for that was a thing between God and themselves. [Afterwards the duchess] sat me down in a long Gallary to wipe my eyes, before I came within sight of any body.'

Blenheim MSS (Gregg, Queen Anne); and Hamilton Diary, drawn from
Churchill, Marlborough, 1933, and other accounts

76

LATER in the Spring, when Sarah was vacating her apartments at St James's Palace, she sent the Queen word through Shrewsbury (Lord Treasurer) that she wished to store her furniture in the palace until Marlborough House was completed; the answer which the Queen (stung by Sarah's financial exactions) returned was that the duchess could rent storage space for ten shillings a week. Infuriated, Sarah removed all portable fixtures from her apartments, down to the mantelpieces and the doorknobs. In retaliation, the Queen ordered a temporary halt to the construction of Blenheim, angrily saying 'that she would not build the Duke a house when the Duchess was pulling down hers'.

Gregg, *Queen Anne*

77

Tory Hospitality

Henry St John (1678–1751), who became Viscount Bolingbroke in 1712, was one of the most colourful of the early Tory Party leaders, celebrated alike for his oratory, prose, political philosophy, deviousness, and debauchery. Here he is in 1704, as Secretary-at-War, writing to a fellow MP, Thomas Coke:

DEAR Tom. . . . I go tomorrow morning to Bucklebury [his country house near Reading] and shall be back on Saturday, on which it would be a great pleasure to meet you in town: but for God's sake do not at furthest stay longer than Sunday, because it is most certain our patriots design some gallant thing to open the session with, and that is what, out of kindness to them, everyone should oppose. Though I believe in a little time all the endeavours of their friends to keep 'em on their legs will prove ineffectual. As to whores, dear friend, I am unable to help thee. I have heard of a certain housemaid who is very handsome: if she can be got ready against your arrival, she shall serve for your first meal. Adieu, ever yours most entirely, Harry.

Sir Charles Petrie, *Bolingbroke*, 1937

78

I WENT this morning with Mr Secretary St John and we were to dine at Mr Harley's alone, about some business of importance; but there were two or three gentlemen there. Mr Secretary and I went together from his office to Mr Harley's and thought to have been very wise; but the deuce a bit, the company stayed and more came, and Harley went away at seven, and the Secretary and I stayed with the rest of the company till eleven; I would then have had him come away, but he was in for't; and though he swore he would come away at that flask, there I left him. I wonder at the civility of these people; when he saw I would drink no more, he would always pass the bottle by me, and yet I could not keep the toad from drinking himself, nor he would not let me go neither.

Jonathan Swift, *Journal to Stella*. Letter xiv, 18 January 1711

79

I DINED today with Lord Treasurer, who chid me for not dining with him yesterday, for it seems I did not understand his invitation, and their Club of the Ministry dined together and expected me. Lord Radnor and I were walking the Mall this evening; and Mr Secretary met us and took a turn or two, and then stole away, and we both believed it was to pick up some wench; and tomorrow he will be at the cabinet with the Queen; and so goes the world.

Ibid. Letter xxviii, 24 August 1711

80

Bolingbroke's Escape

When Queen Anne died in 1714 and George I ascended the throne, Bolingbroke was dismissed as Secretary of State; believing he would be impeached and executed, he decided to leave secretly for France. He went to the theatre and ostentatiously bought tickets for the following night, but left in the interval for Dover, where a Captain Morgan and the brothers Galway had secured a ship for Calais. An eye-witness reported:

AND about 12 at night there came two gentlemen to them post from London, one of them a lord and the other their uncle, Captain Morgan, expecting to go immediately on board, the tide just then serving; but the weather proving tempestuous they were forced to stay, though very uneasily, till the next tide. My Lord was kept locked up all the time and nobody suffered to come near him, except La Vigne, the French courier, who went over with him Sunday, after dinner (though I don't hear they eat any), the tide serving, the officers of the port waiting on them for fees, etc, amongst whom was Mr William Lambe . . . who went abruptly into their chamber, which put them all in the utmost confusion, especially my Lord, who changed his colour and looked as though he thought the Devil was come for him: but Mr Galway immediately took Mr Lambe by the hand and led him out of the room, asked his pardon, told him they were busy and desired him and other officers to go on the pier and they would all come to them and pay the fees . . . But no sooner were the officers gone than they went off in the bay on board the vessel, which was in the road. And now my Lord, whom nobody in the house had seen before, was forced to appear. He had got a very black wig and a riding-coat, which he buttoned over his wig and covered the lower part of his face. He carried on his shoulders a pair of leathern bags and affected a clownish, country air in his walking; though nobody suspected him till he was gone off and then some of the seamen fancied they knew him. He arrived at Calais about 8 o'clock Sunday night and there the Governor's coach attended him on his arrival; and then the man with the riding-coat and black periwig was known to be the Right Honourable the Lord Bolingbroke. Yesterday Captain Morgan and the two Galways returned; and finding it was known they had conveyed over my Lord, they grew very insolent and came to poor George Slater and bullied him and told him, had he not been a Common Councilman, they would have whipped him round the market for an informing rogue.

Letter printed in Petrie, *Bolingbroke*

81

Bolingbroke's Debaucheries

HE himself bragged that in one day he was the happiest man alive, got drunk, harangued the Queen, and at night was put to bed to a beautiful young lady, and was tuck'd up by two of the prettiest young Peers in England, Lord Jersey and Bathurst.

Quoted in G. M. Trevelyan, *England under Queen Anne*, 1934

82

Addison's Modesty

The poet and essayist Joseph Addison (1672–1719) was for many years MP for Malmesbury but never made a speech. It was said that, on the one occasion he rose to make one, he was so abashed by the cries of 'Hear him! Hear him!' that he subsided back on the bench speechless. In fact the Journals *show that, as a government minister, he did briefly declare His Majesty's pleasure on several occasions. In 1717 he was appointed Secretary of State.*

ADDISON took as his senior under-secretary Temple Stanyon, whom he had probably known at Oxford. . . . Their relationship was, however, ruffled by financial transactions. It appears that Stanyon borrowed a sum of money from his superior, and immediately thereafter became acquiescent in everything proposed to him, finally causing Addison to protest: 'Sir, either contradict me or pay me my money.'

Peter Smithers, *Life of Joseph Addison*, 1968

83

Walpole's System

Sir Robert Walpole was First Lord of the Treasury, and in effect Prime Minister, 1721–42, ruling by a judicious mixture of parliamentary skill, man-management and patronage. The Earl of Shelburne recorded:

HE was of a perfectly even temper and the most good-natured man living. Once he lost his temper at a Council, but he broke up the Council immediately after, saying no man was fit for business with a ruffled temper.

Lord Edmund Fitzmaurice, *Life of Shelburne*, 1875

84

His supporters were lavishly entertained at his country-house parties in Norfolk. One of them, Lord Hervey, wrote on 21 July 1731:

OUR company at Houghton swelled at last into so numerous a body that we used to sit down to dinner a little snug party of about thirty-odd; up to the chin in beef, venison, geese, turkeys etc; and generally over the chin in claret, strong beer and punch. We had Lords spiritual and temporal, besides commoners, parsons and freeholders innumerable. In public we drank loyal healths, talked of the times and cultivated popularity; in private we drew plans and cultivated the country.

Earl of Ilchester, *Hervey and His Friends*, 1950

85

Walpole's particular delight was to induce ecclesiatics to participate in his patronage system: he would ask of a bishop, 'Is he mortal?' (i.e. corruptible). He recorded his triumph in persuading Edmund Gibson, Bishop of London, to become the government's adviser on church patronage (1723):

I THOUGHT that I might fairly play the courtier so far as to have the meritte of my good wishes with the Bishop of London, and therefore took an opportunity of telling him what I had thought of that matter. At first he was all *nolo episcopari*; before we parted I perceived upon second thoughts he began to rellish it and the next morning *ex mero motu* he came to me, talked comically, is a mortal man, wants to be ravished, and desired me expressly to write to my Lord Townshend to prevent the King's coming to any resolution about the disposal of the Clerk of the Closetts and Lord Almoner's places. We grow well acquainted. He must be Pope, and would as willingly be *our* Pope as any body's.

Quoted in J. H. Plumb, *Sir Robert Walpole*, 1960

86

Walpole believed that, cleverly managed, patronage could be spread around in such a manner to satisfy all with genuine claims on government: as he put it, 'There is enough pasture for all the sheep.' Typical of the demands made on him was this note (1727) from a senior naval officer, Sir John Jennings:

YOU are senceable when I quitted the Admiralty it was not so much upon account of indisposition as upon the objection I made to serve there with Lord Berkeley and upon these removes I am not at all soolisatouse [solicitous] to retorne to that board again but must desiar if my pattent for Grenwich is to be resuned that it may be for life and that if my Lord Torrington is to be Vice-Admirall of England that I may in my torne be Rare Admirall of the same till the proper time comes for my being created an English barron. This is all the request I have to make being with unfaingd respect, etc.

Ibid.

87

LORD MELCOLME told me several things about Sir Robert Walpole. He said he was inconceivably coarse and low-mannered. He gave me an instance. When he went down with Sir Robert Walpole, which he frequently did, to Houghton, they were obliged to pass a bad common and were more than once benighted on it, which made him represent to Sir Robert how becoming it would be and how suitable to his rank to have flambeaux ready for such occasions. Sir Robert said he would give orders accordingly. The first time the circumstances occurred again, Lord Melcolme reminded Sir Robert. He stopped the coach and inquired of the servants for the *links*. They said they were in the coach; he then obliged them both to get out on a cold, dark night, but the links he obtained were some links of sausages. Such was the vulgarity of Sir Robert's diction and habits that he used the phraseology of Drury Lane and Covent Garden and called the lights links, which the stupidity of the servants interpreted 'links of sausages'.

Fitzmaurice, Shelburne

88

Walpole's Love of Peace

Among Walpole's hardest tasks was managing George II, through his Queen, and restraining the bellicosity of both, which threatened to drag England into Continental conflicts. He told the courtier Lord Hervey:

I SHALL carry my point at last; but you, my Lord, are enough acquainted with this Court to know that nothing can be done in it but by degrees; should I tell either the King or the Queen what I propose to bring them to six months hence, I could never succeed. Step by step I can carry them perhaps the road I wish; but if I ever show that at a distance to what end that road leads they stop short, and all my designs are always defeated. For example, if we cannot make peace and that I can keep this nation out of the war a year longer, I know it is impossible but England must give law to all Europe, yet this I dare not say, since even this consideration would not keep them quiet if they thought peace could not be obtained; and for that reason I graft as yet all my arguments on the supposition that peace will be effected. I told the Queen this morning, 'Madam, there are fifty thousand men slain this year in Europe and not one Englishman, and besides the satisfaction it is to one's good nature to make this reflection, considering they owe their safety and their lives to those under whose care and protection they are, since in point of policy too it is no immaterial circumstance to be able to say that, whilst all the rest of Europe has paid their share to this diminution of their common strength, England remains in its full and unimpaired vigour'.

Lord Hervey's Memoirs, ed. Romney Sedgwick, 1952

89

A Contentious Royal Birth

The King and Queen suspected that the Prince of Wales, with whom they had quarrelled, and who had no heir, would try to manufacture one; so when he announced his wife was pregnant they ordered Walpole to make sure she had the child under their noses in Hampton Court, rather than at the Prince's home in London, where a fraud could be carried out. Hervey related that the Queen told Walpole:

'AT her labour I positively will be, let her lie-in where she will; for she cannot be brought to bed as quick as one can blow one's nose, and I will be sure it is her child' . . . The Queen was every day pressing Sir Robert to have this message sent to the Prince, saying: 'Sir Robert, we shall be catched; he will remove her before he receives any orders for her lying-in here, and will afterwards say that he talked so publicly of his intentions he concluded if the King had not approved of them he should have heard something of it.' Sir Robert said, as the Princess did not reckon till the beginning of October, that it was full time enough; and in this manner from day to day this intended message was postponed, till it never went for on Sunday 31 July the Princess was taken in the evening, after having dined in public that day with the King and Queen, so very ill, with all the symptoms to actual labour, that the

Prince ordered a coach to be got ready that moment to carry her to London. Her pains came on so fast and so strong that her water broke before they could get her out of the house. However, in this condition, M. Dunoyer, the dancing-master, lugging her downstairs and along the passages by one arm, and Mr Bloodworth, one of the Prince's equerries, by the other, and the Prince in the rear, they with much ado got her into the coach; Lady Archibald Hamilton and Mrs Townshend remonstrating strongly against this imprudent step, and the Princess begging, for God's sake, the Prince would let her stay in quiet where she was, for that her pains were so great she could not set one foot before the other, and was upon the rack when they moved her. But the Prince, with an obstinacy equal to his folly and a folly equal to his barbarity, insisted on her going, crying 'Courage! Courage! Ah, quelle sottise!' and telling her, with the encouragement of a toothdrawer or the consolatory tenderness of an executioner, that it would be over in a minute. With these excitations and in this manner, after enjoining all his servants not to say one word what was the matter for fear the news of the Princess's circumstances should get to the other side of the house and their going should be prevented, he got her into the coach. There were in the coach besides him and her Lady Archibald Hamilton and Mrs Clavering and Mrs Paine, two of the Princess's dressers; Vreid, his valet de chambre, who was a surgeon and man-midwife, was upon the coachbox; Mr Bloodworth and two or three more behind the coach; and thus loaded he ordered the coachman to drive full gallop to London. About ten this cargo arrived in town. Notwithstanding all the handkerchiefs that had been thrust one after another up Her Royal Highnesse's petticoats in the coach, her clothes were in such a condition with the filthy inundations which attend these circumstances that when the coach stopped in St James's the Prince ordered all the lights to be put out that people might not have the nasty ocular evidence which would otherwise have been exhibited to them of his folly and her distress. When they came to St James's there was no one prepared for her reception. The midwife came in a few minutes; napkins, warming-pans and all other necessary implements for this operation were sought by different emissaries in different houses in the neighbourhood; and no sheets being to come at, Her Royal Highness was put to bed between two tablecloths. At a quarter before eleven she was delivered of a little rat of a girl, about the bigness of a good large toothpick case, none of the Lords of the Council being present but my Lord President Wilmington and my Lord Godolphin, Privy Seal. . . .

[The King and Queen] went to bed at eleven, without hearing one single syllable of the Princess's being ill or even of her not being in the house. At half an hour after one, which was above two hours after the Princess had been brought to bed, a courier arrived with the first news of her being in labour. When Mrs Titchburne, the Woman of the Bedchamber, came to wake the King and Queen, the Queen as soon as she came into the room asked what was the matter that occasioned their being waked up at so unusual an hour; and as the most natural question, inquired if the house was on fire. When Mrs Titchburne said the Prince had sent to let Their Majesties know the Princess was in labour the Queen immediately cried: 'My God, my nightgown! I'll go to her this moment.' 'Your nightgown, Madam', replied Mrs Titchburne, 'and your coaches too; the Princess is at St James's.' 'Are you mad', interrupted the Queen, 'or are you asleep, my good Titchburne? You dream.' When Mrs Titchburne insisted on its being certainly true, the King flew into a violent passion and in German (as the Queen told me afterwards) began to scold her, saying 'You see now with all your wisdom they have outwitted you. This is all your fault. There is a false child will be put upon you and how can you answer it to all your children?' ... The Queen said little but got up, dressed as fast as she could, ordered her coaches and sent to the Duke of Grafton and Lord Hervey to go with her; and by half an hour after two Her Majesty set out from Hampton Court ... [She] went into the Princess's bedchamber, wished her joy, said she was glad she had escaped so well; and added: 'Apparenement, Madame, vous avey horriblement souffert'. 'Point de tout', replied the Princess, 'ce n'est rien.' Then Lady Archibald Hamilton brought in the child, which had yet no clothes but a red mantle and some napkins, nor any nurse. The Queen kissed the child and said: 'Le bon Dieu vous benisse, pauvre petite creature! Vous voila arrivée dans un disagreeable monde'. ... The Prince being in his undress, the Queen insisted on his not coming out of the house, advised him to go to bed and walked, herself, across the courts to Lord Hervey's lodgings. As soon as she got thither she wrote a short letter to the King and dispatched Lord Essex with it back to Hampton Court. She then said to the Duke of Grafton and Lord Hervey (nobody being present but the two princesses): 'Well, upon my honour, I no more doubt this poor little bit of a thing is the Princess's child, than I doubt of either of these two being mine, though I own to you I had my doubts upon the road that there would be some juggle; and if, instead of this poor, little, ugly she-mouse, there had been a brave, large, fat, jolly boy, I should not have been cured of my suspicions; nay, I believe they would have been so much increased or rather that I should have been so confirmed in that opinion, that I should have gone about his house like a madwoman, played the devil, and insisted on knowing what chairman's brat he had bought'. . . . As soon as Sir Robert [Walpole] came into the room the Queen laughed and only said: 'Here you are, you see; am I in the right? What do you say now?' Sir Robert smiled too but looked vexed and out of countenance and said: 'When anything very improbable happens, Madam, I do not think it is a great disgrace for anybody not to have foreseen it would happen.'

Ibid.

90

Walpole's Regret

SEEING Mr [Henry] Fox reading in the library at Houghton, he said 'You can read. It is a great happiness. I totally neglected it while I was in business, which has been the whole of my life, and to such a degree that I cannot now read a page—a warning to all Ministers.'

Shelburne's autobiographical fragment, printed in Fitzmaurice, op. cit.

91

A Curious Simile

After the failure of the Forty-Five, two Scots peers were executed on Tower Hill in August 1746; the Earl of Kilmarnock suffered first; then came Arthur, 6th Lord Balmerino.

THE scaffold was immediately new strewn with sawdust, the block new covered, the executioner new dressed, and a new axe brought. Then came old Balmerino, treading with the air of a general. As soon as he mounted the scaffold he read the inscription on his coffin, as he did again afterwards: he then surveyed the spectators, who were in amazing numbers, even upon masts of ships in the river; and pulling out his spectacles read a treasonable speech, which he delivered to the Sheriff, and said the Young Pretender was so sweet a prince, that flesh and blood could not resist following him; and lying down to try the block, he said: 'If I had a thousand lives, I would lay them all down here in the same cause.' He said, if he had not taken the sacrament the day before, he would have knocked down Williamson, the Lieutenant of the Tower, for his ill-usage of him. He took the axe and felt it, and asked the Headsman how many blows he had given Lord Kilmarnock; and gave him three guineas. Two clergymen, who attended him, coming up, he said: 'No, gentlemen, I believe you have already done me all the service you can.' Then he went to the corner of the scaffold and called very loud for the warder, to give him his perriwig, which he took off, and put on a nightcap of Scotch plaid, and then pulled off his coat and waistcoat and lay down; but being told he was on the wrong side, vaulted round, and immediately gave the sign by tossing up his arm, as if he were giving the sign for battle. He received three blows, but the first certainly took away all sensation. He was not a quarter of an hour on the scaffold; Lord Kilmarnock above half an hour. Balmerino certainly died with the intrepidity of a hero, but with the insensibility of one too. As he walked from his prison to execution, seeing every window and top of house filled with spectators, he cried out: 'Look, look, how they are all piled up like rotten oranges!'

Horace Walpole, Letter to Horace Mann, in *Letters*, 1840

92

George II Robbed

December 13 1843 . . . Duncannon in the evening told me the story of George II's robbery in Kensington Gardens, which I had heard before but remembered imperfectly. He was walking with William IV, he said, in Kensington Gardens one day, and when they got to a certain spot the King said to him, 'It was here, My Lord, that my great-grandfather, King George II, was robbed. He was in the habit of walking every morning alone round the garden, and one day a man jumped over the wall, approached the King, but with great respect, and told him he was in distress, and was compelled to ask him for his money, his watch and the buckles in his shoes. The King gave him what he had about him and the man knelt down to take off his buckles, all the time with profound respect. When he had got everything, the King told him that there was a seal on the watch-chain of little or no value but which he wished to have back, and requested he would take it off the chain and restore it. The man said, 'Your Majesty must be aware that we have already been here some time, and that it is not safe for me to stay longer, but if you will give me your word not to say anything of what has passed for twenty-four hours, I will place the seal at the same hour tomorrow morning on that stone', pointing to a particular place. The King promised, went the next morning at the appointed hour, the man appeared, brought the seal, and then jumped the wall and went off. 'His Majesty', added King William, 'never afterwards walked alone in Kensington Gardens.'

Charles Greville (1794–1865), *Memoirs*, first pub. 1874–87

93

Newcastle's Freaks

Thomas Pelham Holles, Duke of Newcastle (1693–1768), was Secretary of State for thirty years and managed the government system Sir Robert Walpole had created. Walpole's son, Horace, loved to tell stories about Newcastle's oddities. In 1760 he described the funeral of the old Duke of Cumberland at Westminster Abbey:

WHEN we came to the chapel of Henry the Seventh, all solemnity and decorum ceased; no order was observed, people sat or stood where they could or would; the yeomen of the guard were crying out for help, oppressed by the immense weight of the coffin; the bishop read sadly and blundered in the prayers; the fine chapter, *Man that is born of a woman*, was chanted, not read; and the anthem, besides being immeasurably tedious, would have served as well for a nuptial. The real serious part was the figure of the (new) Duke of Cumberland, heightened by a thousand melancholy circumstances. He had a dark brown adonis and a cloak of black cloth, with a train of five yards. Attending the funeral of a father could not be pleasant: his leg extremely bad, yet forced to stand upon it nearly two hours; his faced bloated and distorted with his late paralytic stroke, which had affected too one of his eyes, and placed over the mouth of the vault into which in all probability he must himself so soon descend; think how unpleasant a situation! He bore it all with a firm and unaffected countenance. This grave scene was fully contrasted by the burlesque Duke of Newcastle. He fell into a fit of crying the moment he came into the chapel, and flung himself back in a stall, the archbishop hovering over him with a smelling-bottle; but in two minutes his curiosity got the better of his hypocrisy and he ran about the chapel with his glass to spy who was or was not there, spying with one hand and mopping his eyes with the other. Then returned the fear of catching cold; and the Duke of Cumberland, who was sinking with heat, felt himself weighed down, and turning round found it was the Duke of Newcastle standing upon his train, to avoid the chill of the marble.

Horace Walpole, Letter to George Montagu, 13 November 1760, *Letters*, 1840

94

THE Duke of Grafton [Lord Chamberlain] still languishes: the Duke of Newcastle has so pestered him with political visits, that the physicians ordered him to be excluded; yet he forced himself into the house. The Duke's gentlemen would not admit him into the bedchamber, saying his grace was asleep. Newcastle protested he would go in on tiptoe and only look at him—he rushed in, clattered his heels to waken him, and then fell upon the bed, kissing and hugging him. Grafton waked: 'God! What's here?' 'Only I, my dear lord'—Buss, buss, buss, buss!—'God! how can you be such a beast to kiss such a creature as I am, all over plaisters! Get along!'—and turned about and went to sleep.

Horace Walpole, Letter to Sir Horace Mann, 20 April 1757. Ibid.

95

The Cornet of Horse

William Pitt, Earl of Chatham (1708–78), was one of the 'Boy Patriots' who formed the opposition to Walpole organized by Bolingbroke in his own age. A cornet in the Blues, he entered parliament as member for the family borough of Old Sarum and in his maiden speech 29 April 1736 infuriated Walpole by supporting the Prince of Wales against his royal father George II. The speech was 'compared favourably with the best orations of Cicero and Demosthenes'.

[PITT] was already a marked man for his constant support of Opposition measures and for the favour he enjoyed from the Prince of Wales; by this display of oratorical capacity and cool impertinence he had shown that he might be dangerous. 'We must muzzle', said Walpole, 'this terrible cornet of horse', and forthwith dismissed him from the Army. No more effective way of unmuzzling the cornet, and giving him the prominence his ambition sought, could have been devised by Pitt's greatest friend. The Army, already alarmed by the removal of Lords Stair and Cobham, saw in this vengeance on a mere subaltern a blow struck at all liberty of opinion in the commissioned ranks, and warmly took up Pitt's cause . . . a member, alluding to Pitt's punishment, said: 'I know the danger I am in by appearing in favour of this motion. I may, perhaps, have a message sent me, I may lose the command I have in the army, as other gentlemen have done for the same reason before me.' Pulteney and Lyttelton attacked Walpole for his action, and especially for descending so low in his vengeance as to cashier a cornet of horse for his vote. But Walpole was quite unabashed and cynically avowed that 'if an officer, of whatever rank or merit, wished to meddle with affairs of State . . . which were outside his sphere, or even show aversion to a minister, that minister would be the most wretched of creatures if he did not cashier him, and left the practice as a legacy to his successors'. . . . Pitt himself showed a becoming spirit. During the summer of 1736 he travelled about the country in a one-horse chaise without a servant, as if to emphasise the narrow straits to which he had been reduced, and to appeal from a corrupt ministry to a generous people. Wherever he went he was received with acclamation.

Basil Williams, *William Pitt, Earl of Chatham*, 1913

96

Pitt's Terrifying Ascendancy

By the mid-1750s Pitt had established such a moral ascendancy in the House of Commons that ministers were afraid to cross swords with him.

HUME Campbell . . . was so terrified of Pitt that once, at an angry glance from him, he implored the Speaker's protection. Pitt could do much with a look or a tone. Turning one day on Murray that awful glance of his, 'I must', said he, 'now address a few words to the Solici-tor; they shall be few, but they shall be daggers'; he paused, but the look continued, and Murray became more and more agitated. 'Judge Festus trembles', said Pitt: 'he shall hear me some other day.' Another day it was Morton, Chief Justice of Chester, who had said: 'King, Lords and Commons, or as that right honourable gentleman would say, Commons, Lords and King.' Pitt sprang up: 'My blood runs cold at such words—I desire they be taken down by the clerk.' 'Nay', sputtered Morton, frightened out of his senses, 'I mean nothing; King, Lords and Commons; Commons, Lords and King—it is all one.' 'I don't wish to push the matter further,' said Pitt in a voice little above a whisper: then higher, 'the moment a man acknowledges his error he ceases to be guilty: but', he added in a colloquial tone, 'whenever that member *means* nothing, I advise him to *say* nothing.' Once when Pitt had concluded a speech and was walking slowly out of the House, just as the doorkeeper was opening the door for him, his ear caught the words: 'I rise to reply to the Right Honourable Gentleman.' Turning round, he gave the Member a look which made him sit down instantly, and began hobbling goutily back to his seat. Then, lowering himself into his seat, he exclaimed: 'Now let me hear what the honourable gentleman has to say to me.' The Member recounting the scene was asked if anybody laughed: 'No, Sir, we were all too much awed to laugh.'

Ibid., quoting Butler's *Reminiscences*

97

Pillow Politics

EVEN during his illnesses Pitt infected his colleagues with some of his contagious energy. One day he asked Newcastle to come to his house to discuss plans. The duke found him ill in bed in a cold room. Pitt had much to say, and the duke found the cold unbearable; at last, spying another bed in the room, he crept into it, and the two statesmen were found talking and gesticulating at one another from under the bed-clothes.

Williams, *William Pitt*

98

Chatham's Death-Speech

Chatham had strongly supported the American colonists in their cry of 'no taxation without representation'; but he was equally opposed to an abject surrender to them and their ally France, and in 1778 arose from his sickbed to make his last speech in the Lords.

ON 7 April Chatham came up to London, accompanied by his three sons and his son-in-law Lord Mahon. To recover from the fatigue of the journey he rested awhile in the Princes' Chamber before entering the House. Here Camden saw him and found him so distempered and agitated that he tried to persuade him not to attend the debate: but it was useless. 'Your Grace knows', wrote Camden to Grafton, 'how obstinate he is, when resolved.' As Chatham entered, supported by William and Lord Mahon, every man in that House, crowded from gallery to floor, seemed conscious that it was a great day in the history of England. The whole assemblage rose and the peers reverentially made way for him as he passed to his seat on the Earls' bench. So shrunk was he with illness and suffering that from his bushy wig little could be seen of his countenance but the great aquiline nose and the flashing eyes. The Duke of Richmond spoke first; next Lord Weymouth for the ministers; then Chatham rose, leaning on his crutches and supported on each side. Taking one hand from his crutch and raising it to heaven, 'I thank God', he said, 'that I have been able to come here this day, to perform my duty. . . . I am old and infirm, have one foot, more than one foot, in the grave—I am risen from my bed to stand up in the cause of my country—perhaps never again to speak in this House.' There was an awed stillness; a handkerchief dropped would have been heard. He went on speaking, but was not like himself; his speech faltered, his sentences were broken, his mind was not its own master. But his words, says Camden, were still shreds of unconnected eloquences, flashes of the same fire which Prometheus-like he had stolen from Heaven, and were then returning from the place whence they were taken: 'Shall a people that fifteen years ago was the terror of the world now stoop so low as to tell its ancient inveterate enemy, "Take all we have, only give us peace?" . . . My Lords, any state is better than despair; if we must fall, let us fall like men.' He sank

down and Temple whispered to him that he had forgotten something—should he get up and say it? 'No, no', said Chatham, 'I will do it
by and by.' The Duke of Richmond answered him with gentle courtesy, then Chatham attempted to rise again. As he rose he fell back on
his seat, to all appearances in the agony of death. At once the House
was in a muffled tumult, peers running hither and thither for salts and
cordials, and crowding round him where he was being tenderly cared
for by William and James Charles, Mahon, Temple and the King's
brother, the Duke of Cumberland. Everyone was astir but Mansfield,
who sat almost as unmoved as the senseless body itself. Then he was
carried to an adjoining chamber and attended by Drs Brocklesby and
Addington, who had been hastily summoned. He revived and after a fit
of sickness recovered enough to be taken for the night to an adjoining
house, and two days later to be driven to Hayes. . . . On the afternoon
of 11 May 1778 he died.

Ibid.

99

A Tory Atheist's Death

*David Hume (1711–76), Britain's greatest conservative philosopher, gave
offence to his would-be political admirers by denying the existence of God.
James Boswell, fascinated by Hume's infidelity, recorded this conversation
which took place on 7 July 1776, six weeks before he died:*

I FOUND him alone, in a reclining posture in his drawing room. He
was lean, ghastly, and quite of an earthy appearance. He was dressed
in a suit of grey cloth and white metal buttons and a kind of scratch
wig. He was quite different from the plump figure which he used to
present. He had before him Dr Campbell's *Philosophy of Rhetoric*. He
seemed to be placid and even cheerful. He said he was just approaching to his end. I think these were his words. I don't know how I contrived to get the subject of immortality introduced. He said he had
never entertained any belief in religion since he began to read Locke
and Clarke. I asked him if he was not religious when he was young. He
said he was, and he used to read *The Whole Duty of Man*; that he made
an abstract from the catalogue of vices at the end of it, and examined

himself by this, leaving out murder and theft and such vices as he had no chance of committing, having no inclination to commit them. This, he said, was strange work; for instance to try if, notwithstanding his excelling his schoolfellows, he had no pride or vanity. He smiled in ridicule of this as absurd and contrary to fixed principles and necessary consequences, not averting that religious discipline does not mean to extinguish but to moderate the passions; and certainly an excess of pride or vanity is dangerous and generally hurtful. He then said flatly that the morality of every religion was bad and, I really thought, was not jocular when he said that when he heard a man was religious, he concluded he was a rascal, though he had known some instances of very good men being religious. This was just an extravagant reverse of the common remark as to infidels.

I had a strong curiosity to be satisfied if he persisted in disbelieving a future state even when he had death before his eyes. I was persuaded from what he now said, and from his manner in saying it, that he did persist. I asked him if it were not possible that there might be a future state. He answered it was possible that a piece of coal put upon the fire would not burn: and he added that it was a most unreasonable fancy that we should exist for ever. That immortality, if it were at all, must be general; that a great proportion of the human race has hardly any intellectual qualities; that a great proportion dies in infancy before being possessed of reason; yet all these must be immortal; that a porter who gets drunk by ten o'clock with gin must be immortal; that the trash of every age must be preserved, and that new universes must be created to contain such infinite numbers . . .

I may illustrate what he has said by mentioning that in a former conversation with me on this subject he used pretty much the same mode of reasoning and urged that Wilkes and his mob must be immortal. One night last May as I was coming up King Street, Westminster, I met Wilkes, who carried me into Parliament Street to see a curious procession pass: the funeral of a lamplighter attended by some hundreds of his fraternity with torches. Wilkes, who either is or affects to be an infidel, was rattling away, 'I think there's an end of that fellow. I think he won't rise again.' I very calmly said to him, 'You bring into my mind the strongest argument that ever I heard against a future state'; and then told him David Hume's objection that Wilkes and his mob must be immortal. It seemed to make a proper impression, for he grinned abashment, as a Negro grows whiter when he blushes. But to return to my last interview with Mr Hume.

I asked him if the thought of annihilation never gave him any uneasiness. He said not the least; no more than the thought that he had not been, as Lucretius observes. 'Well,' said I, 'Mr Hume I hope to triumph over you when I meet you in a future state; and remember you are not to pretend that you was joking with all this infidelity.' 'No, no,' said he. 'But I shall have been so long there before you come that it will be nothing new.' In this style of good humour and levity did I conduct the conversation. Perhaps it was wrong on so awful a subject. But as nobody was present, I thought it could have no bad effect . . . It was amazing to find him so keen in such a state. I must add one other circumstance that is material, as it shows that he perhaps was not without some hope of a future state, and that his spirits were supported by a consciousness (or at least a notion) that his conduct had been virtuous. He said 'If there were a future state, Mr Boswell, I think I could give as good an account of my life as most people.'

Boswell in Extremes, 1776–8, 1971

100

The Young Fox

CHARLES JAMES FOX, born in 1749, was the third son of Henry Fox, Lord Holland, who had made a fortune in politics and proved an exceptionally indulgent father, saying of Charles: 'Let nothing be done to break his spirit. The world will do that business fast enough.' When the child threatened to smash a watch with a hammer, Lord Holland replied: 'Well, if you must I suppose you must.' Aged twelve, he negotiated his first loan, signing a document still in the Holland House papers: 'December 15, 1761. Receiv'd, advanced to me by my Father as part of my Fortune two hundred pounds, C. J. Fox.' Aged fifteen, while at Eton, he was taken by his father on a Continental tour, and at Spa Lord Holland provided him with five guineas a night to spend at dice and cards. His mother, Lady Caroline, feared the consequences of such an upbringing, writing: 'I have been this morning with Lady Hester Pitt, and there is little William Pitt, *not eight years old*, and really the cleverest child I ever saw *and brought up so strictly and so proper in his behaviour* that, *mark my words*, that little boy will be a thorn in Charles's side as long as he lives.'

101

Fox's Maiden

WHEN Fox was elected to parliament in May 1768 he was only nineteen, technically too young to take his seat until the second session in November. There is no record of a maiden speech. His first recorded remark was on 9 March 1769: *Mr Charles Fox*: 'Are we to take the construction from the Sheriff of the order? He might have come up half way, and an express sent to him in return'.

Sir Henry Cavendish's Debates of the House of Commons, 1841

His first speech of note was on Wilkes, 15 April 1769. His nephew, the 3rd Lord Holland, recorded: 'A listener was so impressed that he ripped off part of his shirt and drew a picture of the young orator. It is still preserved in my possession at Holland House, retaining many traits of resemblance to the dark, intelligent and animated features of Mr Fox'.

Lord John Russell, *Memorials and Correspondence of Charles James Fox*, 1853-7

102

Fox's Troubles

Given a ministerial post at the Treasury, Fox nevertheless frequently criticized North's government in his speeches. In 1774 North dismissed him in the following brief letter: 'His Majesty has thought proper to order a new Commission of the Treasury to be made out, in which I do not see your name.' Shortly afterwards, Horace Walpole recorded:

[Fox] did not shine in this debate, nor could it be wondered at. He had sat up playing hazard at Almack's from Tuesday evening, the 4th, till five in the Afternoon of Wednesday 5th. An hour before, he had recovered £12,000 that he had lost, and by dinner, which was at 5 o'clock, he had ended losing £11,000. On the Thursday he spoke in this debate; went to dinner at past 11 at night; from thence to White's where he drank till seven the next morning; thence to Almack's, where he won £6,000; and between three and four in the afternoon he set off for Newmarket. . . . There being a report that Charles was going to be married, it was told to his father who replied: 'I am glad of it, for then he will go to bed at least one night.'

Last Journals of Horace Walpole, 1910

103

On 26 November 1774, a sadder and wiser Lord Holland was obliged to write to his financial adviser:

I DO hereby order, direct and require you to see and dispose of my long annuitys and so much of my other Stock, Estates and Effects as will be sufficient to Pay and Discharge the debts of my son The Honble Charles James Fox, not exceding the sum of one hundred thousand pounds.

Earl of Ilchester, *Henry Fox, First Lord Holland*, 1920

104

Fox's Appearance

By the common consent of contemporaries, Fox's greatest speeches were made in the second half of the 1770s, when opposing the North ministry on the issue of American independence. An eye-witness describes him at this time:

IT was impossible to contemplate the lineaments of his countenance without instantly perceiving the marks of genius. His features in themselves dark, harsh and saturnine, like those of Charles II from whom he descended in the maternal line, derived a sort of majesty from the addition of two black and shaggy eyebrows which sometimes concealed but more frequently developed the workings of his mind. Even these features, however, did not readily assume the expressions of anger or enmity. They frequently and naturally relaxed into a smile, the effect of which became irresistible because it appeared to be the index of a benevolent and complacent disposition. His figure, broad, heavy and inclined to corpulence, appeared destitute of elegance or grace, except the portion conferred on it by the emanations of intellect, which at times diffused over his whole person, when he was speaking, the most impassioned animation. . . . At five and twenty I have seen him apparelled *en petit maître* with a hat and feather over in the House of Commons; but in 1781 he constantly, or at least usually, wore in that assembly a blue frock-coat and a buff waistcoat neither of which appeared in general new and sometimes appeared to be thread-bare . . . These colours . . . then constituted the distinguishing badge or uniform of Washington and the American insurgents. In this dress he took his seat not upon the front Opposition bench but on the third row behind, close to a pillar supporting the gallery and near to the Speaker's chair.

Posthumous Memoirs of Sir Nathaniel William Wraxall, 1884

105

Fox's Duel

Fox's attacks on the North ministry aroused increasing resentment; one of Fox's ministerial victims, William Adam, relying on a garbled newspaper account, demanded from Fox a formal explanation. Horace Walpole reported:

FOX assured him he had meant nothing personal but had a right to dislocate his arguments, and Adam was satisfied; but on Sunday he sent a Scotch major to Fox to complain of the state of the debate in the newspapers and to desire Mr Fox would contradict and declare his good opinion of him. Fox returned for answer that he was not respon-sible for accounts in newspapers; that it was harder still if on their mis-representation he must give a good character of any man they abused: he again declared he had intended no offence, and that Mr Adam was welcome to show that declaration to anybody. After consult had, Adam returned that Mr Fox must print that recantation. 'Hold,' said Fox, 'not so far neither.' Oh, I forgot the principal circumstance of all, Adam added that his *friends* would not be satisfied under anything less than publication. At eight this morning they went into Hyde Park, Fox with Fitzpatrick, Adam with Major Humerstone for seconds: Adam fired and the ball wounded Charles Fox's side, though only slightly: he then fired, missed and said: 'Now, Mr Adam, are you satisfied?' Near as you are to the Tweed you will not guess the reply: 'No,' said Adam, 'you must still print that letter.' Nothing could be more unjust, more unfair; they had fought because Fox would *not* consent to that preten-sion; Fox, with the same firmness and temper with which he had con-ducted himself through the whole affair peremptorily refused, and the bloodhound again fired but missed, and then Fox fired into the air and it ended.

Horace Walpole's Correspondence with William Mason, ed. W.S. Lewis, 1955

Many other anecdotes are told of this affair. Fitzpatrick, comparing Adam's slight form with Fox's bulk, advised his principal to stand sideways. Fox replied: 'Why, I am as thick one way as the other.' He suffered merely a flesh wound in the thigh, and when reports spread that the ball had lodged in his groin and emasculated him for ever, Fox remarked: 'Mr Adam loaded his pistol with government contractor's powder, too weak to penetrate a thick Whig hide.'

106

How Parliament Works

On 3 April 1778 Boswell recorded a conversation at the Club on the House of Commons; the text is partly from his original diary, in which the names of the speakers are given (they were suppressed in his Life of Johnson).

Richard Brinsley Sheridan: 'I don't mean to flatter, Mr Burke, but when posterity reads one of your speeches it will be difficult to believe you took so much pains, knowing for certain it will have no effect, not one vote gained by it.' *Burke*: 'Waiving your compliment to me, I shall say in general that it is very well worth while to speak. A man who has vanity speaks to display his talents. And if a man speaks well, he gradually forms a consequence in the general opinion which sooner or later will have its political reward. Besides, though not one vote is gained, it has effect. We see, though an Act passes, it is modified, it is softened in such a manner that we see plainly the Minister has been told that Members are so sensible of its injustice or absurdity from what they have heard that it must be altered.' *Johnson*: 'And, Sir, there is a gratification of pride. Though we cannot out-vote them, we'll out-argue them. They shall not do wrong without its being shown both to themselves and the world.' *Burke*: 'The House of Commons is a mixed body. I except the Minority which I shall hold to be pure (smiling). But take just the Majority. It is a mass by no means pure, but neither is it wholly corrupt, though there is a proportion of corruption in it. There are many members who will not go all lengths; there are many who are in Parliament only to keep up the consequences of their families.' *Johnson*: 'We are all more or less governed by interest. But interest will not make us do anything whatever. In a case which admits of doubt, we try to think on the side for our interest, and come to act so. But the subject must admit of diversity of colouring. It must receive a colour on that side. In the House of Commons there are Members who will not vote what is grossly unjust or to keep wrong in countenance.' *Boswell*: 'There is surely a majority who have places, or want them.' *Burke*: 'True, Sir; that majority will always follow *Quo clamor vocat et turba faventium*.' *Boswell*: 'Well now, let us take the common phrase, Place-hunters. I thought they had hunted without regard to any thing, just as their huntsman, the Minister, leads, looking only to the prey.' *Gibbon*: 'But taking your metaphor, you know that in hunting there are few so desperately keen as to follow without reserve. Some do not choose to leap ditches and hedges and risk their necks, or gallop over steeps, or even to dirty themselves in bogs and mire.' *Boswell*: 'I am glad there are some good, quiet, moderate political hunters.' *Burke*: 'I believe in any body of men in England I should have been in the Minority; I have always been in the Minority.' *Sir Joshua Reynolds*: 'The House of Commons resembles a private company. How seldom is any man convinced by another's argument; passion and pride rise against it.' *Sheridan*: 'What would be the consequence if a Minister, sure of a majority in the House of Commons, should resolve that there should be no speaking at all upon his side?' *Burke*: 'He must soon go out. That has been tried; but it was found it would not do.'

Boswell in Extremes, 1776–8 and *Life of Johnson*

107

Hastings's Trial

In 1788, Edmund Burke and other leading Whigs succeeded in bringing an impeachment charge against Warren Hastings, Governor-General of Bengal. The trial opened before the House of Lords on 13 February 1788 and lasted until 1795, when Hastings was acquitted. Fanny Burney, one of the Queen's ladies, was present the first day.

THE business did not begin till near 12 o'clock. The opening of the whole then took place, by the entrance of the *Managers of the Prosecution*; all the company were already long in their boxes or galleries. I shuddered and drew involuntarily back when, as the doors were flung open, I saw Mr Burke, as Head of the Committee, make his solemn entry. He held a scroll in his hand and walked alone, his brow knit with corroding care and deep labouring thought—a brow how different to that which had proved so alluring to my warmest admiration when first I met him! so highly as he had been my favourite, so captivating as I had found his manners and conversation in our first acquaintance, and so much as I owed to his zeal and kindness to me and my affairs in its progress! How did I grieve to behold him now the cruel Prosecutor (such to me he appeared) of an injured and innocent man! Mr Fox followed next, Mr Sheridan, Mr Windham, Messrs Anstruther, Grey, Adam, Michaelangelo Taylor, Pelham, Colonel North, etc . . . When the Committee Box was filled the House of Commons at large took their seats on the green benches . . . Then began the procession, the Clerks entering first, then the lawyers according to their rank, and the peers, bishops and officers, all in their coronation robes; concluding with the Princes of the Blood—Prince William, son to the Duke of Gloucester coming first, then the Dukes of Cumberland, Gloucester and York, then the Prince of Wales; and the whole ending by the Chancellor, with his train borne.

Then they all took their seats. A Serjeant-at-Arms arose and commanded silence in the court on pain of imprisonment. Then some other officer, in a loud voice, called out as well as I can recollect words to this purpose: 'Warren Hastings, Esquire, come forth! Answer to the charges brought against you; save your bail or forfeit your recognisance!' Indeed I trembled at these words, and hardly could keep my place when I found Mr Hastings was being brought to the bar. He came forth from some place immediately under the Great Chamberlain's box and was preceded by Sir Francis Molyneux, Gentleman-Usher of the Black Rod; and at each side of him walked his bails, Messrs Sullivan and Sumner. The moment he came in sight, which was not for full ten minutes after his awful summons, he made a low bow to the Chancellor and court facing him. I saw not his face, as he was directly under me. He moved on slowly and, I think, supported between his two bails, to the opening of his own box; there, lower still, he bowed again; and then advancing to the bar he leant his hands upon it and dropped on his knees; but a voice in the same moment proclaiming he had leave to rise, he stood up almost instantaneously, and a third time profoundly bowed to the court.

What an awful moment this for such a man! A man fallen from such height of power to a situation so humiliating—from the almost unlimited command of so large a part of the Eastern World to be cast at the feet of his enemies, of the great tribunal of his country, and of the nation at large, assembled thus in a body to try and to judge him! Could even his prosecutors at that moment look on—and not shudder at least, if they did not blush?

The cryer, I think it was, made in a loud and hollow voice, a public proclamation: 'That Warren Hastings, Esquire, late Governor-General of Bengal, was now on his trial for high crimes and misdemeanours, with which he was charged by the Commons of Great Britain; and that all persons whatsoever who had sought to allege against him were now to stand forth.' A general silence followed and the Chancellor, Lord Thurlow, now made his speech . . . 'Warren Hastings, you are now brought into this court to answer the charges brought against you by the Knights, Esquires, Burgesses and Commons of Great Britain—charges now standing only as allegations, by them to be legally proved, or by you to be disproved. Bring forth your answers and your defence, with that seriousness, respect and truth due to accusers so respectable. Time has been allowed you for preparation, proportioned to the intricacies in which the transactions are involved, and to the remote distances whence your documents may have been searched and required. You will still be allowed bail, for the better forwarding your defence and whatever you can require will still be yours, of time, witnesses and all things else you may hold necessary. This is not granted you as any indulgence: it is entirely your due: it is the privilege which every British subject has a right to claim and which is due to every one who is brought before this high Tribunal.'

This speech, uttered in a calm, equal, solemn manner, and in a voice mellow and penetrating, with eyes keen and black, yet softened into some degree of tenderness while fastened full upon the prisoner—this speech, its occasion, its portent and its object, had an effect upon every hearer of producing the most respectful attention and, out of the Committee Box at least, the strongest emotions in the cause of Mr Hastings. Again, Mr Hastings made the lowest reverence to the court and leaning over the bar answered, with much agitation, through evident efforts to suppress it: 'My Lords—impressed—deeply impressed—I come before your Lordships, equally confident in my own integrity, and in the justice of the court before which I am to clear it' . . .

A general silence again ensued, and then one of the lawyers opened the cause. He began by reading from an immense roll of parchment the general charges against Mr Hastings, but he read in so monotonous a chant that nothing could I hear or understand, than now and then the name of Warren Hastings. During this reading, to which I vainly lent all my attention, Mr Hastings, finding it I presume equally impossible to hear a word, began to cast his eyes around the House, and having taken a survey of all in front and at the sides, he turned about and looked up; pale looked his face—pale, ill and altered. I was much affected by the sight of that dreadful harass which was written on his countenance. Had I looked at him without restraint, it could not have been without tears. I felt shocked too, shocked and ashamed to be seen by him in that place. I had wished to be present from an earnest interest in the business, joined to firm confidence in his powers of defence; but *his* eyes were not those I wished to meet in Westminster Hall . . .

I hope Mr Hastings did not see us; but in a few minutes more, while this reading was still continued, I perceived Sir Joshua Reynolds in the midst of the Committee. He, at the same moment, saw me also and not only bowed but smiled and nodded with his usual good humour and intimacy, making at the same time a sign to his ear, by which I understood he had no trumpet. [She was joined in her box by one of the prosecutors, William Windham MP.] After the first compliments he looked around him and exclaimed: 'What an assembly is this! How striking a *spectacle*! I had not seen half its splendour down there. You have it here to great advantage; you lose some of the Lords but you gain all the Ladies. You have a very good place here.'

'Yes; and I may safely say I make a very impartial use of it: for since here I have sat, I have never discovered to which side I have been listening.'

He laughed, but told me they were then running through the charges.

'And is it essential', cried I, 'that they should so run them through that nobody can understand them? Is that a form of law?'

He agreed to the absurdity; and then, looking still at the *spectacle*, which indeed is the most splendid I ever saw, arrested his eyes upon the Chancellor. 'He looks very well from hence,' cried he, 'and how well he acquits himself on these solemn occasions! With what dignity, what loftiness, what high propriety he comports himself!'. . . . Looking still on, he next noticed the two Archbishops. 'And see', cried he, 'the Archbishop of York, Markham—see how he affects to read the articles of impeachment, as if he was still open to either side! My good Lord Archbishop, your Grace might, with perfect safety, spare your eyes, for your mind has been made up upon this subject before ever it was

investigated. He holds Hastings to be the greatest man in the world—
for Hastings promoted his son in the East Indies!' . . .

   In the midst of the opening of a trial such as this, so important to the
country as well as to the individual who is tried, what will you say to a
man—a Member of the House of Commons—who kept exclaiming
almost perpetually, just at my side: 'What a bore! When will it be over?
Must one come any more? I had a great mind not to come at all. What's
that?—Lady Hawkesbury and the Copes?—Yes. A pretty girl, Kitty.
Well—when will they have done? I wish they'd call the question—I
should vote it a bore at once!'

The Diary of Fanny Burney, 13 February 1788

108

Lord North's Philosophy

WHEN Tommy Townshend furiously referred to Lord North as 'that
thing called a Minister', his Lordship was unruffled. He said: 'To be
sure'—patting his ample form—'I am a thing. So he said what was
true, and I could not be angry with him. But when he added "that they
call a Minister", he called me that thing which of all things he most
wished to be—and therefore I took it as a compliment.'

DENOUNCED for falling asleep during a Whig speech in which he
was termed 'a criminal', Lord North protested that 'it is cruel to deny
me a solace which most other criminals enjoy—a good night's sleep
before their execution'.

OF Alderman Sawbridge, presenting a petition from Billingsgate,
Lord North admitted: 'I cannot deny that the Honourable Gentleman
speaks not only the sentiments but the very language of his constituents.'

Traditional

109

Wilkes and the Press

ON the same evening, when the debate on the India Bill took place,
about eleven at night, Pepper Arden crossed the House, observing that

Wilkes was about to speak, and earnestly entreated him to be silent, as the House was just in the right State for a favourable vote, such as they both wished. 'My dear friend,' said Wilkes, 'I must speak, or I shall otherwise cut a most ridiculous Figure tomorrow morning. For two hours ago I sent the Speech, which I am about to make tonight, to the Press.'

Lord Eldon's Anecdote Book, eds. Anthony Lincoln and Robert McEwen, 1960

110

Silent Gibbon

Some of the greatest Englishmen have failed to make a mark in the House of Commons, or even to find the courage to speak. Edward Gibbon was an MP for eight sessions but never spoke, as his letters to J. B. Holroyd record:

25 February 1775: 'I am still a Mute; it is more tremendous than I imagined; the great speakers fill me with despair, the bad ones with terror.' *8 April 1775*: 'I have remained silent and notwithstanding all my efforts chained down to my place by some unknown invisible power.'

Letters of Edward Gibbon, ed. J. E. Norton, 1956

111

Muttering Gibbon

Friday 7 April (*1775*) I dined with [Johnson] at a Tavern, with a numerous company . . . One of the company suggested an internal objection to the antiquity of the poetry said to be Ossian's, that we do not find the wolf in it, which must have been the case had it been of that age. The mention of the wolf had led Johnson to think of other wild beasts, and while Sir Joshua Reynolds and Mr Langton were carrying on a dialogue about something which engaged them earnestly, he in the midst of it broke out 'Pennant tells of Bears'. They went on, which he being dull of hearing did not perceive or, if he did, was not willing to break off his talk; so he continued to vociferate his remarks, and *Bear* ('like a word in a catch', as Beauclerk said) was repeatedly heard at intervals, which coming from him who, by those who did not know him, had been so often assimilated to that ferocious animal, while we who were sitting around could hardly stifle laughter, produced a very ludicrous effect. Silence having ensued, he proceeded: 'We are told that the black bear is innocent; but I should not like to trust myself with him.' Mr Gibbon muttered, in a low tone of voice, 'I should not like to trust myself with *you*.'

Boswell, *Life of Johnson*

112

Pitt and Fox

SIR FRANCIS [BARING] said a good deal about the comparative abilities of Mr Pitt & Mr Fox as *orators*. He said that in his youth Mr Pitt had listened to *instruction* more than Mr Fox had done & had received great advantages from his father, Lord Chatham, & which Mr Fox, though the Son of a very able man, Lord Holland, had neglected to do. He said the consequence was that, from early habits of attention & correctness, Mr Pitt always spoke with a regular flow of expression, never requiring to go backward to correct Himself but proceeding with an uninterrupted stream of delivery. On the contrary, Mr Fox went *forward & backward*, not satisfied with his first expression, He would put it another way. The *undertone* of Mr Fox's voice was agreeable, almost musical, but when to give force & energy to his delivery He raised the tone of his voice it became squeaking & disagreeable. Sometimes he would speak in his *undertone* for half an hour together and Sir Francis thought with the best effect. On comparing them on the whole, Sir Francis seemed to think that in his oratory Mr Fox occasionally had flashes of genius beyond Mr Pitt, but he said the Character of an Orator was not to be determined by a single speech but by the effect produced in different debates, in two or three years, and then he granted that Mr Pitt had the ascendancy. Lord Dunlo (Earl of Clancarty) told Lawrence that he had sat behind Mr Pitt during debates in the House of Commons & had observed that notwithstanding his apparent coolness & self-possession, when Mr Fox had drawn towards the conclusion of a speech which Mr Pitt meant to answer, he could perceive that *the pulsation* in him had quickened and by its throbbings made the Hairs of His Head to shake.

Joseph Farington, *Diary*, 25 June 1806

113

The Great Economist

Adam Smith (1723–90) Professor of Logic at Glasgow University, published The Wealth of Nations *in 1776 and became one of the most influential economists who ever lived: and the first to be consulted by a British Prime Minister (William Pitt the Younger). But he was absent-minded.*

WHILE the Rt Hon. Charles Townshend was at Glasgow, the Doctor conducted him to see the different manufactures of the place; and particularly to a very flourishing tan-works. They were standing on a plank which had been laid across the tanning pit; the Doctor, who was talking warmly on his favourite subject, the division of labour, forgetting the precarious ground on which he stood, plunged headlong into the nauseous pool. He was dragged out, stripped, and covered with blankets, conveyed home in a sedan chair where, having recovered from the shock of this unexpected cold bath, he complained bitterly that he must leave life with all his affairs in the greatest disorder.

MR DAMER made him a visit the other morning as he was going to breakfast, and falling into discourse, Mr Smith took a piece of bread and butter, which after he had rolled round and round, he put into the teapot; and, when he had tasted it, he said it was the worst tea he had ever met with.

[WHEN Smith was a Commissioner of Customs, the Board of Customs] had in their service as porter a stately person, who, dressed in a huge scarlet gown covered in frogs of worsted lace, and holding in his hand a staff about seven feet high, used to mount guard before the Custom House when a Board was to be held. When each Commissioner entered, the porter went through a salute with his staff of office, and then marshalled the dignitary to the hall of meeting. This ceremony had been performed before the great economist perhaps 500 times.

Nevertheless one day, as he entered the Custom House, the motions of this porter seem to have attracted his eye, and on a sudden he began to imitate his gestures as a recruit does those of his drill sergeant. The porter having drawn up in front of the door, presented his staff as a soldier does his musket. Dr Smith, raising his cane, and holding it with both hands by the middle, returned the salute with the utmost gravity. The porter, much annoyed, levelled his weapon, wheeled to the right, stepping a pace back to give the Commissioner room to pass, lowering his staff at the same time in token of obeisance. Dr Smith, instead of passing on, drew up on the opposite side and lowered his cane to the same angle. The porter, much out of countenance, next moved upstairs with his staff upraised, while Dr Smith followed with his cane in precisely the same posture, and his whole soul apparently wrapped in the purpose of placing his foot exactly on the same spot of each step. At the door of the hall the porter again drew off, saluted with his staff, and bowed reverentially. Dr Smith again imitated his motions and returned his bow with the most profound gravity. Only when the Doctor entered the room was the spell under which he seemed to act broken and he was with some difficulty convinced that he had been doing anything extraordinary.

ACCORDING to Dr Rogers, Smith during his residence in Kirkaldy went out one Sunday morning in his dressing-gown to walk in the garden, but once in the garden he went onto the path leading to the turnpike road, and then to the road itself; along which he continued in a condition of reverie till he reached Dunfermline fifteen miles distant, just as the bells were sounding for church. The strange sound of the bells was the first thing that roused the philosopher from his meditation.

From *The Times*, 24 July 1790; John Rae, *Life of Adam Smith*, 1895; *Autobiography of the Rev Dr Alexander Carlyle of Inveresk 1722–1805*, 1860

114

Pitt, Fox and others frequently quoted from The Wealth of Nations. *But:*

IT was [my] good fortune to spend a day *tête-à-tête* with Mr Fox at St Anne's Hill. I mentioned . . . that I had never read Adam Smith's celebrated work on the Wealth of Nations. 'To tell you the truth', said Mr

Fox, 'nor I neither. There is something in all these subjects which
passes my comprehension; something so wide, that I could never
embrace them myself or find anyone else who did.'

Butler, Reminiscences

115

Pitt and Gibbon

*Chatham's second son, William Pitt, born in 1759, first came to public notice
in 1780, while a student at Lincoln's Inn. During the Gordon Riots, the
Northumberland Militia were quartered on the Inn, and during a dinner
given by its officers, the star guest was the historian Edward Gibbon. Bland
Burges, who was present, records:*

MR GIBBON, nothing loth, took the conversation into his own hands,
and very brilliant and pleasant he was during the dinner and for some
time afterwards. He had just concluded, however, one of his best
foreign anecdotes, in which he had introduced some of the fashionable
levities of political doctrine then prevalent, and with his customary tap
on the lid of his snuff-box was looking around to receive our tribute of
applause, when a deep-toned but clear voice was heard from the bottom of the table, very calmly and civilly impugning the correctness of
the narrative and the propriety of the doctrine of which it had been
made the vehicle. The historian, turning a disdainful glance towards
the quarter whence the voice proceeded, saw for the first time a tall,
thin and rather ungainly-looking young man, who now sat quietly eating some fruit. There was nothing very prepossessing or very formidable in his exterior but as the few words he had uttered appeared to
have made a considerable impression on the company, Mr Gibbon I
suppose thought himself bound to maintain his honour by suppressing
such an attempt to dispute his supremacy. He accordingly undertook
the defence of the propositions in question and a very animated debate
took place between him and his youthful antagonist Mr Pitt, and for
some time was conducted with great talent and brilliance on both
sides. At length the genius of the young man prevailed over that of his
senior who, finding himself driven into a corner from which there was
no escape, made some excuse for rising from the table and walked out
of the room. I followed him, and finding he was looking for his hat, I
tried to persuade him to return to his seat. 'By no means,' said he.

'That young gentleman is, I have no doubt, extremely ingenious and agreeable, but I must acknowledge that his style of conversation is not exactly what I am accustomed to, so you must positively excuse me.' And away he went in high dudgeon.

Selections from the Letters and Correspondence of Sir James Bland Burges,
Bart., ed. James Hutton, 1885

116

The Young Minister

Pitt entered the Commons, aged twenty-one, in January 1781 and his mai-
den speech on 26 February was given impromptu, after Members who were
anxious to test the merit of Chatham's son called on him by name. Afterwards
Burke declared: 'He is not a chip off the old block. He is the old block itself.' In
summer 1782 Pitt became Chancellor of the Exchequer and in December
1783, following the dismissal of the Fox–North coalition, Prime Minister. A
vignette by an eye-witness:

HE was not then much more than twenty-four years and a half old and consequently had not attained the age at which many individuals, under the testamentary dispositions of their parents, are still largely considered to be in a state of tutelage or minority. In the formation of his person he was tall and slender but without elegance or grace. His countenance, taken as a whole, did not display either the fine expression of character or the intellect of Fox's face, on every feature of which mind was more or less forcibly depicted. It was not until Pitt's eye lent animation to his other features, which were in themselves tame, that they lighted up and became strongly intelligent. Fox, even when quiescent, could not be mistaken for an ordinary man. In his manners, Pitt, if not repulsive, was cold, stiff and without suavity or amenity. He seemed never to invite approach or encourage acquaintance, though when addressed he would be polite, communicative and occasionally gracious. Smiles were not natural to him, even when seated on the Treasury bench where, placed at the summit of power, young, surrounded by followers, admirers and flatterers, he maintained a more sullen gravity than his antagonist exhibited who beheld around him only the companions of his political exile, poverty and privations. From the instant that Pitt entered the doorway [of the Commons] he advanced up the floor with a quick and firm step, his head

erect and thrown back, looking neither to the right nor to the left, not
favouring with a nod or a glance any of the individuals seated on either
side, among whom many who possessed £5,000 a year would have
been gratified even by so slight a mark of attention. It was not thus that
Lord North or Fox treated parliament.

Posthumous Memoirs of Sir Nathaniel William Wraxall, 1884

117

Pitt and the Whig Mob

*On 28 February 1784 Pitt was given the freedom of the City of London; his
brother, the Earl of Chatham, records what happened when he returned to the
West End:*

HE was attended by a great concourse of people, many of the better
sort, all the way down the Strand, as well as by a considerable Mob—
the Populace insisting on taking off the Horses and drawing the
Coach. A Mob is never very discreet and unfortunately they stopped
outside Carlton House and began hissing, and it was with some difficulty that we forced them to go on. As we proceeded up St James's
Street, there was a great Cry and an attempt made to turn the Carriage
up St James's Place to Mr Fox's house (he then lived at Lord North-
ington's) in order to break his windows and force him to light [them],
but which we at last succeeded in preventing their doing. I have often
thought that this was a trap laid for us, for had we got up ┼here into a
Cul de Sac, Mr Pitt's situation would have been critical indeed. This
attempt brought us rather nearer in contact with Brooks's, and the
moment we got opposite . . . a sudden and desperate attack was made
on the carriage . . . by a body of Chairmen armed with bludgeons,
broken chair-poles—many of the waiters and several of the gentlemen
among them.

They succeeded in making their way to the carriage and forced open
the door. Several desperate blows were aimed at Mr Pitt and I recollect
endeavouring to cover him as well as I could in his getting out of the
Carriage. Fortunately however by the exertion of those who remained
with us by the timely assistance of a Party of Chairmen and many
Gentlemen from White's, who saw his danger, we were extricated
from a most unpleasant situation and with considerable difficulty got
into some adjacent houses . . . and from thence to White's. The

Coachmen and the Servants were much bruised and the Carriage nearly demolished.

Letter from the Earl of Chatham to George Tomline, 1821, quoted in John Ehrman, *The Younger Pitt*, 1969

118

FOX denied he had played any part in the riot. He said that, at the time, he was in bed with his mistress, Mrs Armistead, 'who was prepared to prove it on oath'.

The Olio: A Collection of . . . Anecdotes . . . by the late Francis Grose, 1796

119

Pitt's Stoicism

In 1786 Pitt had to be operated on.

THE doctors found 'an encysted tumor' (on his face) and the celebrated John Hunter removed it in Downing Street. Pitt showed a sangfroid equal to the standards of a pre-anaesthetic age. He would not let Hunter tie his hands as was normally done, assured him he would not move and asked how long the surgeon would take. On being told six minutes he fixed his eyes on the Horse Guards clock and remained motionless until it was over, where he remarked cheerfully: 'You have exceeded your time by half a minute.'

Ehrman, *The Younger Pitt*

120

Pitt's Drinking

PITT'S apparent insensibility towards the other sex and his chastity formed one of the subjects on which the minority exhausted their wit, or rather their malevolence. . . . If, however, the Minister viewed women with indifference, he was no enemy to wine nor to the social conviviality of the table. His constitution, in which a latent and hereditary gout early displayed itself, which disorder, heightened by political distress, domestic and foreign, carried him off at forty-seven, always demanded the aid and stimulus of the grape. It was not therefore in him so much a gratification or an indulgence as a physical want, though he unquestionably yielded to its seductions without making any great effort at resistance.... Early in the autumn of 1784 he had indeed nearly fallen a victim to one of those festive meetings at which no severe renunciations were enjoined by the host or practised by the guests. Returning by way of frolic very late at night on horseback to Wimbledon from Addiscombe, the seat of Mr Jenkinson [later Lord Liverpool] near Croydon, where the party had dined, Lord Thurlow, who was then Chancellor, Pitt and Dundas found the turnpike gate situate between Tooting and Streatham thrown open. Being elevated above their normal prudence and having no servant near them, they passed through the gate at a brisk pace without stopping to pay the toll, regardless of the remonstrances or threats of the keeper of the turnpike who, running after them and believing them to belong to some highwaymen who had recently committed depredations on that road, discharged the contents of his blunderbuss at their backs. Happily he did no injury.

Wraxall, *Posthumous Memoirs*

121

Burke's Quarrel with Fox

Fox and Burke had been close political allies and personal friends for a quarter of a century; but by early 1791 their violently opposed views on the French Revolution threatened rupture, which came at three o'clock in the morning on 14 April:

FOX rounded off the debate with a sudden fatuous panegyric on the French Revolution. He said that the new French constitution was 'the most stupendous and glorious edifice of liberty which had been erected on the foundations of human integrity in any time or country'. Burke rose at once in a state of visible agitation but he was silenced by a loud and concerted clamour. Fox always regretted that Burke was prevented from replying at once, on the ground that his anger would not then have been bottled up, and permitted to ferment for a period of three weeks. [Finally on 6 May Burke got his opportunity.] In eloquent terms Burke was proceeding to describe the indignities to which the unfortunate King of France was at that moment being subjected when he was interrupted on a point of order. From that time he was continuously interrupted on points of order in a systematic and concerted manner. Fox's followers rose one after another and Burke, in an agony of rage, hurled at them the words of the maddened Lear:

> . . . the little dogs and all,
> Tray, Blanche and Sweetheart, see they bark at me!

Finally Fox himself rose and declared that the French Revolution was one of the most glorious events in the history of mankind. He complained that Burke had come down to the House, not to debate the clauses of the particular Bill which was then before the committee, but to ventilate a private quarrel of his own. He said that Burke himself had taught him that no revolt of any nation ever took place without provocation. The Rights of Man, which Burke ridiculed, were the foundation of every rational constitution, including our own. Why else had Burke and he rejoiced together at every success gained by Washington during the War of American Independence? Now the people of France had risen, as the Americans had risen before them. Why should Burke support the cause of liberty in the one case and not in the other? Why should he now seek to draw up an indictment against an entire people? . . . At hearing his own words and actions publicly twisted in this tendentious manner by a man with whom he had been intimate for nearly a quarter of a century, Burke's indignation reached boiling-point. He had for a long time disliked most of Fox's train of gilded youths, the Greys, the Grenvilles, the Pelhams, the Fitzpatricks, the Cokes, the Lambtons, whose ways of life were so different from his own. They, on their side, had never attempted to conceal the ignorant contempt with which they regarded Burke, whom they were always glad of an opportunity of baiting. At Brooks's, the social headquarters of the Whigs, Burke never touched a card: he left nothing behind him there except twelve years' accumulated arrears of subscription which were outstanding at his death. He was no gambler; he was no sportsman. He neither hunted nor shot; he cared nothing for the turf. He was an Irish upstart from the Catholic underworld across the Bristol Channel who had taken insufficient pains to accommodate himself to English ways and to manage English opinion. His speeches were mercilessly long; his brogue was teasing; his gestures ungainly; his voice harsh; his delivery indifferent. His zeal was offensive and unnatural; his manner violent almost to madness. Even his vaunted disinterestedness was probably hypocrisy. Had he not once been the paid Agent of the Colony of New York? Was he not known to have jobbed in the Funds? Were there not ugly rumours in circulation regarding his brother, and his cousin, whom he so much adored? He had bored the whole country with the politics of India and he had now challenged Fox, the darling of the Whigs, and the best of good fellows, on the subject of the internal affairs of France. What the French chose to do within their own borders was no concern of England and it was intolerable that England should now be dragged into another European war in order to suit one of the latest of Burke's whims.

The friendship between Burke and Fox had been one of the wonders of the age and has left its mark on English history. But it was essentially a political and intellectual friendship: it was often remarked that it appeared to begin and end at the entrance to the House of Commons. With splendid loyalty Burke had been content to see Fox, who was twenty years his junior, preferred over his head. Now it seemed as though the party which he had served so long, so faithfully and so unprofitably, was about to disown him altogether and strip him of the remnants of his reputation. His opinions were thrown back into his face, tortured into lying shapes and perilous misrepresentations. His grey hairs were derided and he was about to be driven in dishonour from a field on which he had battled all his life . . .

By God it was too much! England must at any cost be awakened from her false security. The French Revolution was no mere domestic concern of the French people: it was a plague worse than the Black Death which threatened to sweep the world. Already the first symptoms of infection had appeared in England and Burke felt himself inspired to stand forth once again as the champion of the liberties of Englishmen. When he rose to answer Fox, Burke began soberly and coolly, but most of the time he was speaking at white heat. At one point he turned to the astonished Chairman of Committee and exclaimed: 'I am not mad, most noble Festus, but speak the words of truth and soberness.' Burke complained that Fox had been heard with perfect composure by the whole House, whereas he himself was always being interrupted and called to order. He repudiated the charge of inconsistency: he had fought tyranny at home and in America; he would not fight it in France. The fact that in 1780 he had desired to limit the influence of the English Crown did not mean that he now wished to see that of the French Crown reduced to nothing. He had taken the side of the Americans because he had supposed them to be fighting not for speculative rights with a universal propagandist appeal, but for specific constitutional liberties which were the birthright of every Englishman. He declared that the supreme object of his life had been, and always would be, the defence of the constitutional liberties of Britain. He cited instances in which he had differed from Fox in former years and said that those differences had never threatened their friendship: 'It certainly is indiscretion, at any period, but especially at my time of life, to provoke enemies, or to give my friends occasion to desert me; yet if by a firm and steady adherence to the British constitution I am placed in such a dilemma I will risk all; and as public duty and public prudence instruct me, with my last words exclaim—"Fly from the French Revolution!" '

At that point Fox leant across and whispered audibly: 'There is no loss of friends.' 'I am sorry', Burke replied in a loud voice, 'but there is. I know the price of my conduct. I have done my duty at the price of my friend: our friendship is at an end.' The House was hushed while Burke concluded with a rapturous peroration in the course of which Fox and Pitt were pictured moving across the face of the Heavens like two flaming meteors, while the British constitution glowed like a fixed star, and the arm of the Almighty flung comets from their courses.

When Fox rose it was some minutes before he was able to speak: Tears trickled down his cheeks and he strove in vain to give utterance to feelings which dignified and exalted his nature. There was scarcely a dry eye in the House . . . Fox referred in moving terms to the favours he had received from Burke while he was still almost a boy; to the manner in which time had ripened their friendship; and to the familiar intimacy in which for twenty years at least they had lived: 'Nothing but the ignominious terms which my Right Honourable friend has heaped upon me—.' Here Burke interposed to say that he did not recollect any. 'My Right Honourable friend does not recollect the epithets,' Fox eagerly exclaimed. 'They are out of his mind; then they are completely and for ever out of mine. I cannot cherish a recollection so painfully and from this moment they are obliterated and forgotten.'

Unfortunately, Fox, who possessed a genius for debate, was quite unable to resist the temptation of attacking Burke by the unfair method of quoting from his printed speeches and writings, and giving to the selected contexts a garbled and even opposite meaning from that which they had originally borne. He did more: he even repeated some of the expressions used by Burke in his unguarded and convivial moments; he called them up in the shape of accusations and with a serious meaning attached to them which they were never intended to bear. In the light of such conduct Fox's olive-branch withered in his hands. Burke demanded whether his most inveterate enemy could have acted more unkindly towards him. The debate was closed without any reconciliation and Burke and Fox were thenceforward divided for ever.

Philip Magnus, *Burke: a Life*, 1936

122

Burke left the House that evening with his friend Therry, whose son later recorded:

WHEN the debate concluded, my father accompanied Mr Burke home. In the carriage, Mr Burke observed stern and inflexible silence; and after their arrival he only replied to questions in harsh and abrupt monosyllables. Gradually a strong fit of passion came over him; he threw up the windows of the apartment, flung open his coat and waistcoat and in a paroxysm of passion paced up and down the room until nearly 4 o'clock in the morning.

R. Therry, *A Letter to George Canning*, 1826

123

Burke at Home

Mrs Thrale visited Burke at his country house in Beaconsfield in 1774 and described the scene as one of 'shocking paradox'. The moral defender of Christian chivalry 'was the first man I had ever seen drunk or heard talk obscenely'. The house was filled with great statues and fine paintings but there was dirt and cobwebs everywhere; a liveried footman 'served tea with a cut finger wrapped in rags'. Lord Inchiquin gave another picture of Burke at home:

IN his house Burke is quiet if not contradicted in anything; but walks about it heedless of every concern; knowing nothing of servants, expenses, etc. He is very careless of his papers—would drop on the floor a paper though it contained treason as if it were a newspaper cover. Mrs Burke watches over everything—collects his scraps, arranges and dockets every paper. My dear Jane, will Burke say, I want such a paper—it is produced. As conversation proceeds, he calls for

others. She produces them. He asks sometimes for one which she cannot remember. Yes, yes, yes, my dear Jane—no contradiction, it must
be found. She examines.

Quoted in Dixon Wecter, *Edmund Burke and his Kinsmen*, 1939

124

Sheridan at Brighton

*In a memorandum written in 1821, Thomas Creevey described the Prince of
Wales and Sheridan at the Brighton Pavilion in 1805:*

SHERIDAN entered into whatever fun was going on at the Pavilion as
if he had been a boy, tho' he was then 55 years of age. Upon one
occasion he came into the drawing-room disguised as a police officer
to take up the Dowager Lady Sefton for playing at some unlawful
game; and at another time, when we had a phantasmagoria at the Pavilion and were all shut up in perfect darkness, he sat himself on the lap
of Madame Gerobtzoff, a haughty Russian dame, who made row
enough for the whole town to hear her. The Prince of course was
delighted with all this; but at last Sheridan made himself so ill with
drinking that he came to us soon after breakfast one day, saying he was
in a perfect fever, desiring he might have some table beer and declar-
ing that he would spend that day with us and send his excuses to
Bloomfield for not dining at the Pavilion. I felt his pulse and found it
going tremendously, but instead of beer we gave him some hot white
wine, of which he drank a bottle, I remember, and his pulse subsided
almost instantly . . . After dinner that day he must have drunk at least a
bottle and a half of wine. In the evening we were all going to the Pavilion, where there was to be a ball and Sheridan said he would go home,
i.e. to the Pavilion [where he slept] and would go quietly to bed. He
desired me to tell the Prince, if he asked me after him, that he was far
from well and was gone to bed.

So when supper was served at the Pavilion about 12 o'clock, the
Prince came up to me and said: 'What the devil have you done with
Sheridan today, Creevey? I know he has been dining with you and I
have not seen him the whole day.' I said he was by no means well and
had gone to bed; upon which the Prince laughed heartily, as if he
thought it all fudge, and then taking a bottle of claret and a glass, he

put them both in my hands and said: 'Now, Creevey, go to his bedside and tell him I'll drink a glass of wine with him and if he refuses admit he must be damned bad indeed! . . . When I entered Sheridan's bedroom, he was in bed and, his great fine eyes being instantly fixed upon me, he said: 'Come, I see this is some joke of the Prince and I am not in a state for it.' I excused myself as well as I could and as he would not touch the wine I returned without pressing it and the Prince seemed satisfied he must be ill. About two o'clock, however, the supper having been long over and everybody engaged in dancing, who should I see standing at the door but Sheridan, powdered as white as snow, as smartly dressed as ever he could be from top to toe . . . I joined him and expressed my infinite surprise at this freak of his. He said: 'Will you go with me my dear fellow into the kitchen and let me see if I can find a bit of supper?' Having arrived there he began to play off his cajolery upon the servants, saying if he was the Prince they should have much better accommodation etc, etc, so that he was surrounded by supper of all kinds, everyone waiting upon him. He ate away and drank a bottle of claret in a minute, returned to the ballroom, and when I left it between three and four he was dancing . . .

Among other persons who came to pay their respects to the Prince during the Autumn of 1805 was Mr Hastings, whom I had never seen before excepting at his trial in Westminster Hall. He and Mrs Hastings came to the Pavilion and I was present when the Prince introduced Sheridan to him, which was curious considering that Sheridan's parliamentary fame had been built upon his celebrated speech against Hastings. However, he lost no time in attempting to cajole old Hastings, begging him to believe that any part he had ever taken against him was purely political and that no one had a greater respect for him than himself, etc, upon which old Hastings said with great gravity that 'it would be a great consolation to him in his declining days if Mr Sheridan would make that sentence more publick.' But Sheridan was obliged to mutter and get out of such an engagement as well as he could.

The Creevey Papers, ed. Sir Herbert Maxwell, 1903

125

Byron on Sheridan

THE other night we were all delivering our respective and various opinions on [Sheridan] and other *hommes marquans*, and mine was this. 'Whatever Sheridan has done or chosen to do has been, *par excellence*, always the *best* of its kind. He has written the *best* comedy (School for Scandal), the *best* drama (*The Duenna*, in my mind, far before that St Giles lampoon, the *Beggar's Opera*), the best farce (the *Critic*—it is only too good for a farce) and the best Address (Monologue on Garrick), and, to crown all, delivered the very best Oration (the famous Begum speech) ever conceived or heard in this country.' Somebody told S. this the next day, and on hearing it he burst into tears.

> Byron's Journal for 17 December 1814, *Byron's Letters and Journals*, ed. Leslie A. Marchand, 1974

126

I DOUBT greatly if the English *have* any eloquence. . . . I never heard the speech which was not too long for the auditors—& not very intelligible except here and there—The whole thing is a grand deception—and as tedious and tiresome as may be to those who must be often present. I heard Sheridan only once—and that briefly—but I liked his voice—his manner—and his wit—he is the only one of them I ever wished to hear at greater length. In society I have met him frequently—he was superb!—he had a sort of liking for me—and never attacked me—at least to my face, and he did every body else—high names & wits and orators, some of them poets also. I have seen him cut up Whitbread—quiz Madame de Staël—annihilate Coleman—and do little less by some others (whose names as friends I do not set down) of good fame and abilities. Poor fellow! He got drunk very thoroughly and very soon—it occasionally fell to my lot to convey him home—no sinecure—for he was so tipsy that I was obliged to put on his cock'd hat for him—to be sure it tumbled off again and I was not myself so sober as to be able to pick it up . . . He told me that on the night of his grand success of his *School for Scandal*, he was knocked down and put into the Watch house for making a row in the street & being found intoxicated by the Watchmen. Latterly, when found drunk one night in the kennel and asked his *Name* by the Watchman, he answered: 'Wilberforce' . . .

Once I saw him cry at Robin's the Auctioneer's after a splendid dinner full of great names and high Spirits—I had the honour of sitting next to Sheridan—The occasion of his tears was some observation or other upon the subject of the sturdiness of the Whigs in resisting Office—& keeping to their principles—Sheridan turned round: 'Sir, it is easy for my Lord Grenville, or Earl Grey or Marquis Buckingham or Lord Holland with thousands upon thousands a year some of it either *presently* derived or *inherited* in Sinecures or acquisitions from the public money—to boast of their patriotism—& keep aloof from temptation— but they do not know from what temptations those have kept aloof who had equal pride—at least equal talent, & not unequal passions—& nonetheless—knew not in the course of their lives—what it was to have a shilling of their own'—And in saying this he wept.

I have more than once heard Sheridan say that he never 'had a shilling of his own'—to be sure he contrived to extract a good many of other people's. In 1815 I had occasion to visit my lawyer—in Chancery Lane—he was with Sheridan—After mutual greetings etc Sheridan retired first—Before recurring to my own business—I could not help enquiring that of S. 'Oh (replied the Attorneo) the usual thing—to stave off an action from his wine-merchant—my client.' 'Well (said I) & what do you mean to do?' 'Nothing at all for the present'—said he— 'would you have us proceed against old Sherry? What would be the use of it?' And here he began laughing and going over Sheridan's good gifts of Conversation. Now from personal experience I can vouch that my Attorneo is by no means the tenderest of men, or particularly accessible to any kind of impression out of the Statute or record—And yet Sheridan in half an hour had found a way to soften and seduce him in such a manner that I almost think he would have thrown his Client (an honest man with all the laws and some justice on his side) out of the window had he come in at the moment—Such was Sheridan!—he could soften an Attorney!—there has been nothing like it since the days of Orpheus.

Byron, 'Detached Thoughts', 15 October 1821, *Letters and Journals*

127

Sheridan's Greatest Speech

Though Burke introduced the impeachment proceedings against Hastings, it was Sheridan who ensured that the case was taken to the Lords, his oratory persuading even the Prime Minister, Pitt, and other Tories that there was a case to answer.

THE charge touching the spoliation of the Begums was brought forward by Sheridan, in a speech which was so imperfectly reported that it may be said to be wholly lost, but which was without doubt the most elaborately brilliant of all the productions of his ingenious mind. The impression which it produced was such as has never been equalled. He sat down, not merely amidst cheering but amidst the loud clapping of hands, in which the Lords below the bar and the strangers in the gallery joined. The excitement of the House was such that no other speaker could obtain a hearing; and the debate was adjourned. The ferment spread fast through the town. Within four and twenty hours, Sheridan was offered a thousand pounds for the copyright of the speech, if he would himself correct it for the press. The impression made by this remarkable display of eloquence on severe and experienced critics, whose discernment may be supposed to have been quickened by emulation, was deep and permanent. Mr Windham, twenty years later, said the speech deserved all its fame and was, in spite of some faults of taste, such as were seldom wanting either in the literary or in the parliamentary performances of Sheridan, the finest that had been delivered within the memory of man. Mr Fox, about the same time, being asked by the late Lord Holland what was the best speech ever made in the House of Commons, assigned the first place without hesitation to the great oration of Sheridan on the Oude charge.

Macaulay, *Essay on Warren Hastings*, 1839

128

Sheridan's Morning Dram

IN speaking of Sheridan's eloquence, Lord H[olland] said that the overstrained notions he had of perfection were very favourable to his style of oratory in giving it a certain elevation of tone and dignity of thought. Mr Fox thought his Westminster Hall speech trumpery and used to say it spoiled the style of Burke, who was delighted with it. Certainly in the report I have read of it it seems most trashy bombast. At Holland House, where he was often latterly, Lady H. told me he used to take a bottle of wine and a book up to bed with him always; the *former* alone intended for use. In the morning he breakfasted in bed and had a little rum or brandy with his tea or coffee; made his appearance between one and two and, pretending important business, used to set out for town but regularly stopped at the Adam and Eve public house for a dram. There was indeed a long bill run up by him at the Adam and Eve, which Lord H. had to pay.

Thomas Moore, *Journals*, 7 October 1818

129

Sheridan's Posthumous Arrest

Despite the immense sums he made as a playwright and theatre-owner, Sheridan was perpetually in debt and was hopelessly insolvent when he died in 1816.

THE remains of Sheridan were removed from Savile Row to the residence of his kinsman in Great George Street, Westminster. There they lay in state, to indulge the longing grief of the few friends who clung to his bleak and shattered fortunes. On the forenoon of the day fixed for their interment, a gentlemen dressed in deep mourning entered the house and requested of the attendant, who watched in the chamber of death, to allow him a last look at his departed friend. He professed to have known the deceased early in life; and to have undertaken a long journey in order to seize a parting glance of his pale features. The agony and earnestness with which the application was urged lulled the suspicions of the serving-man if any had arisen in his mind; and after a slight hesitation, it was assented to. The lid of the coffin was removed—the body unshrouded—and the death-chilled frame revealed to view. The gentleman gazed for some minutes upon it; and then, fumbling in his waistcoat pocket, produced a bailiff's 'wand', with which he touched the face and instantly declared, to the horror and alarm of the servant, that he had arrested the corpse in the King's name, for a debt of £500. Before the requisite explanations had been gone through, the funeral group had assembled. The circumstance was instantly made known to Mr Canning, who took Lord Sidmouth aside and begged his advice and assistance. Lest the delay might mar the progress of the sorrowful train, they generously agreed to discharge the debt; and two cheques for £250 each were given over to the bailiff and accepted of by him.

Sheridaniana, 1826

130

Thurlow's Ascendancy

Lord Thurlow (1731–1806), Lord Chancellor for nearly thirteen years, was one of the most ferocious and feared of eighteenth-century legal politicians. He entered the House of Lords as Lord Chancellor when only forty-six and soon made himself resented by frequent and peremptory speeches. In June 1779 the Duke of Grafton attempted to rebuke him, but on the ill-chosen ground of his plebeian extraction and recent admission to the peerage. An eye-witness described Thurlow's response:

HE rose from the woolsack and advanced slowly to the place from which the Chancellor generally addresses the House, then fixing on the Duke the look of Jove when he grasped the thunder, 'I am amazed', he said in a loud tone of voice, 'at the attack the noble Duke has made on me. Yes, my Lords'—considerably raising his voice—'I am amazed at his Grace's speech. The noble duke cannot look before him, behind him or on either side of him, without seeing some noble peer who owes his seat in this House to successful exertions in the profession to which I belong. Does he not feel that it is as honourable to owe it to these, as to being the accident of an accident? To all these noble lords the language of the noble duke is as applicable and as insulting as it is to myself. But I don't fear to meet it single and alone. No one venerates the peerage more than I do—but, my lords, I must say, that the peerage solicited me, not I the peerage. Nay more, I can say and I will, that as a Peer of Parliament, as Speaker of this right honourable House, as Keeper of the Great Seal, as guardian of his Majesty's conscience, as Lord High Chancellor of England, nay even in that character alone in which the noble duke would think it an affront to be considered—as A MAN—I am at this moment as respectable—I beg leave to add—I am at this moment as much respected—as the proudest peer I now look down upon.' The effect of this speech, both within the walls of parliament and out of them, was prodigious. It gave Lord Thurlow an ascendancy in the House which no Chancellor had ever possessed: it invested him in public opinion with a character of independence and honour; and this, though he was ever on the unpopular side in politics, made him always popular with the people.

> Butler's *Reminiscences*, quoted in Lord Campbell's *Lives of the Lord Chancellors*, 1846

131

Thurlow's Giveaway Hat

Thurlow was determined to hang on to the Chancellorship at any cost; and when in 1788 George III's madness made a regency and a change of government seem likely, Thurlow, while ostensibly supporting Pitt's efforts to avoid a regency, was secretly negotiating with the government's arch-enemy, the Prince of Wales.

MR Pitt was at first duped by such artifices, but suddenly came to the full knowledge of his colleague's perfidy. The exact circumstances of the discovery are variously related, although all accounts agree in stating that it took place at a meeting of the Ministers in Windsor Castle and that it arose from a mistake that the Chancellor made respecting his hat. . . . I have received the following account of the discovery from a quarter entitled to the most implicit credit: 'When a Council was to be held at Windsor to determine the course which Ministers should pursue, Thurlow had been there some time before any of his colleagues arrived. He was to be brought back to London by one of them and the moment of departure being come, the Chancellor's hat was nowhere to be found. After a fruitless search in the apartment where the Council had been held, a page came with the hat in his hand, saying aloud and with great *naïveté:* "My Lord, I found it in the closet of

His Royal Highness the Prince of Wales!" The other Ministers were
still in the hall, and Thurlow's confusion corroborated the inference
which they drew.'

Ibid.

132

*Thurlow nonetheless wept copiously when George III's affliction was debated
in the Lords.*

HE declared his fixed and unalterable resolution to stand by a Sovereign who, through a period of 27 years, had proved his sacred regard to
the principles which seated his family on the British throne. He at last
worked himself up to this celebrated climax: 'A noble viscount has, in
an energetic and eloquent manner, expressed his feelings on the
melancholy situation of his Majesty—feelings rendered more poignant
from the noble viscount's having been in habits of personally receiving
marks of indulgence and kindness from his suffering sovereign. My
own sorrow, my lords, is aggravated by the same cause. My debt of
gratitude is indeed ample for the many favours which have been graciously conferred upon me by his Majesty; AND WHEN I FORGET MY
SOVEREIGN, MAY MY GOD FORGET ME!' 'GOD FORGET YOU?' muttered
Wilkes, who happened then to be seated on the steps of the throne—
eyeing him askance with his inhuman squint and demoniac grin—'GOD
FORGET YOU? HE'LL SEE YOU D———D FIRST!'

Ibid.

133

Castlereagh's Suicide

*Lord Castlereagh, who had been Foreign Secretary since 1812, had succeeded
his father as 2nd Marquess of Londonderry in 1821: the following year he
committed suicide, as described by John Wilson Croker in a letter of
25 August 1822 to his friend Sir Benjamin Bloomfield:*

ON Friday he had his parting audience with the King, and his conversation towards the close became so incoherent and unhappy, that the

King that evening wrote to Lord Liverpool at Coombe to come to see him *directly*, but not to tell any one that he was coming, and not to see any soul till he should see him. You may judge of Lord Liverpool's surprise at receiving such a note, and with what strange thoughts he must have hastened to the King. His Majesty told him that Londonderry's mind was gone, and that when so strong and well-regulated an intellect was shaken, the consequences were likely to be proportionately serious. . . . I understand that the Duke of Wellington, who left town on Friday, had also observed something wrong, and had sent Dr Bankhead, Londonderry's favourite physician, to him. Dr Bankhead saw him at St James's Square on Friday evening, and now I shall give you *his* story. He found him labouring under a strong mental delusion, accompanied with fever. He had him cupped, which relieved him, and in the quiet of the evening it was thought he might go down to Cray with Lady Londonderry, Bankhead promising to follow next morning and stay till his Lordship was quite well.

He remained in bed all Saturday, and was kept as tranquil as possible. On Sunday (yesterday) he was much worse, a good deal of fever, heat, thirst, and an increase of delusion and wretchedness. He, however, grew less uncomfortable towards night, and it would seem that his state was not such as to prevent his sleeping as usual in Lady Londonderry's chamber. Dr Bankhead took leave of him about midnight, and retired to his own room, which was close to theirs. About seven this morning Dr Bankhead was called by Lady Londonderry's maid, who said my Lord wished to see him. The Doctor immediately rose and went into the bedroom, when he found Lord Londonderry had just gone into the dressing-room. He followed him and saw him standing with his face to the window (and of course his back to the Doctor) in his dressing-gown, with his head leaned back and his eyes fixed on the ceiling. 'My dear Lord', said he, 'why do you stand so?' 'O Bankhead', he said, 'I am glad you are there, let me fall into your arms; it is all over.' And he fell back into Bankhead's arms who then, for the first time, saw clenched in his right hand a small-bladed pen-knife, with which our unhappy friend had just divided by a deep cut the carotid artery, and with a sudden effusion of blood the body fell forward on the face, and Castlereagh expired without a struggle. Precautions had been taken to remove his pistols and razors from his dressing-room, but with a little nail-knife which he carried in his pocket-book, and which had escaped their vigilance, he executed his fatal purpose with, they tell me, anatomical accuracy.

Croker's Correspondence and Diaries, ed. Louis J. Jennings, 1884

134

How George IV Lived

HE lives a most extraordinary life—never gets up till six in the afternoon. They come to him and open the window curtains at six or seven o'clock in the morning; he breakfasts in bed, does whatever business he can be brought to transact in bed too; he reads every newspaper quite through, dozes three or four hours, gets up in time for dinner, and goes to bed between ten and eleven. He sleeps very ill and rings his bell forty times in the night; if he wants to know the hour, though a watch hangs close to him, he will have his valet de chambre down rather than turn his head to look at it. The same thing if he wants a glass of water; he won't stretch out his hand to get it. His valets are nearly destroyed . . . they cannot take off their clothes at night and hardly lie down. . . .

[Despite his debts and borrowing] He always had money. When he died they found £10,000 in his boxes and money scattered about everywhere, a great deal of gold. There were above 500 pocketbooks, of different dates, and in every one money—guineas, one pound notes, one, two or three in each. There never was anything like the quantity of trinkets and trash that they found. He had never given away or parted with anything. There was a prodigious quantity of hair—women's hair—of all colours and lengths, some locks with the powder and pomatum still sticking to them, heaps of women's gloves, *gages d'amour* which he had got at balls, and with the perspiration still marked on the fingers, notes and letters in abundance, but not much that was of any political consequence, and the whole was destroyed. . . . There are all the coats he had ever had for fifty years, 300 whips, canes without number, every sort of uniform, the costumes of all the orders in Europe, splendid furs, pelisses, hunting-coats and breeches, and among other things a dozen pair of corduroy breeches he had made to hunt in when Don Miguel was here. His profusion in these articles was unbounded because he never paid for them, and his memory was so accurate that one of his pages told me he recollected every article of dress, no matter how old, and that they were always liable to be called on to produce some particular coat or other article of apparel of years gone by. It is difficult to say whether in great or little things that man was most odious and contemptible.

Charles Greville, *Diary*, 19 March 1829, 8 September 1831, 3 August 1830

135

Busy Canning

The brilliant orator George Canning (1770–1827) was Foreign Secretary in 1807 and Prime Minister for four months in 1827.

CANNING'S industry was such that he never left a moment unemployed, and such was the clearness of his head that he could address himself almost at the same time to several different subjects with perfect precision and without the least embarrassment. He wrote very fast, but not fast enough for his mind, composing much quicker than he could commit his ideas to paper. He could not bear to dictate, because nobody could write fast enough for him; but on one occasion, when he had the gout in his hand and could not write, he stood by the fire and dictated at the same time a despatch on Greek affairs to George Bentinck and one on South American politics to Howard de Walden, each writing as fast as he could, while he turned from one to the other without hesitation or embarrassment.

Ibid., 9 August 1827

136

Goderich's Spouse

Frederick Robinson, Viscount Goderich, later Earl of Ripon (1782–1859), was perhaps the silliest Prime Minister and the only one whose government collapsed without meeting parliament.

. . . in the midst of all the squabbles which preceded the breaking up of his Administration [he] went whining to the King and said: 'Your

Majesty don't know what vexation I have at home, with my wife's ill-health etc.' The King, telling the story, said, 'God damn the fellow, what did he bother me about his wife for? I didn't want to hear all the stories about her health.' Lady Goderich was a principal cause of all his follies, she never left him any repose, sent for him twenty times a day, even from the midst of the cabinets, and he was weak and silly enough to give way to her fancies, for she had persuaded him that she should die if she was thwarted, which would have been the best thing that could have happened to him, for she is ridiculous, capricious and tiresome.

Ibid., 23 February 1830

137

Wellington on Pitt

THE Duke and I spoke of Pitt, lamenting his early death. 'I did not think', said the Duke, 'that he would have died so soon. He died in January 1806, and I met him at Lord Camden's in Kent, and I did not think that he seemed ill, in the November previous. He was extremely lively and in good spirits. It is true that he was by way of being an invalid at that time; a great deal was always said about his taking his rides, for he used then to ride 18 or 20 miles every day, and great pains were taken to send forward his luncheon, bottled porter, I think, and getting him a beefsteak or mutton-chop ready at some place fixed beforehand. That place was always mentioned to the party, so that those kept at home in the morning might join the ride there if they pleased. On coming home from these rides they used to put on dry clothes and to hold a Cabinet, for all the party were members of the Cabinet, except me and I think the Duke of Montrose. At dinner, Mr Pitt drank little wine; but it was at that time the fashion to sup, and he then took a great deal of port wine and water. In the same month I also met Mr Pitt at the Lord Mayor's dinner; he did not seem ill. On that occasion I remember he returned thanks in one of the best and neatest speeches I ever heard in my life. It was in very few words. The Lord Mayor had proposed his health as one who had been the Saviour of England and would be the Saviour of the rest of Euope. Mr Pitt then got up, disclaimed the compliment as applied to himself, and added,

England has saved herself by her exertions, and the rest of Europe will be saved by her example. That was all—he was scarcely up two minutes—yet nothing could be more perfect.'

Earl of Stanhope, Notes of Conversations with Wellington, 1831–51, 1888

138

The Iron Duke

LADY SALISBURY asked which was the greatest military genius, Marlborough or Napoleon? 'Why, I don't know—it is very difficult to tell. I can hardly conceive anything greater than Napoleon at the head of an army—especially a French army. Then he had one prodigious advantage—he had no responsibility—he could do whatever he pleased; and no man ever lost more armies than he did. Now with me the loss of every man told. I could not risk so much; I knew that if I ever lost five hundred men without the clearest necessity, I should be brought upon my knees to the bar of the House of Commons.'

Ibid.

139

ASKED what he thought of the Reformed Parliament, when for the first time he surveyed the new Members of Parliament from the Peers' Gallery, the Duke replied: 'I have never seen so many bad hats in my life.'

Sir William Fraser, Words on Wellington, 1889

140

GEORGE JONES RA, painter and Secretary of the Royal Academy, was always delighted when people mistook him for the Duke. When the Duke heard this, he said: 'Mistaken for me, is he? That is strange, for no one ever mistakes me for Mr Jones.' Shortly afterwards, however, he was accosted in Pall Mall by a minor official from a government office, who raised his hat and said: 'Mr Jones, I believe.' The Duke replied: 'Sir, if you believe that, you will believe anything.'

W. P. Frith, Autobiography, 1888

141

Wellington's Sayings

To the blackmailing publisher Joseph Stockdale, threatening to publish Harriette Wilson's Memoirs ('I have stopped the Press for the moment; but as the publication will take place next week, little delay can necessarily take place'): 'Publish and be damned.'

Denying he was Irish: 'Because a man is born in a stable, that does not make him a horse.'

To his officers at Waterloo: 'Hard pounding, this, gentlemen. Try who can pound the hardest.'

Pointing to a British infantryman: 'There, it all depends upon that article whether we do the business or not. Give me enough of it, and I am sure.'

On the army: 'People talk of their enlisting from their fine military feeling—all stuff—no such thing. Some of our men enlist from having got bastard children—some for minor offences—many more for drink; but you can hardly conceive such a set brought together, and it really is wonderful that we should have made them the fine fellows they are.'

In 1811 the Prince of Orange, accompanied by his English tutor, Mr Johnson, joined Wellington's staff. At dinner, the Duke described a moment of danger when he was caught 'like a rat in a bottle', *going on to explain the Indian conjuring trick in which muskrats were sucked into bottles by means of a vacuum created inside. Mr Johnson*: 'Either the rats must be very small or the bottles very large.' *The Duke, fiercely*: 'On the contrary, Sir, very small bottles and very large rats.'

Wellington did not say 'The Battle of Waterloo was won on the playing-fields of Eton.' He said: 'I really believe I owe my spirit of enterprise to the tricks I used to play in the garden' (*of his Eton boarding-house*).

To a mob which forced him to cheer Queen Caroline: 'God save the Queen, and may all your wives be like her!'

To FitzRoy Somerset, urging British military preparedness: 'There is no such thing as a *little War* for a great Nation.'

To the Austrian diplomat Philip von Neumann: 'There is nothing worse than a battle won, except a battle lost.'

After Waterloo: 'By God! I don't think it would have done if I had not been there.'

When Queen Victoria asked him how they should get rid of the sparrows which infested the Crystal Palace: 'Try sparrow-hawks, Ma'am.'

On hearing the names of Palmerston's 1851 Cabinet: 'Who—who?'

Explaining why he supported Peel's repeal of the Corn Laws in 1846: 'I am the retained Servant of the Sovereign of this Empire. A good government is more important than Corn Laws.'

142

Wellington and the Mob

APSLEY HOUSE was stoned for the second time in one year, on 12 October 1831. This time the Duke was at home. In broad daylight the stones came hurtling through the plate-glass windows for fifty minutes before the police arrived on the scene. One narrowly missed the Duke's head as he sat at his writing-table and broke a glass-fronted bookcase behind him; another cut through Lady Lyndhurst's portrait by Wilkie, hanging on the wall. The garden was full of stones, though the stone-throwers themselves were kept outside the railings by the sight of armed men posted round the house. Having withdrawn to the Park, the mob circled menacingly round the Achilles statue but found it too heavy to overturn. 'It is now five o'clock, and beginning to rain a little', the Duke wrote to Mrs Arbuthnot from his beleaguered citadel, giving her a blow-by-blow account of the affair; 'and I conclude that the Gentlemen will now go to their Dinners' . . .

On Waterloo Day, 18 June 1832, a mob lay in wait for the Duke while he was sitting to Pistrucci at the Mint. They greeted him as he emerged with such apt slogans as 'Bonaparte for ever!' and, refusing to be shaken off, gave him the longest five-mile ride of his life. There were critical moments when he sighted loose paving-stones and then a loaded coal-cart. 'Here's the artillery coming up', he joked, 'we must look out.' But the mob were too intent on their quarry to notice the coal-cart and by now he had acquired a small bodyguard to save him from being dragged from his horse. Two Chelsea Pensioners had offered their services. 'Then keep close to me now', he said, ordering them to stand with their backs against his stirrups whenever his horse was stopped. A magistrate and some police joined his escort, a man in a buggy protected his rear, and after failing to give the mob the slip by a diversion through Lincoln's Inn, he reached clubland to find the worst was over. The men in the bay-windows marvelled at the set face looking straight ahead. A *'visage de fer'* was one's only choice, as he told Mrs Arbuthnot two months later, apropos of life in general. They said that the iron mask had slipped a little when an apothecary with whom he had had dealings rushed out of Surgeon's Hall shouting 'Waterloo, Waterloo!' and he himself admitted being touched by the many women who waved their handkerchiefs from upper windows and implored him to come indoors. But he would not stop. 'If I were to get in, in what manner was I to get out again?' At last he reached Apsley House, and turning to Lord St Germans, who had joined him outside the United Services Club, raised his hat: 'An odd day to choose. Good morning!' Each window of Apsley House had its own iron shutter, behind which the broken glass of October 1831 had not been replaced. The glass was mended in time for the Waterloo Banquet of 1833, but the Duke retained the shutters and to the end of his life was apt to raise his hat ironically and point towards them if a crowd began cheering him.

Elizabeth Longford, *Wellington: Pillar of State*, 1972

143

The Passing of the Great Reform Bill

The Reform Bill passed its second reading on 22 March 1831, by 302 to 301. Macaulay describes the scene in a letter of 30 March 1831 to Thomas Flower Ellis:

SUCH a scene as the division of last Tuesday I never saw, and never expect to see again. If I should live fifty years the impression of it will be as fresh and sharp in my mind as if it had just taken place. It was like seeing Caesar stabbed in the Senate House, or seeing Oliver taking the mace from the table, a sight to be seen only once and never to be forgotten. The crowd overflowed the House in every part. When the strangers were cleared out and the doors locked we had six hundred and eight members present, more by fifty than ever were at a division before. The Ayes and Noes were like two vollies of cannon from opposite sides of a field of battle. When the opposition went out into the lobby,—an operation by the bye which took up twenty minutes or more,—we spread ourselves over the benches on both sides of the House. For there were many of us who had not been able to find a seat during the evening. When the doors were shut we began to speculate on our numbers. Every body was desponding. 'We have lost it. We are only two hundred and eighty at most. I do not think we are two hundred and fifty. They are three hundred. Alderman Thompson has counted them. He says they are two hundred and ninety-nine.' This was the talk on our benches. I wonder that men who have been long in parliament do not acquire a better coup d'œil for numbers. The House when only the Ayes were in it looked to me a very fair house—much fuller than it generally is even on debates of considerable interest. I had no hope however of three hundred. As the tellers passed along our lowest row on the left-hand side the interest was insupportable—two hundred and ninety one—two hundred and ninety two—we were all standing up and stretching forward, telling with the tellers. At three hundred there was a short cry of joy, at three hundred and two another—suppressed however in a moment. For we did not yet know what the hostile force might be. We knew however that we could not be severely beaten. The doors were thrown open and in they came. Each of them as he entered brought some different report of their numbers. It must have been impossible, as you may conceive, in the lobby, crowded as they must have been, to form any exact estimate. First we heard that they were three hundred and three—then the number rose to three hundred and ten, then went down to three hundred and seven. Alexander Baring told me that he had counted and that they were three hundred and four. We were breathless with anxiety, when Charles Wood who stood near the door jumped on a bench and cried out, 'They are only three hundred and one'. We set up a shout that you might have heard to Charing Cross—waving our hats—stamping against the floor and clapping our hands. The tellers scarcely got through the crowd—for the house was thronged up to the table, and all the floor was fluctuating with heads like the pit of a theatre. But you might have heard a pin drop as Duncannon read the numbers. Then again the shouts broke out—and many of us shed tears—I could scarcely refrain. And the jaw of Peel fell; and the face of Twiss was as the face of a damned soul; and Herries looked like Judas taking his neck-cloth off for the last operation. We shook hands and clapped each other on the back, and went out laughing, crying, and huzzaing into the lobby. And no sooner were the outer doors opened than another shout answered that within the house. All the passages and the stairs into the waiting rooms were thronged by people who had waited till four in the morning to know the issue. We passed through a narrow lane between two thick masses of them; and all the way down they were shouting and waving their hats; till we got into the open air. I called a cabriolet—and the first thing the driver asked was, 'Is the Bill carried?'—'Yes, by one.' 'Thank God for it, Sir.'

> *Letters of Thomas Babington Macaulay, March 1831–Dec. 1833*, ed. Thomas Pinney, 1974

144

The Sailor King

[William IV's] ignorance, weakness and levity put him in a miserable light, and prove him to be one of the silliest old gentlemen in his dominions; but I believe he is mad, for yesterday he gave a great dinner to the Jockey Club, at which (notwithstanding his cares) he seemed in excellent spirits; and after dinner he made a number of speeches, so ridiculous and nonsensical, beyond all belief but to those who heard them, rambling from one subject to another, repeating the same thing over and over again, and altogether such a mass of confusion, trash and imbecility as made one laugh and blush at the same time . . . While the Duke [of Wellington] and Lyndhurst were with him, he said, 'I have been thinking that something is wanting with regard to Hanover. Duke, you are now my Minister, and I beg you will think of this; I should like to have a slice of Belgium, which would be a convenient addition to Hanover. Pray remember this.'

. . . . The King invited the Duchess of Kent [mother of Princess Victoria] to go to Windsor on the 12 August to celebrate the Queen's birthday . . . She sent word she wanted to keep her own birthday at Claremont on the 15th, took no notice of the Queen's birthday but said she would go to Windsor on the 20th. This put the King in a fury; he made, however, no reply, and on the 20th he was in town to prorogue Parliament, having desired that they would not wait dinner for him at Windsor. After the prorogation he went to Kensington Palace to look about it; when he got there he found that the Duchess of Kent had appropriated to her own use a suite of apartments, seventeen in

number, for which she had applied last year, and which he had refused
to let her have. This increased his ill-humour, already excessive. When
he arrived at Windsor and went into the drawing-room (at about ten
o'clock at night), where the whole party was assembled, he went up to
the Princess Victoria, took hold of both her hands and expressed his
pleasure at seeing her there and his regret at not seeing her oftener.
He then turned to the Duchess and made her a low bow, almost
immediately after which he said that 'a most unwarrantable liberty had
been taken with one of his palaces; that he had just come from Kensington, where he found apartments had been taken possession of not
only without his consent, but contrary to his commands, and that he
neither understood nor would endure conduct so disrespectful to him'.
This was said loudly, publicly and in a tone of serious displeasure. It
was, however, only the muttering of the storm which was to break the
next day. Adolphus Fitzclarence went into his room on Sunday morning and found him in a state of great excitement. It was his birthday,
and though the celebration was what was called private, there were a
hundred people at dinner, either belonging to the Court or from the
neighbourhood. The Duchess of Kent sat on one side of the King and
one of his sisters on the other, the Princess Victoria opposite . . . After
dinner, by the Queen's desire, 'His Majesty's health and long life to
him' was given, and as soon as it was drunk he made a very long
speech, in the course of which he poured forth the following extraordinary and *foudroyante* tirade: 'I trust in God that my life may be spared
for nine months longer, after which period, in the event of my death,
no regency would take place. I should then have the satisfaction of
leaving the royal authority to the personal exercise of that young lady
(pointing to the princess) the heiress presumptive of the Crown, and
not in the hands of a person near me, who is surrounded by evil
advisers, and who is herself incompetent to act with propriety in the
station in which she would be placed. I have no hesitation in saying that
I have been insulted—grossly and continually insulted—by that person, but I am determined to endure no longer a course of behaviour so
disrespectful to me. Amongst many other things I have particularly to
complain of the manner in which that young lady has been kept away
from my Court; she has been repeatedly kept away from my drawing-
rooms; at which she ought always to have been present, but I am fully
resolved that this shall not happen again. I would have her know that I
am King, and I am determined to make my authority respected, and
for the future I shall insist and command that the Princess do upon all

occasions appear at my Court, as it is her duty to do' . . . This awful
philippic (with a great deal more which I forget) was uttered in a loud
voice and excited manner. The Queen looked in great distress, the
Princess burst into tears, and the whole company was aghast. The
Duchess of Kent said not a word. Immediately after they rose and
retired, and a terrible scene ensued; the Duchess announced her
immediate departure and ordered her carriage, but a sort of reconciliation was patched up and she was prevailed upon to stay till the next
day . . . It was an unparalleled outrage from a man to a woman, from a
host to his guest, and to the last degree unbecoming the situation they
both of them fill.

                              Greville, *Diary*, 17 May 1832, 21 September 1836

145

Sacking Ministers, 1834

*When Viscount Melbourne succeeded Earl Grey as Prime Minister in 1834,
he found himself obliged to sack three of his most powerful colleagues, the Earl
of Durham, the Marquess of Wellesley, and the Lord Chancellor, Lord
Brougham.*

DURHAM was packed off to Russia again; Wellesley was fobbed off
with a court appointment; and Brougham was not offered a job at all.
The last two protested violently. Wellesley even talked of challenging
Melbourne to a duel. Melbourne went to see him. 'His language',
related the outraged Wellesley afterwards, 'was rough, vulgar and such
as has never been employed from a person in his station to one in
mine.' However in spite of this there was no more talk of a duel; nor
was Lord Wellesley promoted.

Brougham was a harder nut to crack. The trouble with him had
started as soon as Melbourne left office. Brougham had heard that his
late colleagues were talking against him; he wrote angrily to Melbourne to ask why. He got a plain answer. 'It is a very disagreeable
task', Melbourne said, 'to have to say to a statesman that his character
is injured in the public estimation; it is still more unpleasant to have to
add that you consider this to be his own fault; and it is idle to expect to
be able to convince almost any man, and more particularly a man of
very superior abilities, and with unbounded confidence in those abilities, that this is true. I must, however, state plainly that your conduct

was one of the principal causes of the dismissal of the late ministry; and that it forms the most popular justification of that step.' Brougham demanded details. Not without zest, Melbourne provided them. 'You ask for specific charges. Allow me to observe that there may be a course and series of very objectionable conduct, there may be a succession of acts which destroy confidence and add offence to offence, and yet it would be difficult to point to any marked delinquency. I will, however, tell you fairly that, in my opinion, you domineered too much, you interfered too much with other departments, you encroached upon the provinces of the Prime Minister, you worked, as I believe, with the Press in a manner unbecoming to the dignity of your station, and you formed political views of your own and pursued them by means which were unfair towards your colleagues . . . Nobody knows and appreciates your natural vigour better than I do. I know also that those who are weak for good are strong for mischief. You are strong for both, and I should both dread and lament to see those gigantic powers which should be directed to the support of the state exerted in the contrary and opposite direction.' To soften the blow he ended his letter on a friendlier note: 'I can only add that whatever may be your determination, no political difference will make any change in the friendship and affection which I have always felt and will continue to feel for you.' However, he had already decided not to take Brougham back. 'If left out he would be dangerous,' he said, 'but if taken in he would be simply destructive.' Brougham was so obsessively vain that despite all Melbourne's home-truths, he was dumbfounded when he actually heard he was not going to get a place. His nose twitching more violently than ever, he strode round to Melbourne's house, fulminating wrath and demanding redress. 'Do you think I am mad?' he kept on shouting furiously, 'do you think I am mad?' 'God damn you,' said Melbourne, 'you won't get the Great Seal, and that's the end of it.'

Lord David Cecil, *Lord M: or the Later Life of Lord Melbourne*, 1954

146

Cabinet Solidarity

IT had always been one of [Melbourne's] principles that a wise statesman compromised with a movement once it had become too strong and too widespread to be checked without an explosion. He behaved over the Corn Laws as he had over the Reform Bill. All the same he could not bring himself to feel much interested in how they should be modified. . . . Absent-minded and indifferent, he sat through one Cabinet meeting after another while his colleagues wrangled interminably about fixed duties and sliding scales. At last in March [1841], they came to an agreement and took their leave. As they went downstairs, they heard the Prime Minister's voice calling to them: 'Stop a bit,' he said, 'what did we decide? Is it to lower the price of bread or isn't it? It doesn't matter which, but we must all say the same thing.'

Ibid.

147

Richard Monckton Milnes, Lord Houghton

MONCKTON MILNES was a good-natured fellow, and not naturally bad-hearted; he was highly instructed and very clever. But he was always ridiculous, from an insane vanity . . . When I published *Coningsby*, he complained to me that I had not introduced his character among the Young England group; he spoke to me on this matter with great earnestness—tears in his eyes—I had never appreciated him, and all that sort of thing . . . I at length promised that, if the opportunity offered, I would remember his wish. Accordingly, when I wrote *Tancred*, in which the Young England group reappeared, I sketched the character of Vavasour, and I made it as attractive as I could consistent with that verisimilitude necessary. . . . His passion was office. He wanted to sit on the Treasury Bench, with folded arms, and to be a man of business. He was, unfortunately, short, with a face like a Herculaneum Masque, or a countenance cut out of an orange. He never caught the House of Commons tone. Too easy and familiar in Society, the moment he was on his legs in St Stephens, he was nervous, took refuge in pomposity, and had no flow; a most elaborate style, and always recalling his words. His irresistibly comic face, becoming every moment more serious, produced the effect of some celebrated droll, Liston or Keeley, and before he had proceeded five minutes, though he might be descanting on the wrongs of Poland or the rights of Italy, there was sure to be a laugh.

Disraeli, Memorandum written in 1860s, quoted in W. F. Monypenny and G. E. Buckle, *Life of Benjamin Disraeli, Earl of Beaconsfield*, 1910–12

148

Audacious Palmerston

17 February 1835. The other night I met some clerks in the Foreign Office to whom the very name of Palmerston is hateful, but I was suprised to hear them give ample testimony to his abilities. They said that he wrote admirably and could express himself perfectly in French, very sufficiently in Italian and understood German; that his diligence and attention were unwearied—he read everything and wrote an immense quantity; that the foreign ministers (who detest him) did him justice as an excellent man of business.

Greville, *Diary*

149

Palmerston was in office forty-eight years, probably longer than any other British politician; as a rule he worked from 7 a.m. to midnight and insisted that his staff be equally diligent. Consuls were rebuked for laziness, bad handwriting, and using foreign words; one had his dispatch returned for recopying on the grounds that his ink was inferior; Foreign Office clerks were kept working late into the night to suit his convenience, forbidden to smoke in the office and often terrorized by a man fond of snooping round the corridors; when Palmerston lost his seat as well as his office in 1841, the clerks subscribed to have the Foreign Office illuminated. Foreign diplomats were treated equally harshly. He was three-quarters of an hour late for a dinner given by the Turkish Ambassador, whom he dismissed as 'a greasy, stupid old Turk . . . one of Bluebeard's attendants'; he kept Talleyrand hanging about for over an hour in his ante-room, and the Russian Ambassador, Pozzo di Borgo, had to wait two hours, perhaps because he had once been the lover of Palmerston's mistress, Lady Cowper. It was a London saying 'the Palmerstons always miss the soup'; they kept even the Queen waiting, his excuse being the perfunctory: 'Public business must be attended to, Ma'am'; this was one reason she disliked him so much.

28 August 1853 . . . Nothing will induce Her Majesty to have Palmerston. . . . There are old offences, when he was at the Foreign Office, which sunk deep into her mind, and besides this the recollection of his conduct before her marriage, when in her own palace he made an attempt on the person of one of her ladies, which she very justly resented as an outrage to herself. Palmerston, always enterprising and audacious with women, took a fancy to Mrs Brand (now Lady Dacre) and at Windsor Castle, where she was in waiting and he a guest, he marched into her room one night. His tender temerity met with an invincible resistance. The lady did not conceal his attempt and it came to the Queen's ears. Her indignation was somehow pacified by Melbourne, then all-powerful, and who on every account would have abhorred an *esclandre* in which his colleague and brother-in-law would have so discreditably figured. Palmerston got out of the scrape with his luck, but the Queen has never forgotten and will never forgive it.

Ibid.

150

The Queen and Prince Albert came to believe it was a case of attempted rape. As Albert put it to Lord John Russell:

. . . how could the Queen consent to take a man as her chief adviser and confidential counsellor in all matters of State, religion, society, Court, etc., etc., he who as her Secretary of State and while a guest under her roof at Windsor Castle had committed a brutal attack upon one of her ladies? Had at night by stealth introduced himself into her apartment, barricaded afterwards the door and would have consummated his fiendish scheme by violence had not the miraculous efforts of his victim and such assistance attracted by her screams saved her?

Quoted in *Regina v. Palmerston*, ed. Brian Connell, 1962

151

In fact, Palmerston claimed he went to Mrs Brand's room by mistake, thinking it was occupied by another lady who was eagerly awaiting him; and as soon as he discovered his error left without argument. However, he was quite capable of forcing the pace. Lady Stanley complained of his 'brusque, impudent' way of making love to married women: 'Ha, ha! I see it all—beautiful woman—neglected by her husband—allow me, etc.' Palmerston continued to make passes at women into his eighties, while still Prime Minister, and indulging in a variety of other physical activities, including copious eating.

Speaker Denison noted his appetite, in his eighty-second year, at the pre-Session Dinner.

HE ate two plates of turtle soup; he was then served very amply to cod and oyster sauce; he then took a pâté; afterwards he was helped to two very greasy-looking entrées; he then despatched a plate of roast mutton (two slices) . . . there then appeared before him the largest, and to my mind the hardest, slice of ham that ever figured on the table of a nobleman, yet it disappeared just in time to answer to enquiry of the butler, 'Snipe or pheasant my Lord?' He instantly replied 'Pheasant', thus completing his ninth dish of meat at that meal.

John Evelyn Denison, Viscount Ossington, Notes from My Journal when Speaker of the House of Commons, 1899

152

Disraeli and Lady Sykes

Disraeli's first political patron was the Tory Lord Chancellor, Lord Lynd-hurst, a notorious womanizer, with whom he shared the favours of Henrietta, wife of Sir Francis Sykes, Bart. She was the original of the heroine of Disraeli's novel Henrietta Temple *(1837). Her letters to Disraeli turned up in 1882, after his death, when his solicitor, Sir Philip Rose, was arranging his papers. Rose left this memorandum to Disraeli's secretary and executor, Lord Rowton.*

Very Private and Confidential
For Lord Rowton's Eye alone—and then to be destroyed.
The Sykes and Bolton Correspondence

THE letters in the Dossier relate to the intimacy that existed, from 1833 to 1836, between [Disraeli] and the writer, Lady Sykes, wife of Sir Francis Sykes, Bart., which materially affected D's health, and nearly shipwrecked his career. Few other men could have had the necessary force of will to escape from such an entanglement. There are a mass of letters undated, which is not worth while to put in order, but suff⋅ are dated to show the nature and progress of the connection up to its final denouement, and the disgraceful exposure of the lady. The positive assertion at the time, that Lady Sykes was the mistress both of D. and also Lord Lyndhurst was evidently true, but by which of the two she was introduced to the other, there is no evidence to show. The allegation, at the time, was that D. had introduced her to Lord L. and made use of the influence she acquired over Lord L. to forward his own advancement. I can well remember the scandal in the County at this connection; and especially at the visit of Lady S. to Bradenham, accompanied by Lord L., and the indignation aroused in the neighbourhood at D. having introduced his reputed mistress, and her Paramour, to his *home*, and made them the associates of his *Sister*, as well as his Father and Mother. It did much harm at the time & to shew how unfavourable impressions linger long afterwards, I have had it thrown in my teeth by influential County people within very recent years, that this was an act which never would be forgotten and which all D's subsequent career could never obliterate. The family letters of this period shew, however, that the anxiety for this visit was more on the part of his own family than of himself, and that it was at his Sister's insistence the invitation was given which it would probably have been more embarrassing to him to have refused than accepted.

The correspondence extends up to the final denouement when Lady Sykes, after the intimacy with D. had ceased, was caught in the arms of Maclise, the Artist, in her own Bed, in her Husband's house in Park Lane. I remember reading the crucial announcement of this exposure with Sir F. Sykes's signature attached to it on the front page of the Morning Chronicle or some other London newspaper. No proceedings for a Divorce, however, were persevered in, as Sir F. Sykes had committed himself with Mrs Clara Bolton, the wife of a Doctor of that name, who also lived in Park Lane, and with whom D. was also on intimate terms, and for some time previously to the break-up, Mrs Bolton had been living, on and off, under Sir F. Sykes's protection and, as I understood at the time, with the Husband's knowledge and consent, who was said to derive a pecuniary benefit from the connection. It is unnecessary now to enquire but I think there is some internal evidence in the letters that the nature of the intimacy between D. and 'Henrietta' was also known to and acquiesced in by Sir F. Sykes.

When Sir Robert Peel formed his Govt. [in 1841] I have heard it was currently reported that the notoriety of D's connection with Lady S. and of Lord L's alleged participation in it operated to prevent the offer of office to D.

Clara Bolton: Some letters by this Lady are put up separately in this bundle. By members of D's family she was looked upon as his mistress. She also gained an introduction to Bradenham, but I believe there had been a previous acquaintance between the Boltons and Disraelis in London.

There is, among [Disraeli's] papers a mutilated diary referring to his intimacy with 'Henrietta' and from a very hasty glance at its contents, when the Book was found, I think it will prove how great was his desire to be extricated from the connection, under a conviction that it was injuring his Health, and would, if continued, be fatal to his prospects . . . I submit to Lord Rowton that all the Sykes and Bolton Correspondence and their Memo. should at once be destroyed.

Quoted in B. R. Jerman, *The Young Disraeli*, 1960

153

Rowton did not destroy the letters. One of them gives a candid picture of the Lady Sykes–Disraeli–Sir Francis Sykes–Mrs Bolton quartet; it was written by Henrietta to Disraeli after Mrs Bolton had made a determined effort to exclude Disraeli from the arrangements, and Lady Sykes had gone to her house to have it out:

I WAS vexed, my own Amin, to have such a short minute to write to you. But yesterday was fully occupied as you shall hear. I wrote and destroyed a dozen notes to Madame. None pleased me. Some too hot, others too cold. At last, thinks I, I will walk and tell her my opinion upon the fracas between myself and my Lord. I did so, found *his* cabt at the door, which was open, walked in sans knocking, and up to the drawing room sans being announced. Fancy their consternation! I really thought Francis would have fainted.

Lady S (stiff as a poker and perfectly cool): 'Mrs Bolton I have called upon you in consequence of a scene which I am perfectly aware I owe entirely to you and I am here to have an understanding, as from what has passed there can be no reserve betwixt us three. Sir F. is aware of my role, this intimacy with Disraeli. It has suited all parties to be a great deal together, not certainly from the intimacy of the Ladies, for I have never expressed a friendship for you. I have never been even commonly Ladylike in my conduct to you, and when together Disraeli and I, Francis and you, formed two distinct parties, and it can be *proved* that we did. Consequently in Sir Francis's absence there was no change in me, and should he leave London tomorrow your doors *I would never enter*, nothing should induce me, but I will give Francis the sanction of my acquiescence on the strict condition of his not again

violating by unjust and ungenerous threats ties which he himself has
sanctioned and which both himself and yourself *know* have been
necessary to carry on your own game . . . So chuse. Before I leave this
House the solemn promise must be given *never* to mention Disraeli's
name as a bug bear.' *Mrs Bolton*: 'It was from Disappointment I complained and not from malice. Disraeli is a heartless wretch. I have
stuck up for him for years. Our acquaintance has been of nine years
standing. *Here are his letters*, vowing undying friendship, unspeakable
obligation, but I repay them now with scorn. As for you and I, I have
too much dignity to wish our acquaintance on any other footing than
you have placed it. Disraeli has influenced his *dear* family to desert me,
witness his father never having called upon me, and through him your
character has gone—I heard from good authority. No one would visit
you next year on his account and he will leave you, he has left you, I
know him well and he is everywhere despised.'

I was enraged and contradicted the falsehood but dearest even if
memory would serve of what avail would be the repetition of our eloquence? Suffice for you and I that we are victorious. Madame cried and
wrung her hands. F cried and begged me to be merciful. I did *not cry*
and had apologies from both.   Ibid.

154

An Exchange of Insults, 1835

*The Irish champion, Daniel O'Connell MP, was notorious for his vitupe-
ration. Having killed a man in a duel, he had sworn he would never fight
another; and when Lord Alvanley, whom he had termed 'a bloated buffoon',
challenged him, O'Connell's son Morgan fought a duel in his place. During
the 1835 election, the young Benjamin Disraeli, standing for Taunton, was
reported (mistakenly as he claimed) to have described O'Connell as 'an
incendiary and a traitor'. A few days later O'Connell replied in a speech in
Dublin.*

I MUST confess that some of the attacks made on me, particularly one
by a Mr Disraeli at Taunton, surprised me. Anything so richly deserv-
ing the appellation of superlative blackguardism, or at all equal to that
in impudence and assurance, I never before met with. The annals of
ruffianism do not furnish anything like it. He is an author, I believe, of
a couple of novels, and that was all I knew about him until 1831 or

1832, when he wrote to me, being about to stand for High Wycombe, requesting a letter of recommendation from me to the electors. He took the letter with him to the place, got it printed and placarded all over the place. The next I heard of him was his being a candidate for Marylebone; in this he was also unsuccessful. He got tired of being a Radical any longer after these two defeats, and was determined to try his chance as a Tory. He stands the other day at Taunton, and by way of recommending himself to the electors he calls me an incendiary and a traitor. Now my answer to this piece of gratuitous impertinence is, that he is an egregious liar. He is a liar both in action and words. What! Shall such a vile creature be tolerated in England? Shall the man be received by any constituency who after coming forward on two separate occasions as the advocate of certain opinions, now boldly and unblushingly recants those principles by which his political life had been apparently regulated? He is a living lie; and the British Empire is degraded by tolerating a miscreant of his abominable description. The language is harsh, I must confess; but it is no more than deserved, and if I should apologise for using it, it is because I can find no harsher epithets in the English language by which to convey the utter abhorrence which I entertain for such a reptile. He is just fit now, after being twice discarded by the people, to become a Conservative. He possesses all the necessary requisites of perfidy, selfishness, depravity, want of principle, etc., which would qualify him for the change. His name shows that he is of Jewish origin. I do not use it as a term of reproach; there are many most respectable Jews. But there are, as in every other people, some of the lowest and most disgusting grade of moral turpitude; and of those I look upon Mr Disraeli as the worst. He has just the qualities of the impenitent thief on the Cross, and I verily believe, if Mr Disraeli's family herald were to be examined and his genealogy traced, the same personage would be discovered to be the heir at law of the exalted individual to whom I allude. I forgive Mr Disraeli now, and as the lineal descendant of the blasphemous robber, who ended his career besides the Founder of the Christian Faith, I leave the gentleman to the enjoyment of his infamous distinction and family honours.

Quoted in W. F. Monypenny and G. E. Buckle, *Life of Disraeli*

155

The speech was reported verbatim in the London papers; Disraeli replied by
challenging O'Connell Jr. to a duel; but the son declined to be further answer-
able for what his father might say. So Disraeli wrote O'Connell Sr. a letter
beginning:

MR O'CONNELL,
    Although you have long placed yourself out of the pale of civilis-
ation, still I am one who will not be insulted, even by a Yahoo, without
chastising it. When I read this morning in the same journals your viru-
lent attack upon myself, and that your son was at the same moment
paying the penalty of similar virulence to another individual on whom
you had dropped your filth, I thought that the consciousness that your
opponents had at length discovered a source of satisfaction might have
animated your insolence to unwonted energy, and I called upon your
son to re-assume his vicarious office of yielding satisfaction for his
shrinking sire. But it seems that gentleman declines the further exercise of the pleasing duty of enduring the consequences of your liber-
tine harangues. I have no other means, therefore, of noticing your
effusion but this public mode . . .

Ibid.

156

Disraeli's long letter was sent to the papers and printed. He then wrote to
O'Connell Jr:

I DEDUCE from your communication that you do not consider yourself responsible for any insults offered by your father, but only bound
to resent the insults that he may receive. Now, Sir, it is my hope that I
have insulted him; assuredly it was my intention to do so. I wished to
express the utter scorn in which I hold his character, and the disgust
with which his conduct inspires me. If I failed in conveying this
expression of my feelings to him, let me more successfully express
them now to you. I shall take every opportunity of holding your father's
name up to public contempt. And I fervently pray that you, or some of
his blood, may attempt to avenge the unextinguishable hatred with
which I shall pursue his existence.

Ibid.

157

Three days later, in a letter to his sister Sarah, Disraeli recounted the upshot.

THIS morning as I was lying in bed, thankful that I had kicked all the O'Connells and that I was at length to have a quiet morning, Mr Collard, the police officer of Marylebone, rushed into my chamber and took me into custody. . . . We all went in a hackney coach to the office, where I found that the articles were presented by a Mr Bennett, residing in some street in Westminster, and an acquaintance of the O'Connells. We were soon dismissed, but I am now bound to keep the peace in £500 sureties. As far as the present affair was concerned, it was a most unnecessary precaution, as if all the O'Connells were to challenge me I could not think of meeting them *now*. I consider, and everyone else, that they are lynched.

Ibid.

158

Disraeli summarized the affair in his diary: 'Row with O'Connell in which I greatly distinguish myself.'

Ibid.

159

Mrs Disraeli's Devotion

FROM the time that they were married, [Mrs Disraeli] always said that she would not go into the House until he was Prime Minister, but one evening she drove to Westminster with him. She knew that, that night, he had a very important speech to make. When Disraeli was leaving, her fingers got trapped in the carriage door. She suffered excruciating pain but never uttered a word because she did not want to upset him and thereby spoil his speech. Once, travelling to Hatfield, she fell and cut her face. Disraeli was to follow later and she knew that he was preparing a great speech. She told Lady Salisbury this when she arrived, adding: 'If he finds out I have had an accident he will be quite upset. I want you to take me straight to my room and say I have a headache. He has lost his eye-glass and if you put me a long way from him at dinner he will never see what a condition I am in.' Her request was complied with and it was at least two days before Disraeli himself discovered what had happened . . .

However late the House sat, Mary Anne never went to bed before Disraeli got home. He never had to come back to dark rooms and a cold, cheerless atmosphere. The place was always a blaze of light, there was a fire burning and a hot meal ready for him. One night, after a very late sitting, he was invited by a number of his supporters to supper at the Carlton Club. But he insisted on going home. There he found waiting for him a delicious pie and a bottle of champagne. He turned to his wife, embraced her and said: 'My dear—you are more like a mistress than a wife.'

D. H. Elletson, *Maryannery: Mary Ann Lincoln and Mary Anne Disraeli*, 1959

160

An Adventurer and a Gentleman

The clash between Disraeli and Sir Robert Peel over the latter's repeal of the Corn Laws in 1846 was one of the most dramatic episodes in British political history. Peel got his policy through but in the process Disraeli destroyed the government. What MPs did not know was that, five years earlier, when Peel became Prime Minister, Disraeli had written to him on 5 September 1841, begging for office:

DEAR Sir Robert,

I have shrunk from obtruding myself upon you at this moment, and should have continued to do so if there were anyone on whom I could rely to express my feelings.

I am not going to trouble you with claims similar to those with which you must be wearied. I will not say that I have fought since 1834 four contests for your party, that I have expended great sums, have exerted my intelligence to the utmost for the propagation of your policy, and have that position in life which can command a costly seat.

But there is one peculiarity in my case on which I cannot be silent. I have had to struggle against a storm of political hate and malice which few men ever experienced, from the moment, at the instigation of a

member of your Cabinet, I enrolled myself under your banner, and
I have only been sustained under these trials by the conviction that
the day would come when the foremost man in this country would
publicly testify that he had some respect for my ability and my
character.

I confess to be unrecognised at this moment by you appears to me to
be overwhelming, and I appeal to your own heart—to that justice and
that magnanimity which I feel are your characteristics—to save me
from an intolerable humiliation.

Believe me, dear Sir Robert,
Your faithful servant,
B. Disraeli.

Monypenny and Buckle, *Life of Disraeli*

*Mary Anne Disraeli, unknown to her husband, had also written to Peel
begging that Disraeli be given a job: 'My husband's political career is for ever
crushed, if you do not appreciate him. . . . Do not destroy all his hopes, and
make him feel his life has been a mistake.'*

161

*Peel declined to comply with the Disraelis' request, and five years later when
he changed his policy on the Corn Laws, Disraeli took the opportunity for
revenge. His philippics against Peel culminated on 15 May 1846, on the
third reading of the Corn Bill, when he savagely accused Peel of dishonesty
throughout his political career.*

WHEN I examine the career of this Minister, which has now filled a
great space in the Parliamentary history of this country, I find that for
between thirty and forty years the right hon. gentleman has traded on
the ideas and intelligence of others. (Loud cheering.) His life has been
a great appropriation clause. (Shouts of laughter and cheers.) He is a
burglar of others' intellect. Search the index of Beatson, from the days
of the Conqueror to the termination of the last reign, there is no statesman who has committed political petty larceny on so great a scale.
(Renewed laughter.) I believe, therefore, when the right hon. gentleman undertook our cause on either side of the House, that he was perfectly sincere in his advocacy; but as, in the course of discussion, the

conventionalism which he received from us crumbled away in his grasp, feeling no creative power to sustain him with new arguments, feeling no spontaneous sentiments to force upon him conviction, the right hon. gentleman, reduced at last to defending the noblest cause, one based upon the most high and solemn principles, upon 'the burden peculiar to agriculture'—the right hon. gentleman, faithful to the law of his nature, imbibed the new doctrines, as he had imbibed the doctrines of every leading man in this country for thirty or forty years, with the exception of the doctrine of Parliamentary reform, which the Whigs very wisely led the country upon, and did not allow to grow sufficiently mature to fall into his mouth. . . . After the day that the right hon. gentleman made his first exposition of his [Corn Laws] scheme, a gentleman well known in this House, and learned in all the political secrets behind the scenes, met me and said: 'Well, what do you think of your chief's plan?' Not knowing exactly what to say, but taking up a phrase which has been much used in the House, I observed: 'Well, I suppose it's a "great and comprehensive" plan.' 'Oh,' he replied, 'we know all about it! It was offered to us! It is not his plan; it's Popkins's Plan!' (Peals of laughter from all parts of the House.) And is England to be governed, and is England to be convulsed, by 'Popkins's Plan'? (Cheers and laughter.) Will he go to the country with it? Will he go with it to that ancient and famous England that once was governed by statesmen—by Burghleys and by Walsinghams; by Bolingbrokes and by Walpoles; by a Chatham and a Canning—will he go to it with this fantastic scheming of some presumptuous pedant? (Great cheering).

Ibid.

162

Peel had not hitherto replied to Disraeli's personal attacks, but on this occasion he asked why, if Disraeli had always held such a low opinion of his capacity and character, had he been 'ready, as I think he was, to unite his fortunes with mine in office?' Disraeli promptly replied with a flat lie.

I CAN assure the House nothing of the kind ever occurred. I never shall—it is totally foreign to my nature—make any application for any place. . . . I never ask a favour of the government, not even one of those mechanical things which persons are obliged to ask . . . and as regards myself I never directly or indirectly solicited office . . . It is

very possible if, in 1841, I had been offered office, I dare say it would
have been a very slight office, but I dare say I would have accepted
it . . . But with respect to my being a solicitor for office, it is entirely
unfounded.

Ibid.

163

Disraeli's latest biographer takes up the story:

IT is inconceivable that Disraeli had forgotten what he had written to
Peel. Nor is it plausible to suggest, as Miss Ramsay does in her life of
Peel, that he knew his man and reckoned on Peel being too gentle-
manly to produce the letter. It is true that Disraeli knew of Peel's refusal to read out a damaging letter from Joseph Hume in 1830 in
somewhat similar circumstances, but no one would have dared, in the
light of cool reason, to gamble upon a repetition; even though, as
events turned out, the gamble would have come off. Disraeli had
indeed denied asking for office once before—to his constituents at
Shrewsbury in 1844. He had not been contradicted then, but that was
a different matter from confronting in person the very minister to
whom he had written an almost abject letter of solicitation. The most
likely explanation is panic, rare though such lapses were in Disraeli's
life. He possibly knew that in some circles his reputation was none too
good. He may well have been flustered, and he probably blurted out
his unconvincing denial without fully considering the risk. He certainly
asked for trouble by not only denying that he ever solicited office, but
also, and equally untruthfully, that he had ever asked for a favour. Had
he forgotten the applications that he made to Graham and Stanley for
his brother? It is unlikely that they had.

Peel did not read out Disraeli's letter, but there is no truth in the
story apparently believed by Buckle [Disraeli's official biographer] that
he was unable to find it. Goldwin Smith in his reminiscences declares
that he had first-hand information on this point from Lord Lincoln,
who had walked with Peel to the House in the morning and actually
saw the letter in Peel's dispatch-case. Why, then, did he miss such a
splendid opportunity? We will never know for certain. Perhaps Peel,
who had the hypersensitivity on points of honour of a man only half
belonging to the patrician world, refrained because it would be unfair
to read out a personal communication. If so it is to his credit. One cannot easily imagine Palmerston or Russell or Stanley showing a similar

delicacy. Disraeli was lucky, but the general impression of his conduct seems to have been adverse. No doubt much was said in the Lobbies and the Carlton that has not survived to posterity, and people drew their own conclusions. It is not an episode on which his admirers care to dwell.

Robert Blake, Disraeli, 1969

164

Disraeli and Salisbury

Though both were Tories, Disraeli and Robert Cecil, 3rd Marquess of Salisbury (1830–1903) began as political enemies. In April 1860 Lord Robert Cecil (as he then was) published a celebrated attack on his party leader in the Quarterly Review. *The next week he went to Hatfield.*

ON arriving he heard, to his consternation, that Mr Disraeli was among the guests assembled there. What was to be done? How was the first meeting to be got over? Should he shirk the difficulty by keeping out of the way or should he risk a snubbing by going boldly to meet it? He was young enough to feel the embarrassment of such questions and fled into the garden to meditate upon them in solitude. At a turn of a path in the shrubbery he found himself suddenly face to face with the object of his anxieties and at a distance too short for avoidance. He had scarcely realised the situation when Mr Disraeli advanced rapidly to meet him, exclaiming, 'Ah Robert, Robert, how glad I am to see you!' and before the horrified young Englishman could make even a gesture of protest, enfolded him in his embrace.

Lady Gwendolen Cecil, Life of Robert Marquis of Salisbury, 1931

165

In time the two men became close colleagues and friends; one thing they had in common was devotion to Jane Austen; Salisbury knew all six of her novels 'almost by heart'; Disraeli told Benjamin Jowett he had read Pride and Prejudice *seventeen times. Disraeli told Salisbury's daughter there was another reason for the friendship:*

THE strongest cement to the new understanding was the courage for which both men were preeminent. Lord Salisbury would comment admiringly upon his chief's quality in this respect. He found a constant refreshment in working with a man who never hampered counsel by hesitating doubts or shrinking avoidance of large decisions. . . . The satisfaction was mutual. Speaking to the present writer not long before his death, Lord Beaconsfield dwelt on the disabilities which he had suffered throughout his career from the timidity of colleagues. He mentioned one or two names but said that the evil had been continuous. Never until now, at the end of his life, had he known what it was to work with a man of nerve. 'You will find as you grow older', he insisted, 'that courage is the rarest of all qualities to be found in public men.' 'Your father', he repeated, 'is the only man of real courage that it has ever been my lot to work with.'

Ibid.

166

On 7 January 1896, Salisbury was giving a dinner-party at Hatfield when a red dispatch box was brought to the table. He asked the permission of Princess Christian, a daughter of Queen Victoria, to open it, and studied the short message it contained. Then he scribbled for a moment or two and had the box removed. The Princess asked him what it was. He replied that the German Emperor had landed 150 men at Delagoa Bay, in Portuguese East Africa, the only access of the Boers to the sea other than through British territory. 'What answer have you sent?' the Princess enquired. 'I haven't answered,' Salisbury said, 'I have sent ships.'

Kenneth Rose, *Superior Person*, 1969

167

Disraeli's Rise

Some Disraeli stories did not reach print until long after his death. One such was told by Harold Macmillan in January 1962.

It was told to me by the late Duke of Portland, and I went away and wrote it all down. It began with his father. Shortly before Disraeli became Leader of the Party, the old Duke's sons, Lord George

Bentinck and Lord Henry Bentinck, came to him and said: 'Father, there is only one man who can lead the Tory Party—and he is a fancy little Jew.' 'But is he a country gentleman?' asked the Duke. 'No', they said, 'he is a fancy little Jew.' 'Only a country gentleman can lead the Tory Party', said the Duke. 'We'll make him one,' said the sons. Straight away they bought Hughenden for Disraeli—the Bentinck family bought Hughenden for Disraeli. But they didn't give it to him: they kept it in their own ownership for eighteen years, and then the Lord Rothschild of the day got the deeds and presented them to the Earl of Beaconsfield (as Disraeli had become).

Then a remarkable thing happened towards the end of Disraeli's life. There was another duke by now—the one who told me the story. He was twenty-three, and he had only just succeeded. He had been a young officer in the Blues, on £500 a year, and now he had come into all the vast Portland estates. He was inexperienced in public affairs and politics, and was quite unnerved one day when Disraeli's private secretary sent for him and said that Disraeli wanted to see him at Hughenden.

To his horror he discovered that he was the only guest. He was asked to put on a white tie for dinner (he was to stay the night). When he came down to dinner, there were just the three of them, Disraeli, the private secretary, and himself. Disraeli said good evening to him, and not a single word was spoken by anyone throughout that long Victorian dinner, not one single word. Disraeli sat there impassive, glittering with all his orders, wearing the lot—the Star of India and all the rest. His face was white, and tight like a drum; he was an old, old man.

Then at the end of dinner he spoke, and he said: 'My lord duke, I have asked you here tonight because I belong to a race that never forgives an insult and never forgets a benefit. Everything I have I owe to the house of Bentinck. I thank you.'

Related by George Hutchinson, *The Last Edwardian at Number Ten: An Impression of Harold Macmillan*, 1980. [There is a more prosaic, and accurate, version in the Duke of Portland's own memoirs, *Men, Women and Things*, 1937]

168

A Visiting Fireman

The Earl of Lytton (1831–91) was Viceroy of India during the years 1876–80, and during his reign was host at dinner to the ex-president of the United States, General Ulysses Grant, during his world tour. He related to John Morley what happened:

ON this occasion, 'our distinguished guest', the double ex-President of the 'Great Western Republic', who got as drunk as a fiddle, showed that he could be as profligate as a lord. He fumbled Mrs A., kissed the shrieking Miss B., pinched the plump Mrs C. black and blue, and ran at Miss D. with intent to ravish her. Finally, after throwing all the . . . female guests into hysterics by generally behaving like a must elephant, the noble beast was captured by main force and carried (quatre pattes dans l'air) by six sailors, which relieved India of his distinguished presence. The marine office . . . reports that, when deposited in the public saloon cabin, where Mrs G. was awaiting him . . . this remarkable man satiated there and then his baffled lust on the unresisting body of his legitimate spouse, and copiously vomited during the operation. If you have seen Mrs Grant you will not think this incredible.

Quoted in Mary Lutyens, *The Lyttons in India*, 1979

169

Gladstone and Disraeli

16 December 1852: . . . The debate [on the budget] languished until Disraeli rose, at about 10.30 pm, and delivered I think the most remarkable speech I remember to have heard in the Commons. He took little notice of other critics but applied himself seriously to answer Graham and Wood. The latter he attacked again and again, demolishing him at each onset, and closing with a personal invective which maddened the House with excitement. Never did one parliamentary speaker receive a severer infliction at the hands of another. Gladstone replied at past one in the morning: he rose choked with passion, for which he could find no vent in words, and his first utterances were the

signal for fresh explosions from each side of the House alternately . . .
Gladstone's look when he rose to reply will never be forgotten by me:
his usually calm features were livid and distorted with passion, his
voice shook, and those who watched him feared an outbreak incompat-
ible with parliamentary rules. So stormy a scene I have never witnessed. I went to the Carlton after the division: those who had voted
with Gladstone prudently kept away: they could not have escaped
insult.

18 April 1853: Gladstone's budget, which occupied five hours, an
extraordinary effort of rhetorical skill: no fault could be found except
too great length, and a hackneyed quotation from Virgil spoiling a fine
peroration: it was said that for three nights before this display he was
unable to sleep from excitement, but the success was worth the suffering.

4 March 1865: . . . Talk, inter alia, of Gladstone, whose social
unpopularity appears to be increasing. His colleagues detest him, and
make little scruple in saying so—Wood and Clarendon more particularly. He is complained of as overbearing and dictatorial beyond what
is permitted even to men of his eminence, while his eccentricities
attract some ridicule. At a country house last Sunday (I think Lord
Chesham's) he passed the evening in singing hymns with his wife, the
Bishop of Oxford, who was also present, reluctantly compelled to join
but revenging himself afterwards by telling the story.

16 July 1869: Gladstone's own temper is visible and audible whenever
he rises to speak . . . the mixture of anger and contempt in his voice is
almost painful to witness. With all his splendid talent, and his great
position, few men suffer more from the constitutional infirmity of an
irritable nature: and this is a disease which hard mental work, anxiety
and the exercise of power, all tend to exacerbate. Disraeli is quite
aware of the advantage which he possesses in his natural calmness: and
takes every opportunity to make the contrast noticeable.

*Disraeli, Derby and the Conservative Party: the Political Journals of Lord
Stanley 1849–69* ed. J. R. Vincent, 1978

170

Gladstone Opts for Home Rule

IMMEDIATELY on making up my mind about the ejection of the government, I went to call upon Sir William Harcourt and informed him as to my intentions and the grounds of them. He said: 'What! Are you prepared to go forward without either Hartington or Chamberlain?' I answered 'Yes'. I believe it was in my mind to say, if I did not actually say it, that I was prepared to go forward without any body. That is to say without any known and positive assurance of support. This was one of the great Imperial occasions which call for such resolutions.

Gladstone, autobiographical fragment, printed in *The Prime Ministers' Papers: Gladstone*, HMC 1971

171

Gladstone and Harcourt

Where Gladstone was an enthusiast on the Irish issue, his lieutenant Sir William Harcourt (1827–1904) was a cynic. The latter's son Lewis recorded a dinner-party exchange between the two at the time of the first Home Rule Bill, 1886.

HARCOURT mentioned the 'loyal' Irish. The word seemed to stir Gladstone's wrath extremely, and he said sarcastically: 'Was there ever such a noble race as that! What a beautiful word—loyalist. How much they have done for their country! You say that the Nationalists care for nothing but money, but have not the loyalists the same tastes?' *Harcourt*: 'Certainly. The only difference is that where you can buy a Nationalist for £5, you must pay £6 for a Loyalist.' (Turning to Lady Airlie, their hostess): 'I once asked your father (Lord Stanley of Alderley) what was the smallest sum he had ever paid for a vote in the House of Commons, and he replied that he had once bought an Irish Member for £5 on the morning of the Derby.' *Gladstone*: 'You think Ireland is a little Hell on earth.' *Harcourt*: 'Yes. I think the only mistake Cromwell ever made was when he offered them the alternative of Connaught.'

A. G. Gardiner, *Life of Sir William Harcourt*, 1923

172

Gladstone's Last Government

November 23 1892. Cabinet . . . A painful scene at the end. Harcourt demands prompt cabinets—falls on Fowler as a faithless accomplice, on Spencer as a 'wretched peer'—Mr G. resists. Rembrandt *Monte Carlo* scene which Asquith & I viewed from the side table. Excited men round table—pale old croupier in midst with passion seething in his face—a memorable and painful scene.

Diary of Lord Rosebery, quoted in Robert Rhodes James, Rosebery, 1963

173

His Last Cabinet Meeting

HE held his last Cabinet on 1 March [1894] and informed his colleagues of his resolve. Lord Kimberley began an impromptu valedictory address, but he broke down and could not continue. Gladstone, who seemed as hard and upright as a rock, was about to reply when Sir William Harcourt called 'Stop!' He had been forestalled by Lord Kimberley, but he now pulled a manuscript from his pocket and began to read a formal valedictory address, gulping at intervals and dabbing his eyes with his handkerchief. Gladstone, in thanking his colleagues spoke for about four minutes. He ended with the words, 'God bless you all!' He then went out at one door while the rest trooped out at the other. Lord Rosebery thought that he was disgusted, but Gladstone was, in truth, more than half indifferent. He noted 'a really moving scene', but he liked afterwards to refer to 'that blubbering cabinet'.

Philip Magnus, Gladstone: A Biography, 1954

174

Gladstone's Eye

[LLOYD GEORGE] longs for a fight, he says. He says Gladstone was the same. Ostensibly a man of peace, & working for peace, nevertheless when the fight came the Old Man warmed to it. D. said he had a terrible eye even to the last. He & Sam Evans once baited the Old Man in the House of Commons, & he glared across at them in reply. Sam Evans nudged D. & whispered: 'I wish he would take that terrible eye off us.'

Frances Stevenson, diary, 17 April 1935

175

Gladstone's Night Walks

Gladstone's habit of accosting prostitutes and attempting to reform them was comparatively widely known even during his lifetime; quite unknown was his pious (not vicious) practice of scourging himself to atone for sins of the flesh; the two were sometimes connected.

IT was in January 1849—before he embarked on his regular associations with prostitutes—that he started to scourge himself, or in his own words: 'during the week I made a slight application in a new form of discipline', an application which was henceforward marked in his diaries by a sign resembling a whip. . . . Gladstone himself was aware of the dubious nature of some of his acts and of the ambivalent motives which might underpin them. [In July 1851] after he had spent a couple of hours in Elizabeth Collins's lodgings in 'a strange and humbling scene' he immediately returned home and scourged himself; two days later he recorded: 'Fell in with E. C. and another mixed scene somewhat like that of 48 hours before', and he again returned home to scourge himself. A week later he spent a further two strange and questionable hours with her and after again returning home to scourge himself he wondered 'whether or not I have been deluded in the notion of doing good by such means, or whether I have sought it

through what was unlawful I am not clear'. With girls other than the
beautiful Elizabeth Collins, whom he described as 'half of a lovely
statue, lovely beyond measure', he wrote of treading on the edge of
danger and of being guilty of weakness, 'nor can I truly say mere weakness' . . .

The proclivity reached a crisis point on the night of Lord Frederick Cavendish's murder, when both a member of the public who ido-
lised Mr Gladstone and a Conservative MP who did not saw him
with a young prostitute near the Duke of York steps at 11.30 pm.
The MP was Colonel Tottenham who said he was about to cross the
road to offer Mr Gladstone his deepest condolences on the news of
Lord Frederick's murder when he witnessed the Prime Minister
accost, get into conversation with and move off in the direction of
Piccadilly Circus in the company of 'an abandoned woman'. The
member of the public was the Bermondsey Workhouse master and
he finished his corroborative account of what he had seen with the
words: 'For years that statesman has been my idol—so much for
human frailty and credulity . . . I almost disbelieved my own eyes
and knowledge.' Colonel Tottenham told the story everywhere he
could, including a dinner party attended by a Mrs Louisa Pepys, who
wrote to Eddy Hamilton (Gladstone's secretary) asking if he could
not flatly and openly contradict what she believed to be a foul
calumny against Mr Gladstone.

Unfortunately Hamilton could not; but what he could and did do
was to write to the workhouse master and Mrs Pepys telling them
that if they had been within earshot of the scene it would have
acquired a different complexion from the obvious interpretation
which had been put upon it. Hamilton told Mrs Pepys: ' . . . he has
at different times been the means of retrieving unfortunate women
from a fallen position. The prudence of such conduct in a man of his
position may be questionable, but of the high, unselfish and kind
motives which guide his conduct there can be no doubt.' After consultation with Lord Rosebery and Lord Granville, Hamilton decided
to show the letter to Mr Gladstone (as he told Mrs Pepys he had).
He noted that Gladstone was 'perfectly frank about the affair, as I
knew he would be, and promptly related everything he remembered
of the incident'. The devoted secretary also begged Gladstone to
stop 'the practice of parleying with people in the streets', and temporarily he did. On 13 June 1882 Hamilton was happy to note in his
diary that he had spoken to Howard Vincent, who was the head of

the recently created Criminal Investigation Department, and 'that since the 6th ult., no further reports of any incidents concerning the night walks'.

Joyce Marlow, Mr and Mrs Gladstone: An Intimate Biography, 1977

176

Our Gracious Queen

27 February 1868: It seems the Queen has given [Lord Derby] much annoyance, in his weak state, by her way of writing, which was curt and totally without expressions of sympathy or regret. Knowing her disposition, I am not surprised, but he has always entertained some illusions about her. She seems to have told him he had better resign at once, in order to save her trouble.

1 March: [Derby] talked to me of the Queen's way of writing to him, about which he was at first very sore: but I think he now understands her nature. She is civil to persons in power under her, whose good will contributes to her comfort (and not always to them): but sees no reason for wasting civility on those who can no longer be of use to her.

Political Journals of Lord Stanley 1849–69

177

On 3 March 1894 Gladstone finally resigned, having served Queen Victoria four times as Prime Minister and for a total of some thirty-five years in ministerial office.

HE received not one syllable of thanks for all his years of faithful and honourable service, and the Queen's letter was so curt as to be almost insulting. He wrote to Ponsonby [the Queen's Private Secretary], in reply to a generous letter, that he had found it necessary to harden his heart 'into a flint'. But that heart refused to harden, and on 2 January 1896, Gladstone placed on record in his diary 'my strong desire that after my decease my family shall be most careful to keep in the background all information respecting the personal relations of the Queen and myself during these later years down to 1894, when they died a kind of natural death. Relations sad in themselves, though absolutely unattended with the smallest ruffle on the surface. It was the kind and generous farewell from Ponsonby which had to fill for me the place of a farewell from my Sovereign.' A few days later, in a private memorandum, he wrote: 'Granted that the absence of any act and word of regard, regret or interest, is absolutely deserved. But then I have a wife. Of her, H. M., in her concluding letter wrote in terms (which conveyed some implication of reproach to me) of warm interest and praise'. He thought the Queen might have presented her portrait to Mrs Gladstone or 'some voluntary offering. . . . But there was nothing of the kind. For I cannot reckon as anything what appeared to be a twopenny-halfpenny scrap, photographic or other, sent during the forenoon of our departure by the hand of a footman.'

Magnus, Gladstone

<h1 align="center">178</h1>

<h2 align="center">A Liberal Cabinet 1885</h2>

The last days of the 1880–5 government were sardonically recorded by Lord Rosebery in his diary.

April 20: Cabinet at 2 on budget. Childers stated his case wretchedly ('bitched it' said W. E. G.!) and got unmercifully handled. It was a Childers Bait (as we should have said at Eton) for 2 hours. Dilke threatened to resign (taking I suppose Chamberlain with him) if the beer duty of $\frac{1}{3}d$. is persisted in, as it will alienate the new voters for ever . . .

May 7: At 2, Cabinet. It was agreed to resign if we were beaten on the question of the Registration payment. It was announced we shd certainly be beaten on the budget & if not shd break up on Ireland. I thought they were not enjoining Dick Grosvenor (who was present) to whip zealously enough so I remarked 'We appear to contemplate a course of conduct which on the Turf wd bring us under the notice of the Jockey Club'. May 10: Cabinet at nine. A Childers worry. Childers wants to amend his budget. Says he must resign if we won't amend it. If we can endure the odium of it surely the author can. He won't resign, nor would it matter if he did. After his statement Harcourt simply remarked: 'So far as I know the budget is as good a question to go out upon as any other, and Tuesday as good a day.' June 5: Cabinet at 11 . . . Discussion on budget. Childers proposed an increased wine duty—everyone against it. At last, saying 'I am sorry to say I cannot agree' he stalked from the room. Harcourt the official pacificator hurried after him, followed shortly afterwards by Gladstone amid general mirth. They came back in 20 minutes saying he required an hour's thought. Then Granville and the Chancellor were sent. Shortly after the cabinet separated C withdrew his resignation.

(On June 8, to the inexpressible relief of most members of the Ministry, the government were defeated by twelve votes in the House of Commons on the beer duties. Rosebery recorded the epitaph of the Ministry thus:

> Here lies a Cabinet, I'll tell you why;
> It spelt its funeral bier without an 'i'.)

Rhodes James, *Rosebery*

179

Rosebery's 'Evil-Smelling Bog'

Lord Rosebery (1847–1929) was credited with three ambitions: to marry the greatest heiress in England, to become Prime Minister, and to win the Derby. He achieved all three, marrying Hannah Rothschild and winning the Derby twice while Prime Minister. Yet his life was very unhappy, as he recorded in a private memorandum written at the end of it.

THE secret of my life, which seems to me sufficiently obvious, is that I always detested politics. I had been landed in them accidentally, by the Midlothian election, which was nothing but a chivalrous adventure. When I found myself in this evil-smelling bog I was always trying to extricate myself. That is the secret of what people used to call my lost opportunities, and so forth. If you will look over my life you will see that is quite obvious. But nothing is so obvious as the thing which one does not wish to see.

I saw in some book the other day that I was described as a failure, and this led me into a train of thought which whirled me from myself. But let me say at once that according to the usual apprehension of the word the description is sufficiently accurate. What! a man who has been more or less in public life for a quarter of a century, who has never enjoyed an instant in power, and has now been long in seclusion without a follower and almost forgotten, what can be a greater failure?

Ibid.

180

Rosebery's government, 1894–5, was probably the most absurd of modern times. He become Prime Minister as Gladstone's successor simply because his colleagues could not bear the thought of the only alternative, Sir William Harcourt. Once installed, he found he could command no loyalty from his ministers. His supposed chief supporter, John Morley, Irish Secretary, wrote to him:

I HOPE that I shall not be asked or expected to take part in such councils as those of this morning. I propose to confine myself strictly and absolutely to the business of my department, *plus* attendance at Cabinet councils, *plus* steady obedience to the call of the whips for my vote.

Rosebery replied:

I have no choice but to accept your 'conditions'. I won't disguise from you that I am deeply pained by them. You would not have imposed them on Mr Gladstone or, I believe, on anybody else. It is because your perhaps most intimate political friend undertakes the Government, largely because of your action, that you insist on a pound of flesh bond which sets forth an absolute want of confidence and a cold denial of all assistance or cooperation. Had I known that this was to be your definite attitude I certainly would have not undertaken the government, and if I could honourably now, I would give it up.

He discussed Morley's behaviour with Asquith:

Asquith: Yes, he is difficult to manage. But at least he's a perfect gentleman.

Rosebery: Yes but I am not sure that he might not be best described as a perfect lady.

181

As for Harcourt, though Chancellor of the Exchequer, Leader of the House and official leader of the Liberal Party in the Commons, he refused to make speeches supporting the government, and set out his position in a remarkable letter of 21 September 1894 to his cabinet colleague Lord Spencer:

I DON'T know why you should suppose I shall depart from my fixed resolution not to make any public speech. Why should I? You and your friends have informed me sufficiently frankly you do not regard me as fit to lead. Why then should I take the initiative only in order that you may repudiate me? As you know I am not a supporter of the present Government. I have a great personal regard for you and contemplate your proceedings with an impartial curiosity and a benevolent neutrality. I quite agree that your position is a difficult one, and I wish you well out of it. But I see that your leader is announced for a good many speeches in which he will no doubt develop his policy with his accustomed clearness—and then you will know what to think and do. It will be quite time enough when your plans are declared for me to consider how far I can support them.

> Letter to Earl Spencer printed in A. G. Gardiner, *Life of Sir William Harcourt*

182

By 19 February 1895 Rosebery could stand it no more, summoned the Cabinet and read them a prepared statement:

I CANNOT call to mind a single instance in which any individual in the party or the Ministry has spoken even casually in my defence within the walls of Parliament. I limit myself to the walls of Parliament, though so far as my knowledge goes that limitation is almost superfluous . . . I have waited patiently and I hope uncomplainingly for a year in order to see whether there would be any change. There has been none. On the contrary, the last two nights have been taken up with a debate on a vote of want of confidence directed obviously and especially against the head of the government. The discussion has been marked with more than the usual violence against the Prime Minister, and there has been no defence and only one word of association with him. There was not even an indication that the government and the Liberal Party did not share the hostility expressed towards the Prime Minister . . . God knows I never sought my present office and would have done anything consistent with honour to avoid it and I renounce it to say the least without regret.

This bombshell shocked the cabinet into a display of loyalty, and the government staggered on for a few more months. On 21 June 1895 it was defeated in the Commons and Rosebery and Harcourt decided they should resign immediately—the only point on which they saw eye-to-eye in the whole government. At the subsequent General Election, a Liberal majority of 43 was converted into a Unionist majority of 152, and Harcourt and most of his friends lost their seats.

The only pleasure Rosebery got from the premiership was the chance to give jobs to old friends. To the Regius Professorship of Modern History at Oxford, in succession to Froude, he appointed an eccentric nonentity, Frederick Yorke Powell, who had been law tutor at Christ Church in Rosebery's time. Powell left the letter of invitation unopened for weeks, believing it to be an Income Tax demand. When finally installed, he scandalized Oxford by his inaugural lecture. Sir Charles Oman recorded (Memories of Victorian Oxford): *'He came in very late and looking rather bored, with two or three scraps of paper in his hand. He made a few disjointed remarks for about twenty minutes, intimated that he had never known his predecessor Froude, so could not speak about him, and complained that Oxford was destitute of the proper apparatus for original research. When we were expecting him to warm up to some eloquent thesis, he suddenly slapped down the last of his scraps, observed that he had no more to say, and departed.'*

Even odder was the promotion of Rosebery's old Eton friend George Kennion. He had just returned from Australia, where he had held the bishopric of Adelaide. On Derby Day 1894 he was sitting in the Athenaeum when a group of friends told him, as a joke, that colonial bishops returning from duty were always expected to call on the Prime Minister. Believing them, Kennion went to Downing Street, where he was directed to Rosebery's palatial town residence, 38 Berkeley Square. There, naturally, he was told that Rosebery was at Epsom, so left his card. In the evening the Prime Minister returned in triumph from the Derby, which had been won by his horse Ladas. *A large crowd cheered in the square, while Rosebery drank a glass of champagne. It was at this moment of euphoria that Kennion's card was brought to him. Rosebery was delighted to be reminded of an old school chum. The bishopric of Bath and Wells happened to be vacant, and it was promptly bestowed on Kennion, who held it until his death 28 years later.*

183

Rosebery's Grandeur

Thanks to his Rothschild wife, Rosebery enjoyed one of the largest incomes in Britain, and the great palace built by the family at Mentmore; though if, while staying there as his guests, his Rothschild relatives bored him in the evening, he would call out: 'To your tents, O Israel!' Sir Edward Grey recorded in his diary:

9 February 1896. Mentmore. I am in a large house and my room looks out on a courtyard with four walls and a huge iron gate. I heard the birds singing this morning but the sound came faintly from beyond the outer walls and I felt they were freer than I. . . . There are many large glass doors, but some are locked, others open with difficulty—and egress and regress are more or less formal; you may go out or in but not slip out or in.

31 July 1900. I saw Rosebery off to Durdans. I drove with him to Waterloo, [and] have now been returned to Brooks's alone in R's brougham. The obsequiousness of the station officials to R. was wonderful; his neat little man in black had gone ahead, bought a ticket, engaged a compartment and put the whole station on the alert, and the head station-master consoled obsequiously with R. upon the death of Prince Alfred of Coburg, which is just announced by telegram. It seemed as if the train would hardly be able to start, so great was the occasion, but the engine-driver, with great nerve and presence of mind, kept his head and started the train at the usual time.

Printed in G. M. Trevelyan, Grey of Fallodon, 1937

184

HIS moods were always varied and frequently disconcerting throughout his life and became increasingly perplexing as he grew older. He was known to ignore guests almost entirely, and his secretary vividly recalls one weekend party at Dalmany which only saw their host once—when he had to go into the library to get a paper-knife. Conversation stopped at once, and the male guests rose from their chairs; Rosebery walked to his desk, got his paper-knife, and withdrew. Some visitors to his houses noticed that in spite of the splendour, in each room there was only one chair which could be called comfortable, and which was exclusively reserved for Rosebery.

Rhodes James, *Rosebery*

185

On the other hand he could be friendly, writing to J. A. Spender of the Westminster Review*:*

38 Berkeley Square, W.
19 May 1904

I AM off to the Durdans tonight for Whitsuntide. If you and Mrs Spender want to see the blossom and breathe the air of heaven, you will know where to come.

AR

You have only to telegraph
Well-aired beds
Obliging manager.

Printed in Wilson Harris, *J. A. Spender*, 1946

186

D. [LLOYD GEORGE] told us he discovered the secret of Rosebery's limitations one night when there was an important debate in the House of Lords. He overheard Rosebery's valet say to him, 'Your grouse is done to a turn, my lord', and Rosebery disappeared, leaving the debate to take care of itself.

Frances Stevenson, diary, 16 November 1934

187

Forgetting Goschen

Lord Randolph Churchill (1849–95), creator of 'Tory Democracy', was the most reckless politician of his age. Lord Salisbury felt he had no alternative but to take Churchill into his 1886 government, as Chancellor of the

Exchequer; but he was not displeased when, before the end of the year, Churchill—in a bid to assert his mastery over the government—staged the most sensational resignation in modern English politics. On 22 December, having secretly sent his resignation (which, to Queen Victoria's displeasure, was written on Windsor Castle writing-paper), Churchill took his wife and his crony Drummond Wolff to see The School for Scandal.

BOTH his wife and Wolff had noticed his lack of interest in the play, and neither was surprised when Churchill said that he would go round to his club in the interval. In fact he went to Printing House Square to see the editor of *The Times*. . . . he showed Buckle copies of the letters and when Buckle saw the last one he said, 'You can't send that.' 'It has gone', replied Lord Randolph. According to one account, Churchill then asked Buckle to support him in his leading article and when he refused, Churchill protested that 'there is not another paper in England that would not show some gratitude for such a piece of news'. Buckle replied by saying that 'you cannot bribe *The Times*'. The full truth of what was said at this interview will in all probability never be known, but when Churchill left Buckle he had his full permission to publish the news of his resignation.

Lord Salisbury was talking to the Duchess of Teck in the middle of the ball at Hatfield shortly before half-past one in the morning of the 23rd when a red dispatch box was brought to him; excusing himself, he opened it, read the one letter (from Churchill) it contained, and then resumed the conversation with unbroken composure. The ball continued until the early hours; Salisbury told no one of the nature of the single letter in the dispatch box; he did not communicate with the Queen; he did not warn the editor of *The Times*; he simply went to bed.

He was woken early by Lady Salisbury, who reminded him that they must get up to see the Duchess of Marlborough off, as she was catching an early train. 'Send for *The Times* first', was the sleepy response. 'Randolph resigned in the middle of the night, and if I know my man, it will be in *The Times* this morning.' It was. The Duchess of Marlborough, to her intense indignation, was allowed to leave Hatfield without seeing either her host or hostess. Some idea of the passion engendered by politics in those days is revealed when the emotions at Hatfield on that morning are examined. The young George Nathaniel Curzon, who felt keenly the fact that Lord Randolph had snubbed him in the January of the same year at Hatfield, was one of the guests, and he wrote to Godley some fifteen years later that Churchill 'did not know that [Salisbury] would be only too pleased to get rid of him. I was at

Hatfield that night and I remember the thanksgivings and hosannas that went up'. . . . On the 26th Lord Randolph lunched with the Jeunes in company with the Lord Chief Justice, Sir James Stephen and Lord Arthur Russell. The conversation was mainly about the resignation, and Churchill was subjected to a severe lecture from Stephen on his lack of patriotism and dereliction of duty which he bore cheerfully enough. He then startled the company by saying in reply that he never thought his offer to resign would be accepted; he said also that he thought Salisbury would be glad to get rid of him and would do nothing to enable him to return. He dwelt somewhat bitterly on the 'coldness and indifference' with which he had been treated by the Prime Minister. The subject of his replacement then arose. Mrs Jeune suggested Hartington; this was dismissed as extremely unlikely; she then mentioned Goschen [a former Liberal minister and financial expert, now a Liberal Unionist]. 'I had forgotten Goschen', Lord Randolph said, but then scoffed at the idea. . . . Some months after the crisis she was driving up Brook Street when she saw Lord Randolph walking towards her. She stopped to talk to him; he was very cheerful and gay, but at the end of the conversation he suddenly said to her, 'You were quite right; I forgot Goschen.'

Robert Rhodes James, *Lord Randolph Churchill*, 1959

188

Tory Democracy

IN 1885 Lord Randolph Churchill urged Wilfrid Scawen Blunt to stand for Parliament as a Tory Democrat. 'But what is Tory Democracy?' asked Blunt. Lord Randolph confessed to dreading the question in public. Being now in private he replied with commendable honesty: 'To tell the truth I don't know myself what Tory Democracy is. But I believe it is principally opportunism.'

Quoted in Elizabeth Longford, *A Pilgrimage of Passion: A Life of Wilfrid Scawen Blunt*, 1979

189

Dying in Public

Churchill had contracted syphilis, perhaps at a bachelor party on the eve of his wedding. By the early 1890s the symptoms of general paralysis had begun to appear, but he carried on with his political life; as Lord Rosebery put it, 'there was no retirement, no concealment. He died by inches in public, sole mourner at his own protracted funeral'. Churchill's son recorded:

WHAT experience can be more painful than for a man who enjoys the fullest intellectual vigour, and whose blood is quite unchilled by age, to feel the whole apparatus of expression slipping sensibly from him? He struggled against his fate desperately, and at first with intervals of profound depression. But, as the malady progressed, the inscrutable workings of Nature provided a mysterious anodyne. By a queer contradiction it is ordained that an all-embracing optimism should be one of the symptoms of this fell disease. The victim becomes continually less able to realise his condition. In the midst of failure he is cheered by an artificial consciousness of victory. While the days are swiftly ebbing, he builds large plans for the future; and a rosy glow of sunset conceals the approach of night. Therefore as Lord Randolph's faculties were steadily impaired, his determination to persevere was inversely strengthened; and in spite of the advice and appeals of his family, by which he was deeply wounded, he carried out in its entirety the whole programme of speeches he had arranged . . . But the crowds who were drawn by the old glamour of his name, departed sorrowful and shuddering at the spectacle of a dying man, and those who loved him were consumed with embarrassment and grief.

Winston Churchill, *Lord Randolph Churchill*, 1906

190

An Unparliamentary Scene

On the night of 27 July 1893, to cries of 'Herod!' and 'Judas!' the Commons voted on the Committee Stage, under a parliamentary guillotine, of the Home Rule Bill; in the excitement, the entrance to the voting lobbies become blocked.

SOME Liberal Members were standing in the centre of the Chamber, and this provoked Carson and some of his friends to shout 'Bar, Bar!' meaning that they should retire below the Bar. At this Mr J. W. Logan, Liberal MP for Market Harborough, crossed over to the Opposition Front Bench and addressed its occupants in strikingly unparliamentary language. 'Hold your bloody row', he said. To this unexpected salutation Carson replied in equally spirited terms: 'Get out, you gagger!' ... Logan, who appeared flushed and excited, thereupon seated himself in a threatening attitude beside Carson on the Front Bench. But any offensive action which Logan contemplated taking was promptly anticipated by another Member, normally a most quiet and respectable individual, named Hayes Fisher, afterwards Lord Downham. He sat immediately behind Carson and now leaned forward, seizing Logan under the chin and pulling his head back over the bench. Logan then struck out at Carson, but was overpowered by several of Carson's colleagues who interfered. The Irish Nationalists thereupon joined in with a yell, hitting out right, left and centre, the principal object of their attentions being the redoubtable Colonel Saunderson. That stalwart Unionist was soon in his element, distributing blows on all sides against his attackers. When little Dr Tanner approached him from behind and struck him on his bald head, Saunderson turned round and sent him flying with a sweep of his long arm. The fracas now became general and soon fights were seen to be going on in every corner of the Chamber. At least forty Members—what is known in quieter times as a quorum— were inextricably mingled below the gangway. One Member was knocked down and dragged out of the scuffle by his heels. John Ross, who was watching the scene from the Bar, ran forward to assist an elderly gentleman who had been felled to the ground by a particularly severe blow. He was forcibly restrained by a fellow Member who was convinced he was intent on further revenge. 'No you don't!

No you don't!' murmured the restraining Member as he held Ross fast.

The scrimmage lasted for nearly twenty minutes, hats being blocked, coats torn and faces bruised. Thick clouds of dust arose throughout the Chamber as the fighting became fiercer. A rail on one of the benches was dislodged in the turmoil and suddenly stood upright—a strange omen, as Tim Healy noted, like a dead arm thrusting itself from a corpse in *rigor mortis*. Meanwhile the Serjeant-at-Arms strode about doing his best to induce Members to enter the division lobbies, but his efforts were unheeded. The onlookers in the galleries, shocked at the spectacle of elderly frock-coated MPs belabouring each other, began to hiss, and their admonition had some effect on the disorderly groups below. Suddenly the uproar ended, as swiftly as it had begun.

Mr Speaker Peel, who had been sent for, was observed standing beside the Chair, surveying the extraordinary scene with an Olympian frown. The noise died down. In a few moments everything was quiet. 'Will some Member tell me what has occurred?' The Speaker spoke in the sternest tones. For a moment or two there was silence as honourable Members eyed each other uncomfortably. Then Mr Gladstone rose in his place, like the head boy of a class who has failed to keep order in his teacher's absence. He looked embarrassed as he gave his explanation. His embarrassment was increased by an old Member from the Opposition side who kept interrupting, 'All your fault! All your fault!' Suddenly, everyone began to laugh.

Montgomery Hyde, *Carson*, 1953

191

Pigott

In 1887 The Times published a facsimile letter, signed by Parnell, which condoned the Phoenix Park murders; the next year other incriminating letters from Parnell were produced. The Times had bought the letters for £30,000 after authentication by a handwriting expert. The government set up an inquiry by three judges, and the original vendor of the letters, an Irish journalist called James Pigott, broke down under cross-examination. He then went to the home of Henry Labouchere MP, editor of Truth, and confessed to forging them, a scene recorded by George Augustus Sala.

IN February 1889 I was the occupant of a flat in Victoria Street, Westminster and one Saturday, between one and two pm, a knock came at my study door, and I was handed a letter which had been brought in hot haste by a servant who was instructed to wait for an answer. The missive was of the briefest possible kind and was from my near neighbour Mr Henry Labouchere MP whose house was then at 24 Grosvenor Gardens. The note ran thus: 'Can you leave everything and come here at once? Most important business—H.L.' I told the servant that I would be in Grosvenor Gardens within a quarter of an hour, and ere that time had expired I was ushered into a large library on the ground floor, where I found the senior member for Northampton smoking his sempiternal cigarette but with an unusual expression of animation on his normally passive countenance.

He was not alone. Ensconced in a roomy fauteuil, a few paces from Mr Labouchere's writing-table, was a somewhat burly individual of middle stature and more than middle age . . . his elderly aspect was enhanced by his baldness, which revealed a large amount of *os frontis* fringed by grey locks. The individual had an eye-glass screwed into one eye, and he was using this optical aid most assiduously; for he was poring over a copy of that morning's issue of *The Times*, going right down one column and apparently up it again; then taking column after column in succession; then harking back as though he had omitted some choice paragraph; and then resuming the sequence of his lecture, ever and anon tapping that ovoid frontal bone of his, as though to evoke memories of the past, with a little silver pencil-case. I noted his shabby-genteel attire, and I observed that the hand which held the copy of *The Times* never ceased to shake. Mr Labouchere, in his most courteous manner and his blandest tone, said 'Allow me to introduce you to a gentleman of whom you must have heard a great deal, Mister—'. I replied: 'There is not the slightest necessity for naming him. I know him well enough. That's Mr Pigott.'

The individual in the capacious fauteuil wriggled from behind *The Times* an uneasy acknowledgement of my recognition; but if anything could be conducive to putting completely at his ease a gentleman who, from some cause or another, was troubled in his mind, it would have been the dulcet voice in which Mr Labouchere continued: 'The fact is that Mr Pigott has come here, quite unsolicited, to make a full confession. I told him that I would listen to nothing he had to say save in the presence of a witness and, remembering that you lived close by, I

thought that you would not mind coming here and listening to what Mr
Pigott has to confess, which will be taken down word by word from his
dictation in writing' . . . At length Mr Pigott stood up and came forward into the light, by the side of Mr Labouchere's writing-table. He
did not change colour; he did not blench; but when—out of the fulness
of his heart, no doubt—his mouth spake, it was in a low, half-musing
tone, more at first as though he were talking to himself than to any
auditors. By degrees, however, his voice rose, his diction became more
fluent. It is only necessary that, in this place, I should say that, in substance, Pigott confessed that he had forged the letters alleged to have
been written by Mr Parnell; and he minutely described the manner in
which he, and he alone, had executed the forgeries in question.
Whether the man with the bald head and the eyeglass in the library at
Grosvenor Gardens was telling the truth or was uttering another batch
of infernal lies it is not for me to determine. No pressure was put upon
him, no leading questions were asked him, and he went on quietly and
continuously to the end of [his story] . . . He was not voluble, but he
was collected, clear and coherent; nor, although he repeatedly confessed to forgery, fraud, deception and misrepresentation, did he seem
overcome with anything approaching active shame. His little peccadil-
loes were plainly owned, but he appeared to treat them more as
incidental weakness than as extraordinary acts of wickedness.

When he had come to the end of his statement Mr Labouchere left
the library for a few minutes to obtain a little refreshment. It was a
great relief to me when he came back for, when Pigott and I were left
together, there came over me a vague dread that he might disclose his
complicity with the Rye House Plot or admit he had been the
executioner of King Charles I. The situation was rather embarrassing;
the time might have been tided over by whistling, but unfortunately I
never learned to whistle. It would have been rude to read a book; and
besides to do so would have necessitated my taking my eyes off Mr
Pigott and I never took them off him. We did get into conversation but
our talk was curt and trite. He remarked, first taking up that so-often-
conned *Times*, that the London papers were inconveniently large.
This, being a self-evident proposition, met with no response from me,
but on his proceeding to say in quite a friendly manner that I must have
found the afternoon's interview rather stupid work, I replied that on
the contrary so far as I was concerned I had found it equally amusing
and instructive. Then the frugal Mr Labouchere coming back with
his mouth full, we went to business again. The whole of Pigott's

confession, beginning with the declaration that he had made it unin-
vited and without any pecuniary consideration, was read over to him
line by line and word by word. He made no correction or alteration
whatsoever. The confession covered several sheets of paper and to
each sheet he affixed his initials. Finally at the bottom of the completed
document he signed his name, beneath which I wrote mine as a witness.

George Augustus Sala, *Life and Adventures*, 1895

192

Labby and Joe

*Henry Labouchere and Joe Chamberlain were close Radical friends; when
Chamberlain left the Gladstonian Liberals over Home Rule, became a
Liberal Unionist and subsequently a leading Imperialist, the two men became
bitter political enemies.*

MR Labouchere remarked once that he had on only one occasion been
asked by a constituent for a pledge with regard to his parliamentary
action. He had unhesitatingly given it, and been unflinchingly true to
his word. The elector's injunction had been: 'Now mind, I say, and
keep your hi on Joe.'

Algar Thorold, *Life of Henry Labouchere*, 1913

193

WE were both the guests of Lady St Helier; who had a pleasant house
upon the Thames; all the afternoon we cruised along the river in a
launch. [Chamberlain] was most friendly to me, talked to me as if I
were a grown-up equal, and afterwards—as Austen used to recount—
gave me all kinds of commendation. The negotiations with President
Kruger were then in an extremely delicate condition. I was no doubt
keen that a strong line should be taken, and I remember his saying, 'It
is no use blowing the trumpet for the charge, and then looking around
to find nobody following.' Later we passed an old man seated upright
in a chair on his lawn at the brink of the river. Lady St Helier said,
'Look, there is Labouchere.' 'A bundle of old rags' was Chamberlain's
comment as he turned his head away from his venomous political
opponent. I was struck by the expression of disdain and dislike which

passed swiftly but with intenseness across his face. I realised as by a lightning-flash how deadly were the hatreds my agreeable, courteous, vivacious companion had contracted and repaid.

Winston Churchill, Great Contemporaries, 1937

194

Dilke Unavailable

Sir Charles Dilke (1843–1911), MP for Chelsea, and the rising star of the Liberal Party was in Gladstone's second cabinet, but his political career was shattered when a young married woman, Mrs Crawford, accused him of seducing her, of 'teaching me every French vice' and even persuading her to share a bed with his young servant, Fanny. Dilke was cited as co-respondent, and even before the case came on, Gladstone excluded him from his third cabinet, recording in his notebook: 'Dilke (unavailable).' The letter he wrote to Dilke on 2 February 1886 was a Victorian masterpiece:

My Dear Dilke,

I write to you, on this first day of my going regularly to my arduous work, to express my profound regret that any circumstances of the moment should deprive me of the opportunity and the hope of enlisting on behalf of a new Government the great capacity which you have proved in a variety of spheres and forms for rendering good and great service to Crown and country.

You will well understand how absolutely recognition on my part of an external barrier is separate from any want of inward confidence, the last idea I should wish to convey.

How can I close without fervently expressing to you my desire that there may be reserved for you a long and honourable career of public distinction?

Believe me always,
Yours Sincerely,
W. E. Gladstone

195

Dilke's attempt to clear his name before a special jury failed, chiefly because he proved such an inept witness. One of the most telling points against him was the condition of his diary, which (he said) he was accustomed to lacerate by the excision of large segments or by cutting neat little circular holes out of its pages. Mrs Crawford's counsel, Henry Matthews QC, made the most of this while cross-examining Dilke about his appointments and movements:

Matthews: I suppose these pieces have been cut out since?

Dilke: I always reduce it in bulk as much as possible. It is done in the morning, and I cut it so as to make it as small as possible.

Matthews: Do you mean you cut holes like that?

Dilke: Yes. It would be an engagement that has gone off.

Matthews: You mean that when an engagement goes off you cut a hole like that?

Dilke: Yes—you will find it done everywhere.

Matthews: What do you mean by an engagement going off?

Dilke: I mean to say if I have made an engagement to see a person, and that person did not come, I should cut it out.

The President of the Court: Do I understand you to say that you carried that very book, which we see, out with you?

Dilke: No.

The President: Then I do not very well see why it is necessary to cut it so as to reduce it in bulk as you say.

Dilke: Because it goes into my letter-box; if you like to send to my house now you can get any of my boxes.

Matthews: When was it you cut the holes?

Dilke: If any of my engagements go off, I take the scissors and cut it out.

Matthews: You sit down with scissors or a penknife and cut it out and cut holes in your diary?

Dilke: I should naturally cut it out, not cutting the diary through—cutting the part off—I should cut it out.

Matthews: If I really understood you rightly that because an engagement goes off, instead of just striking a pen or pencil through it, you would sit down with a penknife and cut a hole in it like that?

Dilke: I sometimes strike a pencil through it, but the blot of a pen is a trouble. I always sit with scissors by my side.

Printed in Roy Jenkins, *Sir Charles Dilke*, 1958

196

After the jury found against Dilke, a music-hall song circulated (it was also translated into French and Latin):

> MASTER DILKE upset the Milk,
> Taking it home to Chelsea,
> The papers say that Charlie's gay,
> Rather a wilful wag.
> This noble representative,
> Of everything good in Chelsea
> Has let the cat, the naughty cat,
> Out of the Gladstone bag.

197

Seeking to make a political comeback (he returned to parliament as MP for the Forest of Dean in 1892 but never again received office), Dilke was given sensible advice by his friend Joe Chamberlain:

IT is not to your interest to arouse the prejudices of the society in which you hope one day again to take your place. I do not mean fashionable society—but political society or the great majority of cultivated politicians. I think you go out of your way to offend them when you advocate evacuation of Egypt, and I ask you to consider if it is worth while . . . Therefore my advice is: Be as Radical as you like. Be Home Ruler if you must. But be a little Jingo if you can.

Jenkins, *Dilke*

198

Dilke did not abandon his amorous propensities. Staying at Glen, the famous Scottish home of the Tennant family, he made a pass at Margot Asquith's beautiful younger sister, Laura Tennant.

ON his second night in the house he met Laura in the passage on her way to bed, and said: 'If you will kiss me, I will give you a signed photograph.' She replied: 'It is awfully good of you, Sir Charles, but I would rather not, for what on earth should I do with the photograph?'

Margot Asquith, *Autobiography*, 1920

199

Gladstone's Funeral

*A. C. Benson, Eton master and son of the Archbishop of Canterbury E. W.
Benson, described Gladstone's funeral at Westminster Abbey, 28 May 1898.*

MRS GLADSTONE entered on the arm of Neville Lyttelton, looking
very frail but gallant—an almost painful attempt to smile. She seemed
a little dazed. All the Gladstones looked very worn and white, at the
end of their forces. Then a funeral march was played—Beethoven—
very fine; a certain amount of wind instruments and drums in organ
loft. Bridge (organist) rushing about and talking—I have no doubt
making jokes. Then the processions arrived. The Speaker first, preceded by heralds with white staves but in morning dress. The Speaker
was quite splendid. He walked slowly and firmly, looked very impassive
and dignified; an almost Egyptian face, though a high colour. Having a
train carried makes anyone who is not very stately look silly. The gold-
laced gown he wore was fine. The mace carried before him. One of the
clerks in a wig, hollow-eyed, bushy grizzled eyebrows also impressive.
Ministers first—Chamberlain (Colonial Secretary) very dapper
indeed. George Curzon (Viceroy of India) looks well again. Richie
(President of Board of Trade) looks the wickedest of the human
race—I believe he is a very good man—as if writhing under a load of
disreputable guilt. They observed a sort of precedence. Old Mowbray,
father of the House, whose chin had almost disappeared into his upper
lip, first. Then the House of Lords. The Lord Chancellor (Halsbury)
absolutely grotesque and made more so by the tremendous figure of
Sir Wellington Talbot (Serjeant-at-Arms) with a silver chain and large
white silk bows on his shoulders for mourning. But it is a poor thing to
have a noble head, a worn and stately expression and silver hair,
acquired by drawing £1500 a year from the public for fifty years and
sitting in a pew like an upper footman. The Archbishop of York (Mac-
lagan) very pale and upright with a pectoral cross, walking behind the
Lord Chancellor, was *magnificent*—most dignified. The Bishops,
especially Salisbury (Wordsworth) who was white, elephantine and
what the Scotch call *creishy*, were not great. Lichfield (Legge) looked
25. The Duke of Devonshire looked younger and leaner and lighter
than I had imagined. Lord Dufferin very splendid. There were a

number of red-nosed people, like half-pay officers, who shambled in—Earls, I think. Among the barons the leanest and shiftiest person I ever saw, in threadbare clothes like a sexton. . . . The two most striking figures were the Archbishop (Temple), very haggard, pale and dusty-looking with his huge whiskers. He had no hood I think; at all events he looked all black and white—very tired and old, and so blind that he was merely led. He seemed to walk with closed eyes. The Bishop of Durham (Westcott) with leonine white hair, such a bowed little figure, deeply affected. He has lost, I imagine, his teeth as his face was all crumpled together.

The Coffin . . . came solemnly along, the bearers holding feebly on to it. Lord Salisbury with a skull-cap, huge, shabby, tear-stained and a heavy, brooding look, most impressive. A. Balfour languid and weary, figure slim and young. The Duke of Rutland, a nobly bowed figure with dark complexion and silky white hair. The Prince of Wales, healthier and more wholesome than I have ever seen him, but with the old look, half insolence and half timidity. He was kept waiting, I hear, just in the doorway and damned and swore at the draught. The Duke of York a poor little figure. Lord Kimberley like a respectable Nonconformist tradesman. Harcourt, large, looming and mournful . . .

An interesting dinner at Ainger's. Sate next L. V. (Loulou) Harcourt who talked much of Gladstone. He said that Mrs Gladstone used to come tripping into the room when Mr G. was dying, with the intention always foremost in her mind of keeping his spirits up, and say 'You're ever so much better. Next week you will be about again and in a month quite well!' He used at last to send for Mrs Drew and say 'I cannot stand this! I want to prepare my mind for the end and cannot bear these terrible misconceptions.' He went on to say that Lady Frederick Cavendish (who left Hawarden in April because it was too great a trial to her faith) treated him very harshly. Used to tell him it was all imagination, and when someone was mentioned whose name Mr G. could not catch, saying 'I don't understand', hand to ear, she screamed out, 'Oh, don't you know Uncle William—the man who always calls you Gordon's murderer.' He went on to say that when he went with the Brasseys to Norway with Mr and Mrs Gladstone, he was sitting in a chair near Mr G. Mr G. was just recovering from sea-sickness and Mrs G., very lively, came out of her cabin, came up to Mr G. who was reading, and stroked the three hairs that lay across his forehead. Mr G.'s face assumed an expression of diabolical rage, and he was just going to say something strong when he saw that Loulou was looking.

The look of wrath died down, was succeeded by a flat and dull apathy which presently broke into wreathed smiles, but with rage still beaming from the corner of his eye. He said: 'I am wonderfully long-suffering, Mr Harcourt.'

> *Edwardian Excursions: From the Diaries of A. C. Benson, 1898–1904*, ed. David Newsome, 1981

200

Harty Tarty

The 8th Duke of Devonshire (1833–1908), better known as the Marquess of Hartington, or 'Harty-Tarty', was the greatest political grandee of his age. In the 1860s and 1870s, his affections were fought over by two remarkable women, the society whore Catherine Walters ('Skittles') and the German adventuress Louisa von Alten, Duchess of Manchester. Hartington gave Skittles a house in Mayfair and £2,000 a year; but the Duchess won the battle, becoming his principal mistress and, after the death of her husband in 1892, his wife.

DURING all these years of scheming and working and keeping her fingers in important places everyone feared Louisa Manchester—feared her and coveted her invitations. Although she failed in her largest ambition, she learned how to make and break men. She wielded power and used it without pity. She had no women friends—the feminine sex disliked her—but she could hold her man. Once she got her manacles on the good-natured Harty-Tarty, she never let go. She must have kept him in unplatonic tow for nearly thirty years before she became widowed and was able to marry him, thus earning the nickname of the Double Duchess . . . The Prince of Wales knew of and enjoyed the love affairs of his friends, and in 1876, when Louisa had determinedly made Hartington her property, H. R. H. devised one of his most famous practical jokes. During an official tour of Coventry the Prince instructed his equerry to ask the Mayor to make certain the party inspected the bowling-alley because Lord Hartington was so keen on that game. When they reached the alley Hartington showed no particular interest, so the Mayor explained: 'His Royal Highness asked specially for the inclusion of this alley in the tour in tribute to your Lordship's love of skittles.'

> Anita Leslie, *Edwardians in Love*, 1972

201

FAR from being intimidated by Court etiquette, he had been known to display an unprecedented independence of character. Dining one night with his Sovereign, he was enjoying a saddle of four-year-old mutton, a specialty of the Windsor kitchens. But he had forgotten that as soon as the Queen had finished her own plate, it was the custom of the footmen to remove those of her guests. Pausing in the middle of his conversation, the Duke realised that his barely-touched dinner had vanished. 'Here', he said sharply, 'bring that back!'

Rose, *Superior Person*

202

May 26 1903: The Duchess of Devonshire is much disturbed because the Prime Minister has asked the Duke to give a dinner on the King's Birthday to relieve his list of a number of Privy Councillors in both Houses. 'That Mr Sandars' [Balfour's secretary], she says, 'is always interfering', and she has some cause to complain that, at the moment the Lord President is denied a salary, he is asked quite contrary to any precedent to take some of his official guests off the hands of the Prime Minister. However, the Duke was never known to refuse his good offices at the request of a colleague, and the dinner is to be given. . . .
June 26: The Duke's dinner at Devonshire House was attended by thirty peers and Privy Councillors . . . After dinner Mr Chaplin, who was on the Duke's left, informed me that he had never had a better dinner but there was one point he had ventured to criticise, and asked the Duke to convey a message to the Duchess, viz, that the grapes with ortolans were not stoned. Jesse Collings, just before he left, button-holed the Duke on tariff reform. He was a little bit the better for the banquet and very full of the great things Mr Chamberlain was to do and the activity that the Birmingham organisation was displaying on the subject. The Duke heard him in absolute silence, and at the end of the conversation, by which time they had reached the top of the stair-case, said grimly: 'Good night, Mr Collings; take care of the first step.'

Almeric FitzRoy, *Memoirs*, 1929

203

The Duke of Devonshire owned what was then the finest private collection of paintings and books in England, at Chatsworth. The Librarian there described his last visit to the house:

HE came in while I was arranging one of the cases that contained the rarer books, and asked me to show him some of the more precious among these. I took out the first edition of *Paradise Lost*, which he seemed not to know. The Duke sat down with the book and, to my astonishment, began to read the poem aloud from the first line. He read on for quite a time, stopping once to say, 'How fine this is! I had forgotten how fine it was'; when the Duchess came in and, poking her parasol into the Duke, whimsically remarked, 'If he begins to read poetry he will never come out for his walk.'

Bernard Holland, Life of the Duke of Devonshire, 1911

204

Skittles's Memories

Among Catherine Walters's younger lovers was Wilfrid Scawen Blunt, and in her old age (1905) she confided in him.

WHEN Blunt sent her a present of rabbits for the pot, she thanked him with a story of Disraeli and Gladstone: how Dizzy was 'a kind old fellow but very dull . . . I loved old bully Gladstone far more than "Dizzy", old G. had a lot of fun in him and was a more powerful man to me than old Dizzy.' [Lord Clanricarde] had once lent her £500 on the security of her jewels, 'but he always refused to let her have them back except on a certain condition and that it should be in her riding hat'. He used to come 'sneaking outside the house at night', so that the then Prince of Wales and Lord Hartington were forced to empty a *pot de chambre* on his head.

Elizabeth Longford, Wilfrid Scawen Blunt

205

A Scientific Premier

Lord Salisbury, premier three times, was an amateur scientist of some distinction and a Fellow of the Royal Society. His house, Hatfield, frequently caught fire.

THE cause was the primitive system of electric light which Salisbury installed at Hatfield in 1881, one of the first two houses in England to have it. The need for fuses was not yet recognised and occasionally an overloaded wire ignited the panelling. The family was well trained to deal with the emergency and would hurl cushions at the fire until it was extinct. Salisbury's practical interest in science caused other interruptions to the rhythm of domestic routine. Once he almost died from chlorine poisoning. On another occasion there was a loud report and he staggered out of his private laboratory streaming with blood and observing with some satisfaction that he knew the exact cause of the explosion: experimenting with sodium in an insufficiently dried retort. He introduced an early model of the telephone, its wire running loose across the floor. From every corner of the house startled visitors would hear the voice of their host testing the instrument with a reiterated: 'Hey, diddle diddle, the cat and fiddle, the cow jumped over the moon.'

Kenneth Rose, *The Later Cecils*, 1975

206

SALISBURY, as he got older, often failed to recognise people. At a dinner party, he enquired who was the gentleman sitting opposite him. His startled host replied it was Mr W. H. Smith, his closest cabinet colleague. Salisbury excused himself by saying that as Smith sat next to him in cabinet, he was used to seeing him in profile. When he resigned office for the last time, King Edward VII gave him a signed photograph of himself. Salisbury scrutinised it closely, shook his head sorrowfully, and said: 'Poor Buller.'

Anon.

207

Lord Salisbury and Patronage

Lord Salisbury's Lord Chancellor, Halsbury, was often accused of favouritism and political bias in the use of his legal patronage; asked when a particularly juicy appointment came up whether, ceteris paribus, *the best man would get it, he replied:* 'Ceteris paribus *be damned, I'm going to appoint my nephew.' But when Tories got the judgeships, he was not always to be blamed, as Salisbury's daughter and official biographer admitted:*

WITH regard to many non-political posts, [Salisbury] would be frankly partisan in his selections. Legal promotions did not come under his direct appointment, but he would never apologise for the practice of making them a reward for political 'right thinking'. Within certain limits of intelligence, honesty and knowledge of law, one man would make as good a judge as another, and a Tory mentality was, *ipso facto*, more trustworthy than a Liberal one. 'We must pay our debts first in the way of judgeships', he wrote to Lord Randolph when the farewell distribution of places on leaving office in 1885 was being prepared for: 'Legal partisans are as bad as duns even when it is not judgeships they want. Gorst lies heavy on my soul; I dare not look Clarke in the face; and I am round the corner if I see Stavely Hill; while the thought of Webster keeps me awake at night.' An incident recorded by Mr Buckle witnesses to the same point of view. The *Times* editor called at Arlington Street for the express purpose of impressing upon the Prime Minister the disrepute which the Lord Chancellor was bringing upon the Government by certain partisan legal appointments. Lord Salisbury listened to his budget and then observed, with meditative detachment, that it was hard on his colleague that he should be so much abused for what was, in fact, his own responsibility: 'I believe it was I who pressed most strongly on him the claims of those who are considered the worst'.

Lady G. Cecil, *Life of Lord Salisbury*, 1931

208

Lady Londonderry

Lady Londonderry, daughter of Viscount ('the Squire') Chaplin, was not only London's leading political hostess but sometimes usurped her husband's political role. When he was made Lord President of the Council in 1903, the Clerk of the Privy Council noted in his diary:

October 28th: This morning, while occupied at my table in the Privy Council Office, the door stealthily opened for the admission, first, of the upper part of a woman's headgear, then of her hair, a pair of amused eyes which I still failed to recognise, and then the revelation of Lady Londonderry's head. . . . *November 23rd*: A curious scene was to be witnessed in the bow-window of the Lord President's room this morning. For more than two hours Lady Londonderry presided over a departmental consultation as to the steps to be taken in dealing with the Durham County Council in its treatment of the voluntary schools of the county. It is true that the Lord President was nominally a party to the conference, but he remained at one end of the table in isolated dignity, while Lady L. held the Permanent Secretary and the subordinate official immediately concerned in close communion. . . . It is certainly a new departure when a Minister's wife undertakes to look into matters of departmental administration in the very seat of her husband's authority, and leaves to him the simple functions of an interested listener.

FitzRoy, *Memoirs*

209

Balfour's Indifference

A. J. Balfour, Salisbury's nephew, made his reputation as Irish Secretary. He was later Leader of the House and Prime Minister (1902–5).

HE was quite fearless. . . . Once I saw a furious scene in the House of Commons when an Irish Member, rushing across the floor in a frenzy, shook his fist for a couple of minutes within a few inches of his face. We young fellows behind were all ready to spring to his aid upon a physical foe; but Arthur Balfour, Leader of the House, regarded the frantic figure with no more and no less than the interest of a biologist examining through a microscope the contortions of a rare and provoked insect. Once during the War when we were rather dissatisfied with the vigour of Sir Edward Grey's policy, I, apologising for him, said to Mr Lloyd George, who was hot, 'Well, anyhow, we know that if the Germans were here and said to Grey, "If you don't sign this Treaty, we will shoot you at once", he would certainly reply, "It would be most improper for a British Minister to yield to a threat. That sort of thing is not done." ' But Lloyd George rejoined, 'That's not what the Germans would say to him. They would say, "If you don't sign this Treaty, we will scrag all your squirrels at Fallodon." That would break him down.' Arthur Balfour had no squirrels.

Churchill, *Great Contemporaries*

210

It was not lack of courage: he showed that in abundance during the Boer War; not lack of ability; he had that in a superlative degree; not onesidedness: he would also listen to any arguments. It was sheer intellectual indolence, a never-knowing his case, an instinctive love for compromise and a trust in the mental agility which would enable him at the last moment to extricate himself from any complication however embarrassing . . . The truth is that Balfour with his scintillating intellectual exterior had no depth of feeling, no profound convictions, and strange to say (in spite of his fascination of manner) no real affection. We all knew that, when the emergency came, he would drop or desert or sacrifice any one of us without a pang, as he did me in India, as he did George Wyndham over Ireland. Were any one of us to die suddenly he would dine out that night with undisturbed composure, and in the intervals of conversation or bridge, would be heard to murmur: 'Poor old George.'

Memorandum by Lord Curzon, printed in Rose, *Superior Person*

211

The 1906 Election

The January 1906 elections produced a Liberal landslide and, for the first time, a block of 50 Labour MPs. The former Tory Prime Minister, A. J. Balfour, and six of his cabinet colleagues lost their seats.

[ON returning home, Balfour] found waiting for him a note from Lady Salisbury which ran thus:

My dear A. J. B.: Damn, damn, damn!

He answered:

My dear Alice,
   I am delighted at the pithiness and vigour of your language . . . I am horribly ashamed at feeling a kind of illegitimate exhilaration at the catastrophe which has occurred. It has made me more violently and pleasurably interested in politics than I remember having been since the Home Rule Bill. If I read the signs aright, what has occurred has nothing whatever to do with any of the things we have been squabbling over the last few years. Campbell-Bannerman is a mere cork, dancing on a torrent he cannot control, and what is going on here is the faint echo of the same movement which has produced massacres in St Petersburg, riots in Vienna and Socialist processions in Berlin.

Blanche Dugdale, Arthur James Balfour, 1939

212

The Relugas Compact

In 1905 the leaders of the Liberal Imperialists, Grey, Asquith, and Haldane, determined to emasculate Sir Henry Campbell-Bannerman, the nominal leader of the Liberal Party, when they all came into office. R. B. Haldane (1856–1928) described how they planned to do it:

WE resolved to take some step. Here Asquith and I were more practical than Grey, who hated to have to make any move. I went to Asquith at a country house he and his wife had taken at Glen of Rothes in the north-east of Scotland. Grey had a fishing at Relugas, only about fifteen miles off. After consultation, Asquith and I decided to go over to confer with Grey. This was at the beginning of September, 1905. We talked the situation over with him. It was decided that it was of great importance that the King, who would soon have to summon a Prime Minister, should be cognizant of the situation. Asquith thought that as I had been much in contact with the King over London University, I would be a natural channel of communication. Grey did not dissent, but he thought that Asquith should also see Campbell-Bannerman as early as possible and tell him our difficulties. What we agreed on was . . . that if Campbell-Bannerman became Prime Minister he should take a peerage, and that Asquith should lead in the Commons as Chancellor of the Exchequer. Unless our scheme were in substance carried out we resolved that we could not join Campbell-Bannerman's government. What we thus resolved on we used afterwards at times to speak of among ourselves as the 'Relugas Compact'.

Viscount Haldane, *Autobiography*, 1929

213

But politicians in opposition propose; Prime Ministers in office dispose. Once charged by Edward VII with forming a government, Campbell-Bannerman soon put the plotters in their place.

C. B. . . . said with a laugh, 'Do you know it was the comicality of it that I could hardly get over. They were to serve *under* me, but on condition that they were not to be *with* me! . . . This thing began on Monday; and I let it go on for three days; and then I said to each and all of them, "Now look here, I have been playing up till now. . . . But now let me just say—*that it is I who am the head of this Government: it is I who have the King's Command: I am on horseback*, and you will be all pleased to understand that I *will not go to the House of Lords*; that I *will not have any condition of the kind imposed upon me*." 'So', says C. B., 'they all came in—no conditions; no nothing; and there they are.'

Lord Shaw, *Letters to Isabel*, 1921

214

Shrewd and Simple 'C-B'

Campbell-Bannerman and his wife Charlotte, the dominant member of the pair, were both enormous eaters and each weighed nearly 20 stone. He once described his favourite meal as 'mutton broth, fresh herring or salmon, haggis, roast mutton, grouse, apple tart and strawberries' and he finished off every meal with gingerbread and butter.

C-B talked over everything with her. He gave all his colleagues nicknames, or if he couldn't think of a suitable nickname referred to them by the name of their houses or their constituency. This enabled him to preserve discretion when talking political gossip in front of the servants. Lord Salisbury was 'Old Sarum'; John Morley (most appropriately) 'Priscilla'; Haldane 'Schopenhauer'; the massive W. V. Harcourt, after his house in the New Forest, 'Malwood', 'The Malwood Philosopher', 'The Nymph of Malwood' or just 'The Nymph'; Rosebery 'Son Eminence Grise' or 'Barnboogle' after his castle on the Forth; Dilke 'The Forest of Dean'; Spencer 'Spec'; and King Edward VII 'Jupiter' . . . [When away] he wrote to Charlotte every day and sometimes two or three times a day. These letters are extremely affectionate. He addressed her as 'Dearest Mouse', 'My own darling diddy', or 'My own pet' and signed them 'Your loving true Poo Ole', 'Your loving bin D' or 'Your old homespinbin D'.

John Wilson, Sir Henry Campbell-Bannerman, 1973

215

C-B observed his colleagues shrewdly:

IN 1894, when Rosebery in his first speech as Prime Minister caused a storm by describing England in relation to Ireland as 'the predominant partner', he asked C. B., in some perplexity, why this remark had stirred up such a shemozzle. He pointed out that it was, after all, true. C. B. used to enjoy telling this story afterwards. It showed, he said, how little political and parliamentary education Rosebery had had if he thought it a sufficient defence of any public utterance that it was true.

Ibid.

216

On Haldane: 'No more tact than a hippopotamus . . . Haldane always prefers the backstairs. But it does not matter. The clatter can be heard all over the house.'

C-B was amused by John Burns's colossal vanity. He told Lord Rendel in 1907 that when he sent for Burns he said, 'John, I want you to join the Cabinet and take the Local Government Board.' Burns replied: 'Sir 'Enry, you never did a more popular thing in your life.'

217

But C-B was not always tactful himself. Augustine Birrell KC records how C-B appointed him Chief Secretary to Ireland.

C. B., always the frankest of men, at once confirmed my suspicions by telling me that he wanted me to go to Ireland. I instantly demurred to the proposal and indicated that it was not at all to my mind. 'Of course it is not', said C. B., 'but tell me, if it is not you, who is it to be?' I had my answer ready and named a colleague (Tommy Shaw) who I had reason to believe would not be unacceptable to our Irish friends. 'Good gracious', replied C. B., 'why Tommy is a great friend of mine.' I answered this with as much hauteur as I ever have been able to command in the crises of life: 'I hoped I was also one of your friends.' C. B. laughed heartily, and assured me he meant no more than that Tommy, being a particular friend of his, he knew that as a lawyer his ambitions lay in the direction of his own profession. I confess, when I heard this, I thought somewhat ruefully of the years between 1873 and 1906 spent by me in daily attendance at New Square, Lincoln's Inn, studying and practising, both in stuff and silk, the mysteries of an Equitable Jurisprudence. Was I not a lawyer? Had I no right to be mildly ambitious in the direction of my profession? However, I had the good sense to perceive that this was not an occasion to enlighten the ignorance of my chief or to try to excite his interest in my biography, so after a few further protestations I accepted the office.

Augustine Birrell, *Things Past Redress*, 1937

218

The Last Whig

I REMEMBER a story told me by the Duke of Devonshire which was very typical of Lord Lansdowne. The Duke had succeeded (to his title) in 1909, much to his disgust, for he had to leave the House of Commons, of which he had been a member for many years. He then became a Whip in the House of Lords, under Lord Lansdowne's leadership, the Conservative and Unionist Party being in opposition. One day they were walking back from the House of Lords on what had seemed a brilliant, warm, sunny afternoon. The House had risen early.

It was about five o'clock. Then it began to rain heavily. They were accoutred in the uniform of the day—frock-coat, top hat, walking-stick. They had no protection. When they got to the top of the Duke of York steps, the Duke said to his father-in-law, 'Let's get into the Carlton Club out of this drenching rain.' (The old Carlton Club before its destruction by bombing in the Second World War stood next to the Reform in Pall Mall.)

Lord Lansdowne looked at him with horror. Although he had resigned from a Liberal government in 1873, held the highest offices in successive Unionist governments and was now the actual leader of the Unionist Party in the Upper House, such a proposal was most distasteful to him. The Duke told me that Lord Lansdowne gave him the kind of look as if he had suggested something utterly disgraceful or as if he had committed some unforgivable act. 'What do you mean, Victor, go in here? Not at all.' Drenched as they were, he insisted in walking all the way along Pall Mall, up St James's Street, until they got to Brooks's Club. Here was a Whig Club, where the portrait of Charles James Fox still presided over a collection of noblemen and gentlemen, some still working for the Liberal Party, some with the Conservatives, but all by adoption or inheritance undoubted Whigs.

Harold Macmillan, *The Past Masters*, 1975

219

Asquith after Dinner

22 April 1911 . . . On Thursday night the PM was vy bad: & I squirmed with embarrassment. He could hardly speak: & many people noticed his condition. He continues most friendly & benevolent, & entrusts me with everything after dinner. Up till that, he is at his best— but thereafter! It is an awful pity, & only the persistent freemasonry of the House of Commons prevents a scandal. I like the old boy & admire both his intellect & his character. But what risks to run. We only got him away the other night just before Balfour began the negotiations wh I conducted but wh otherwise wd have fallen to him—with disastrous consequences. The next day he was serene, efficient, undisturbed . . .

Winston Churchill to his wife, quoted in Randolph Churchill, *Winston S. Churchill*, 1967

220

The Hughligans

When Asquith, as Prime Minister, went to the Commons on 24 July 1911 to announce that the government was determined to push through the Parliament Act, he was made the object of a demonstration organized by Lord Hugh Cecil:

THE Speaker's Gallery was packed to suffocation with female friends and foes, those in the back rows standing upon their chairs. Below, the House was more densely crowded than I had ever seen it, and my father got a tremendous reception as he walked to the floor, members on our side waving hats and handkerchiefs. But through the deafening cheers I began to hear shouts of 'Traitor' and when he rose to speak he was greeted by an organised uproar. For half an hour he stood at the box while insults and abuse were hurled at him by a group of Tory members led by Lord Hugh Cecil and Mr F. E. Smith. There was a background chorus of 'Divide, divide' against which articulate shouts and yells rang out—'Traitor!'—'Redmond!'—'Who killed the King?' I could not take my eyes off Lord Hugh Cecil, who screamed: 'The King is in duress!' and in his frenzied writhings seemed like one possessed. His transformation, and that of many other personal friends, was terrifying. They behaved, and looked, like mad baboons.

Violet Bonham Carter, Winston Churchill as I Knew Him, 1965

221

Grey's War Speech

The speech of Sir Edward Grey, the Foreign Secretary, on 3 August 1914 was decisive in persuading the House of Commons to go to war against Germany.

GREY'S speech was very wonderful—I think in the circumstances one may say the greatest speech delivered in our time or for a very long period, taking the importance of the occasion, the necessity of persuading many doubtful persons, the extraordinary success which it had in that direction, its great dignity, warm emotion and perfect taste. . . .

I could deliver quite a lecture on the merits of the speech—its admirable arrangement, its perfect taste and the extraordinary dexterity with which he dealt with the weak spot of his argument. This was the nature of our obligation to France, under the Entente. With wonderful skill he did not argue the point, but he changed to a note of appeal to the individual conscience, thereby disarming criticism in the one matter where he was weak, without any departure, real or apparent, from perfect sincerity. All these substantial merits set off by his wonderful manner go to make his speech the greatest example of the art of persuasion that I have ever listened to.

Letter of 3 August 1914 from Lord Hugh Cecil MP to Wilfred Ward

222

THAT night, as the lamps were being lit in the summer dusk, Grey, standing in the windows of his room in the Foreign Office overlooking St James's Park, said to a friend: 'The lamps are going out all over Europe; we shall not see them lit again in our lifetime.'

G. M. Trevelyan, *Grey of Fallodon*, 1937

223

Though Grey committed Britain to a Continental policy and war, he only once went abroad and disliked foreigners; yet he was not the most insular of his colleagues. He recorded what happened when the French reconstructed their government on a wartime basis:

To greet this cabinet Asquith, Lloyd George and I went to Paris. We attended a meeting of it, and there beheld with great interest and respect the living forms of men whose names had been familiar to us in our youth as of high repute in French politics. It was a very large Council; the proceedings were complimentary and formal rather than important, but there was some discussion and it was naturally all in French. Such part as was taken by us was left to, or it would be more correct to say thrust upon myself. Asquith would not, Lloyd George could not and I *had* to speak French. In French I know my vocabulary to be limited, my grammar to be imperfect and my genders to be at the mercy of chance; further, I am told my accent is atrocious. But with my back really against a wall, something relevant could always be made forthcoming. When the Council was over and we three British Ministers were safely outside, Lloyd George said to me: 'You know, your French was the only French that I could understand.'

Lord Grey of Fallodon, *Twenty-Five Years*, 1929

224

Lord Kitchener

THE question of enemies came up; somebody said to K, 'How do you treat yours?' He said quite simply: 'Oh, I have *no* difficulty; you see, such awful things happen to them quite independently of me.' So we said: 'How do you mean?' and he said: 'Well, George Curzon lost his wife; Sir Edmund Ellis lost his and his son was eaten by a crocodile; and Sir Denzil Ibbetson died of cancer.'

Letter from Lady Desborough to A. J. Balfour, quoted in Nicholas Mosley, *Julian Grenfell*, 1976

225

Bringing Down the Government

Early in 1915, Lord Kitchener, the War Minister, was still the public hero. But the Commander of the Expeditionary Force, Sir John French, privately reported that he was being starved of shells. The Press Lord, Northcliffe, determined to shake the government.

LATE in the afternoon of 20 May, Northcliffe arrived at Carmelite House and, giving orders that he was not to be disturbed, himself wrote the leader for the next morning's *Daily Mail*. His secretary said that when he had finished writing it in his own hand 'his face was white and set'. He went over the article with Wilson, who warned him that it might bring upon his head the utmost wrath of the authorities. Wilson mentioned prison. 'I don't care what they do to me,' Northcliffe said.

'The circulation of the *Daily Mail* may go down to two and the circulation of *The Times* to one—I don't care. The thing has to be done! Better to lose circulation than to lose the war.' The leading article was sent to the printer. While he waited for proofs, Northcliffe called for the sub-editor who wrote the contents bills. For the next day, 21 May, he ordered one bill for all editions: KITCHENER'S TRAGIC BLUNDER. In a few minutes a proof of the leading article was in his hands. He took it into Marlowe's room. Having read it, Marlowe said to him: 'You realize, I suppose, that you are smashing the people's idol?' Northcliffe's reply was: 'I don't care. Isn't it all true?' 'Quite true,' Marlowe said, 'but it will make the public very angry. Are you prepared for the consequences?' To which Northcliffe retorted: 'I don't care tuppence for the consequences. That man is losing the war!'

After seeing Marlowe, Northcliffe drove down to Totteridge, taking the leading article with him to read it over to his mother. She suggested certain changes of emphasis. He made them and then telephoned instructions to Carmelite House that the article was to 'go in' that night. Wickham Steed, who was with him in the evening, recorded that he looked 'more grim' than he had ever seen him . . . The attack on Kitchener shocked the public, shook Whitehall and threw Northcliffe's critics into new paroxysms of rage. At 11 am that morning he telephoned to the *Daily Mail* circulation manager, Valentine Smith. 'What do you think of the contents bill this morning?' Smith answered: 'It will cause us a lot of trouble. We're bombarded with orders reducing supplies.' Northcliffe asked him how many readers the paper might lose. 'A hundred thousand at least,' was the reply. 'I don't care,' said Northcliffe in his quietest tone . . .

The service clubs of Pall Mall banished *The Times* and the *Daily Mail* from their midst. Individual readers cancelled their subscriptions. Fifteen hundred members of the London Stock Exchange burnt copies of both papers to a chorus of cheers for Kitchener and jeers for Northcliffe. The Liberal *Westminster Gazette* praised 'the manly and honourable impulse' of the stockbrokers who, it was surmised at Carmelite House, were also working off an old score against the *Daily Mail* for having established the 'Daily Mail Exchange' to assist readers in their share transactions. The paper was denounced and burnt by members of the Liverpool Provision Exchange. Envelopes containing bits of charred *Daily Mail* were sent to Northcliffe. Similar demonstrations were staged at the Baltic Exchange in London and at the Cardiff Coal and Shipping Exchange . . . The *Daily Mail* sale on the day of the

Kitchener attack was 1,386,000 copies. By the end of the campaign the circulation had fallen by 238,000 copies.

Reginald Pound and Geoffrey Harmsworth, *Northcliffe*, 1959

(On 26 May the Liberal government fell, and Lloyd George was made Minister of Munitions in the new national coalition.)

226

The PM at Cards

The drowning of Lord Kitchener on 5 June 1916 provoked a political crisis over who was to succeed him as War Minister.

BONAR LAW now endeavoured to get in touch with Asquith, only to be informed that if he wanted to see the Prime Minister he must go to the latter's house at Sutton Courtenay in Berkshire. Bonar Law was naturally irritated at this news. It was too late to go that evening and the next morning he and Aitken were due to leave for Paris together. However, he could not risk Asquith making the appointment before he had time to put the case for Lloyd George. Accordingly early on Monday morning he motored with Aitken from Leatherhead to Sutton Courtenay. Bonar Law went into the house leaving his companion in the car. He found the Prime Minister engaged in a rubber of bridge with three ladies. Asquith genially requested him to wait till the game was finished. Bonar Law, by now considerably annoyed, declined to wait and informed him of the discussion with Lloyd George. Asquith immediately offered the War Office to Bonar Law. Bonar Law replied that it was too late: he would have taken it, had it been offered before his discussion with Lloyd George, but by now he was committed to the latter; and in any case he considered Lloyd George the best man for the job. Faced with this situation Asquith agreed to offer the post to Lloyd George.

The episode left a lasting impression upon Bonar Law. His doubts about Asquith were more than confirmed. It seemed to him that the Prime Minister displayed a levity which was inexcusable in so serious a matter. Moreover, fond of bridge as he was himself, he regarded it as wrong that the leader of a nation engaged in a struggle for its existence should be playing cards on a Monday morning, and should oblige one of his principal colleagues to put off all arrangements in order to visit him at his country house fifty miles away from London. Earlier in the year Bonar Law had observed in a letter to Asquith: 'In war it is necessary not only to be active but to seem active.' These were words Asquith would have been prudent to heed.

Robert Blake, *The Unknown Prime Minister*, 1955

227

Curzoniana

More stories are told about Lord Curzon than any other modern British statesman, Churchill alone excepted. He was the last to live and behave like a nineteenth-century grandee, at Carlton House Terrace in London, and at his many and vast country houses, Kedleston, Hackwood, Montacute etc. He had the endearing but risky habit of telling stories against himself.

To a fellow member of the cabinet, on observing the attire of one of their colleagues: 'Gentlemen never wear brown in London.'

On first taking a bus: 'This omnibus business is not what it is reported to be. I hailed one at the bottom of Whitehall and told the man to take me to Carlton House Terrace. But the fellow flatly refused.'

On seeing soldiers on leave in a swimming pool: 'Good heavens! I never knew that the working classes had such white skins!'

Instructing his second wife on the subject of love-making: 'Ladies never move.'

Once, at Kedleston, he was summoned by his butler to the telephone. His private secretary at the Foreign Office, Robert Vansittart, wished to tell him that a certain foreign statesman had died suddenly. *Curzon*: 'Do you realise that to convey to me this trivial piece of information, you have forced me to walk the length of a mansion not far removed from the dimensions of Windsor Castle?'

Curzon's behaviour often attracted the asperities of his colleagues:

Winston Churchill, complaining of the unavailability of the Foreign Secretary during the 1922 Chanak Crisis: 'In spite of the momentous situation, Lord Curzon had left London on Friday night for one of his country seats, and did not propose to return till Tuesday. On Sunday Lord Curzon was definitely requested by Mr Lloyd George and Mr Chamberlain to return to London. He replied that he was remaining in the country because his house in London was not properly prepared for his reception. He was finally induced to return on Monday. To this day I do not know how the problem of his lordship's accommodation in the metropolis was ultimately solved.'

The 17th Earl of Derby: 'He makes one feel so terribly plebeian.'

In March 1917, Derby complained to Bonar Law, head of the Tory Party and War Minister, in charge of official army cars, of Curzon's misuse of government transport: 'There was a car placed at the disposal of the Air Board but when I was Chairman I never once used it. When Curzon came to the Air Board he calmly took it for himself. He talks about it being for general use but I should doubt a single soul having been in it except himself and his guests. He motors them down to Hackwood and uses the car for sending to the station for his Saturday-to-Monday parties, and I should like to have asked him whether it is not true on the occasion of his Dance the other night the car came backwards and forwards to London three times. . . . The real truth is he is just what he *says* he is not. He is one of the meanest men that I know. He was a tenant of mine at one time and I have good reason for knowing it.'

On one occasion Curzon kept the cabinet waiting, without sending any message of explanation or apology. At long last an office messenger arrived, bearing an antique footstool, covered in green baize, on which Curzon was accustomed to rest his leg (he suffered from phlebitis). Derby said: 'The Marquess himself has not yet arrived but we see premonitory symptoms.' And he rose and bowed to the footstool.

Lord Beaverbrook: 'In 1898 he was created Viceroy of India, an office filled with pomp and ceremony, at the youthful age of thirty-nine. In his train followed long strings of elephants and retinues of gaily colourful servants. But his years of semi-kingship came to an end in 1905, when at forty-six years of age he left India an angry and embittered man. For all the rest of his life Curzon was influenced by his sudden journey to heaven at the age of thirty-nine and then by his return seven years later to earth, for the remainder of his mortal existence. Lloyd George treated him roughly but gave him compensation in the form of a Marquisate, in which he took pride. Curzon changed sides on almost every issue during his long career. Often undecided whether to desert a sinking ship for one that might not float, he would make up his mind to sit on the wharf for a day. He had many intimates, but none of them deplored his reverses in public life.'

A few days before Curzon's death, he was described by a young architect, A. S. G. Butler, employed on work at Kedleston: 'He was lying in the State bed, that superb design by Robert Adam with tall carved and gilded columns upholding a canopy, tufted with smoke-blue feathers at each corner. The high bed-head was heavily embroidered with heraldry—an effect of acid blues and gold—and the counterpane matched it. He was lying there wearing grey gloves in the cold, silk-lined room and reading a magazine of adventure stories.'

Curzon went to great trouble to adorn the tomb of his first wife and to prepare his own in Kedleston church. Not long after his death, his widow went down into the vault to look at his coffin. On a nearby ledge she noticed a postcard. It bore, in his handwriting, the words: 'Reserved for the second Lady Curzon.'

Lord Beaverbrook, *Men and Power*, 1956; Rose, *Superior Person*, Leonard Mosley, *Curzon: The End of an Epoch*, 1960

228

Lord Curzon's Trousers

The Marquess Curzon, as Foreign Secretary, attended the 1922 Lausanne Conference accompanied by a new valet, who turned out to be a drunk. His antics culminated in a scene in the ballroom of the Beau Rivage Hotel in which, wearing Curzon's evening clothes, he reeled around with the delegates' wives. He was told to take the first train back to England, and Harold Nicolson, one of Curzon's staff, recorded the sequel. He calls the valet 'Arketall':

I DID not witness his departure. I merely heard next morning that he had gone. While having breakfast I received a message that Lord Curzon wished to see me urgently. I found him in his dressing-gown. He was half angry and half amused. 'That indefinite Arketall', he said, 'has stolen my trousers.' 'Not all your trousers?' I asked in some confusion. 'Yes, all of them except these.' Lord Curzon was wearing his evening trousers of the night before. I glanced at my watch. There was still

another hour before the meeting of the conference but by this time
Arketall must have reached Pontarlier. I rang for Bill Bentinck and
told him to telephone to the frontier police. 'Don't say trousers', I
shouted after him, 'say "quelques effets".' I then secured the manager
and proceeded to Arketall's room. We looked in, over and under the
cupboard and into the chest of drawers; I peered under the bed; there
were three bottles of Benedictine against the wall but otherwise the
space was empty. The manager and I looked at each other in despair.
'*C'est inénarrable*', he muttered, '*complètement in-é-narrable*.' I sat down
wearily on the bed to consider our position. I jumped up again
immediately and pulled back the bedspread. Upon the crumpled bed-
clothes lay a trouser-press bursting with Lord Curzon's trousers. I sent
the manager to stop Bill Bentinck telephoning; myself I clasped the
trouser-press and returned in triumph to Lord Curzon. He was seated
at his writing-table, his pencil dashing across sheets of foolscap, his
lips moving. I stood there waiting. When he had finished four or five
sheets and cast them from him he turned to me indignantly. His face
relaxed into a smile and then extended into that irresistible laugh of
his, that endearing boyish sense of farce. 'Thank you', he said, 'I shall
now complete my toilet. There will only be Leeper at dinner tonight,
and as a reward I shall give my celebrated imitation of Tennyson recit-
ing "Tears, idle tears".'

He kept his promise. It was an amazing performance. We expressed
our admiration and our gratitude. A sudden wave of depression descended upon Lord Curzon. 'Ah yes', he sighed, 'ah yes. I know. All
that was years ago when I was young and could still laugh at my elders.
But all young men are remorseless. You will go upstairs this evening
and chaff me behind my back. You will give imitations in after life of
the old buffer imitating Tennyson. And so it continues.' He sighed
deeply. And then he grinned. 'I am sorry', he said, 'for Arketall. I liked
that man.'

Harold Nicolson, Some People, 1927

229

Lord Curzon's Anguish

When Andrew Bonar Law resigned as Prime Minister in May 1923, Lord Curzon and most other people assumed he would be the automatic choice as Bonar Law's successor.

THERE was no telephone installed at Montacute. Throughout that Whit Monday Lord Curzon remained in the country, a prey to excited impatience. Towards the evening a policeman was observed approaching the front door upon a bicycle. A telegram was delivered to Lord Curzon. He opened it with trembling fingers. It contained a message from Lord Stamfordham [George V's Private Secretary], summoning him to London without delay. He regarded that message as equivalent to an offer of the premiership.

On the morning of Tuesday, 22 May, he travelled up from Somerset with Lady Curzon. During the journey he discussed their future plans. 'I shall use Number Ten', he said, 'only for official purposes. We shall still live and entertain at Carlton House Terrace. I shall remain Curzon, even though Prime Minister.' During the rest of the journey he discoursed upon ecclesiastical appointments. They arrived in London. The photographers with their cameras were busy at the railway station and a further group awaited them at Carlton House Terrace. They lunched expectantly. They waited: they waited. At 3.30 Lord Stamfordham was announced. With some embarrassment he explained that the King had decided to send for Mr Baldwin. Curzon insisted that so ludicrous a decision should immediately be reversed. Lord Stamfordham explained that at that very moment Mr Baldwin was being received at Buckingham Palace. Curzon gasped. The dream of his lifetime lay shattered at his feet. Lord Stamfordham left him. In an agony of mortification he collapsed into a chair. Lady Curzon tried to console him. He wept like a child. He had forgotten Baldwin. Nobody had ever thought of Baldwin. 'Not even a public figure,' sobbed Curzon. 'A man of no experience. And of the utmost insignificance.' He repeated: 'Of the utmost insignificance.'

Harold Nicolson, *Curzon: The Last Phase*, 1934

The former Prime Minister, Arthur Balfour, who cherished a grudge against Curzon, was instrumental in depriving him of the premiership.

When Bonar Law resigned, Balfour was ill with phlebitis at Sheringham in Norfolk; he nevertheless struggled to London to advise the King to appoint Baldwin, and on his return could not resist a sneering reference to Curzon's financial dependence on his second wife Grace. The house party was agog to hear the news, and one of the ladies asked: 'And will dear George be chosen?' 'No', replied Balfour with some satisfaction, 'dear George will not.' 'Oh—I am so sorry', said the lady, 'he will be terribly disappointed.' 'Oh, I don't know,' said Balfour. 'He may have lost the hope of glory but he still retains the means of Grace.'

230

'F. E.'

Like Curzon, F. E. Smith, Earl of Birkenhead (1872–1930), loved to tell stories against himself. One of them concerned an incident when he had just begun his career as a barrister on the Northern Circuit in Liverpool:

HE was on a tram in Liverpool. A young woman sitting opposite him was about to alight when a man boarded the tram and jostled her. F. E. promptly intervened, struck the man on the jaw and sent him flying into the roadway, where he struck his head on the kerb. Instinctively, F. E. knew the man was dead. He leapt off the tram and ran as fast as his legs would carry him to a friend in shipping whom he begged to get him out of the country at once. The friend obliged and put him on a boat *en route* for the Mediterranean. The moral of the rest of the story, F. E. interpolated, was: 'Never take your boots off if you're having fun with a woman.' After a fortnight at sea the ship called at Malta, where F. E. went ashore and picked up an extremely attractive girl who took him home with her. They went upstairs and he foolishly removed his boots as well as his trousers, fortunately as it turned out, noticing that there was a chamber-pot under the bed. At the crucial moment in came the infuriated husband, armed with knife and revolver. Despite the unpromising circumstances, the wife at once began to protest her innocence. F. E. induced her to keep her husband talking until he located the chamber-pot, which he brought down on the man's head.

Then he ran all the way back to the ship in his stockinged feet over the cobblestones, which he described as one of the most agonising experiences of his life.

William Camp, *The Glittering Prizes*, 1960

231

On 12 May 1906, F. E. Smith, newly elected Conservative MP for Birken-head, and faced by an overwhelming and triumphant Liberal majority, made perhaps the most famous maiden speech in parliamentary history. Some eye-witness comments:

T. P. O'Connor: 'They might have been the eyes of a man who watched with sleepless though furtive vigilance all the great drama that was being unfolded in that astonishing new House of Commons, or they might have been just beautiful and shallow eyes that concealed no depths because there were no depths to conceal. He stood for a moment, aloof and silent, and the eyes retained their strange look of sombreness; on his face was a look of supreme boredom and contempt.

Philip Snowden: 'It was a piece of comedy more admirably acted than can be seen on the stage for many long moons. The speaker was abso-lutely impassive and immobile. The roars of laughter, which nearly every sentence called forth, brought not the faintest ripple of a smile into the look of supreme contempt which covered the speaker's face. The Tories were sent into ecstasies of hilarious joy. The members of the Front Bench, Balfour, Chamberlain and Wyndham, lost all the restraint of dignity and gave themselves up to convulsions of enjoy-ment.'

J. L. Garvin: 'He spoke for an hour, and put the House in his pocket.'

G. D. Faber MP: 'Light badinage and cutting sarcasm came with equal dexterity in that even magnetic voice which never faltered or failed. It was a long, sustained, *tour de force*, which captivated and held friend and foe alike. His logic was inexorable, his denunciations were won-derful, his satire played like forked-lightning. I had heard many mai-den speeches, and have heard many since, but this one stood and stands alone in my memory. The young new member who had been sitting beside me with his parliamentary fortunes to make, sat down a new member with his parliamentary fortunes made. He had not to wait till next morning to wake and find himself famous. He became famous there and then.'

Tim Healey, master of parliamentary shock-tactics, sent F. E. a note as soon as he sat down: 'I am old, and you are young, but you have beaten me at my own game.' The next evening an old lady was heard to ask at dinner: 'Who is this Effie Smith? She can't be a modest girl to be talked about so much.'

Earl of Birkenhead, *F. E.*, 1959

232

F. E. in Court

HIS worst insults were reserved for Judge Willis, a worthy, sanctimonious County Court Judge, full of kindness expressed in a patronizing manner. F. E. Smith had been briefed for a tramway company, which had been sued for damages for injuries to a boy who had been run over. The plaintiff's case was that blindness had set in as a result of the accident. The judge was deeply moved. 'Poor boy, poor boy,' he said, 'blind. Put him on a chair so that the jury can see him.'

F. E. said coldly: 'Perhaps Your Honour would like to have the boy passed round the jury box.' 'That is a most improper remark,' said Judge Willis angrily. 'It was provoked', said F. E., 'by a most improper suggestion.'

There was a heavy pause, and the judge continued: 'Mr Smith, have you ever heard of a saying by Bacon—the great Bacon—that youth and discretion are ill-wed companions?' 'Indeed I have, Your Honour; and has Your Honour ever heard of a saying by Bacon—the great Bacon—that a much-talking judge is like an ill-tuned cymbal?' The judge replied furiously: 'You are extremely offensive, young man,' and F. E. added to his previous lapses by saying: 'As a matter of fact we both are; the only difference between us is that I'm trying to be and you can't help it. I have been listened to with respect by the highest Tribunal in the land and I have not come down here to be browbeaten.'

He had a particular objection to a judge saying that he had read his case and thought little of it. One such judge said to him: 'I have read your case, Mr Smith, and I am no wiser now than I was when I started.' 'Possibly not, my Lord, but far better informed.'

Ibid.

233

Churchill on F. E.

FOR all the purposes of discussion, argument, exposition, appeal or altercation F. E. had a complete armoury. The bludgeon for the platform; the rapier for a personal dispute; the entangling net and unexpected trident for the Courts of Law; and a jug of clear spring water for an anxious perplexed conclave.

Churchill, Great Contemporaries

234

F. E. and Carson

In the years 1909–14 F. E. had been Carson's lieutenant in encouraging Ulster to resist Home Rule. In 1921, as Lloyd George's Lord Chancellor, he was one of the principal architects of the Irish Treaty, the completion of which he marked by a celebrated exchange with the Irish leader Michael Collins. Birkenhead: 'I may have signed my political death-warrant tonight.' Collins: 'I may have signed my actual death-warrant.' (He had.) When the Treaty was debated in the Lords, Carson savaged F. E.:

OF all the men in my experience that I think are the most loathsome it is those who will sell their friends for the purpose of conciliating their enemies, and, perhaps still worse the men who climb up a ladder into power of which even I may have been part of a humble rung, and then, when they have got into power, kicked the ladder away without any concern for the pain, or injury, or mischief, or damage that they do to those who have helped them to gain power. To which Birkenhead replied: 'As for the speech of Lord Carson, his constructive effort at statesmanship would be immature on the lips of a hysterical schoolgirl.'

235

F. E.'s Extravagance

AT the end of his life, when he had left politics for the City, he had his
yacht, six motor-cars, only three of which were normally used, three
chauffeurs, eight horses with three grooms, a large London house in
Grosvenor Gardens and a house in Oxfordshire. He refused to attend
to his income-tax returns, exercised no control over his agents and
gradually incurred an enormous overdraft. This rake's progress was
prompted by the same *hubris* which led to the downfall, in a different
way, of Oscar Wilde. When protests were made to him he bought
another car or a new motor-launch, and this selfishness and indifference to the interests of his family was undoubtedly the least attractive
feature of his character.

Lord Birkenhead, *F.E.*

236

L. G. at Bay

While preparing his famous 1909 budget, Lloyd George was accused by the
People of having an affair with a married woman. The story was true; but
Lloyd George had either to sue and deny it on oath, or abandon his career.
His eldest son, the 2nd Earl Lloyd George, related how he persuaded his wife
to commit perjury too:

FATHER knew that win or lose, his career was greatly endangered. He
had an unerring instinct about the public temper. 'You must stand by
me, Maggie. Otherwise it's all over with me.' My father was forty-six,
holding a post second in importance only to that of the Prime Minister.
He knew that he would be attacked mercilessly if my mother expressed
open doubt as to his innocence, if it were shown that she did not support him in his rejection of the accusation. There was great danger
even if she remained uncommitted to his cause. I know that my
mother, a deeply religious woman, was in torment in giving support to
the lie to be sworn on oath. As a woman, she had been mortally hurt by

his infidelities. As a wife she had been gravely wronged. I know exactly the extent of her conflict.

'You must help me Maggie. If I get over this, I give my oath you shall never have to suffer this ordeal again.' 'You will go into the witness box?' 'Yes.' 'And you will give your oath that this story is untrue?' 'I have to. And you give *me* your oath that I shall not have to suffer this sort of thing again. How can I rely on your "oath"?' 'I can make it true. Maggie, I put my life in jeopardy for my beliefs. One day I shall be Prime Minister. I shall be a force for the public good. If you help me, you shall never regret your decision.'

My mother told me much about the conversations she had with father at this time. (She was never to forget them.) She did not want him to plead with her to save his career 'for the public good'. She did not care about that; she wanted simply to help him because he was hurt and frightened and in grave trouble. She could not deny him help then.

On 12 March 1909 the Chancellor of the Exchequer drove to the Law Courts in the Strand. . . . There were rumours that Mrs Lloyd George was leaving her husband, that papers had been submitted to solicitors. Her carriage, packed with trunks, had been seen bound for the station where she was to take the train to Criccieth. Others believed that she was at home, but estranged from her husband and waiting the outcome of the case before filing a suit against him. Mr Lloyd George alighted from his car, and it was then seen that his wife had accompanied him. Together they entered the courtroom. Throughout the hearing she sat at his side.

He was called into the witness box. 'Have you read the allegations made in the *People?*' his counsel asked him. 'Yes.' 'Are they true in substance or in fact?' 'The paragraphs are an absolute invention', he said firmly, 'every line of them.' Cross-examination? None. Carson, for the defence, offered 'a sincere and frank apology' for the allegations, saying that they were without foundation or justification. The case was over, and damages for the plaintiff were put at £1,000, a modest sum indeed for an 'unfounded and unjustified' attack on the reputation of the Chancellor of the Exchequer. But father was glad to settle the matter without further parley. This money too went to a local Welsh cause. Even my father's worst enemies were silenced by mother's presence at his side during the hearing, and the anticipated aftermath of privileged sniping in the Commons did not take place; nor did anyone refer to the meagre estimate of damages awarded the Chancellor. The general feeling was that, innocent or not, if Maggie stood by him, that was good enough. The chapter was closed.

Earl Lloyd George, *Lloyd George*, 1960

237

Lloyd George's Lie

21 November 1916. D. had a great row in the Cabinet with McKenna today. The question of Sir W. Robertson going to Russia was discussed. D. said that he left the decision in the hands of the Cabinet, that he did not wish to press for it, but that what he objected to was the impression that one of his colleagues in the Cabinet was trying to give Sir W. Robertson, that D. was urging the proposal in order to get rid of Robertson. Immediately all the others demanded to know the name of the person he was alluding to. D. demurred and said that he would prefer to disclose it to the PM alone. But the others would not have it: several of them, they said, had been in Robertson's company, & it was only fair to them that they should be absolved from the accusation. 'Very well', said D., 'then I will tell you. It is the Chancellor of the Exchequer!' Of course McKenna denied it flatly, but D. insisted, saying 'One of two people then is lying, and I think I know which to believe.' Eventually D. wrung it out of him in the end that 'perhaps he had not denied the suggestion that Robertson was being sent because D. wanted to get him out of the way'. That was enough for the others. The prestige of McKenna is now lower than it was before. D. literally hates him, & I do not think he will rest until he has utterly broken him. I said to D.: 'Who was it who actually told you that McKenna had said this to Robertson?' 'No one', he said, 'but I guessed that he had said it.' 'Then whom did you mean when you said that one of two people was lying? Who was the second person?' 'That was pure bluff', said D. laughing, 'but I was right, and that was how I got it out of him.'

Frances Stevenson, diary

238

L. G. and George V

3 February 1922. Yesterday he saw the King. The latter does not like the idea of the Genoa Conference. 'I suppose you will be meeting Lenin & Trotsky?' he asked. 'Unfortunately, Sir', D. replied, 'I am not able to choose between the people I am forced to meet in your service. A little while ago I had to shake hands with Sami Bey, a ruffian who was missing for the whole of one day, & finally traced to a sodomy house in the East End. He was the representative of Mustapha Kemal, a man who I understand has grown tired of affairs with women & had lately taken up unnatural sexual intercourse. I must confess I do not think there is very much to choose between these persons whom I am forced to meet from time to time in Your Majesty's service.' D. said the King's only reply was to roar with laughter.

Frances Stevenson, diary

239

8 September 1911—[Lord Loreburn] told a naughty story. A year ago Lloyd George was opposed to keeping on the 3*s.* 9*d.* spirit duty, to which the Irish were opposed, in the held-up budget of 1909/10, and was outvoted in the cabinet. A month or two later on the 1910/11 budget, he quite forgot this, and publicly declared that to abandon the duty would be 'a crime against civilisation'.

The Political Diaries of C. P. Scott, ed. Trevor Wilson, 1970

240

The Welsh Wizard

HOW can I convey to the reader, who does not know him, any just impression of this extraordinary figure of our time, this siren, this goat-footed bard, this half-human visitor to our age from the hag-ridden magic and enchanted woods of Celtic antiquity? One catches in his company that flavour of final purposelessness, inner irresponsibility, existence outside or away from our Saxon good and evil, mixed with

cunning, remorselessness, love of power, that lend fascination, en-
thralment and terror to the fair-seeming magician of North European
folklore. . . . Lloyd George is rooted in nothing; he is void and without
content; he lives and feeds on his immediate surroundings; he is an
instrument and a player at the same time which plays on the company
and is played on by them too; he is a prism, as I have heard him described, which collects light and distorts it and is most brilliant if the
light comes from many quarters at once; a vampire and medium in one.

J. M. Keynes, *Essays in Biography*, 1933

241

Lloyd Georgeisms

On the 1905 Tory government: 'They died with their drawn salaries in
their hands.'

On Kitchener as War Minister: 'One of those revolving lighthouses
which radiate momentary gleams of revealing light far out into the sur-
rounding gloom, and then suddenly relapse into complete darkness.
There were no intermediate stages.'

On Field Marshal Haig: 'Brilliant—to the top of his boots.'

On Churchill: 'He would make a drum out of the skin of his mother in
order to sound his own praises.'

Balfour's impact on history: 'No more than the whiff of scent on a lady's
pocket-handkerchief.'

On Northcliffe: 'An alliance with him is like going for a walk with a
grasshopper.'

On Curzon: 'In Cabinet, he is worth his weight in brass—sounding
brass.'

On Austen Chamberlain: 'Standing like a stork on the shores of Locarno.'

On Sir John Simon: 'He has sat on the fence so long the iron has
entered his soul.'

On Éamon de Valera: 'Negotiating with him is like trying to pick up
mercury with a fork.'

242

Lucky Geordie

IT happened early in 1921. I was dining at the Criterion Restaurant, then the popular resort, occupying the top floor of a tall Piccadilly building. My guests were Sir Matthew Wilson and the Dolly Sisters, famous theatrical stars from New York. They appeared in London with overwhelming success. It is right to say that the Dolly Sisters also attained fame in Government circles when Lord Birkenhead referred, in the House of Lords, to the late Lord Salisbury and also Lord Selborne of that generation, who always worked together, as the Dolly Sisters of the Tory Party.

During dinner I received a message to go to 10 Downing Street. On arrival I was shown into the Cabinet Room where Lloyd George was talking with Bonar Law. Lloyd George then offered to make me High Commissioner to the General Assembly of the Church of Scotland. The offer was indeed attractive to me, for my father was a Scottish minister serving in Canada, under the Augmentation Scheme of that great institution of widespread influence in Dominions and Colonies throughout the Empire. However, I replied that I would not be suited to the office. It was my intention to continue my practice of sitting up late into the night. Indeed I had just come from dining with the Dolly Sisters at the Criterion Restaurant.

Lloyd George then turned to Bonar Law and said: 'Geordie gets it'. Of course 'Geordie' was the Duke of Sutherland.

So I went back to the Criterion Restaurant intending to make the most of my freedom, which I had retained by paying such a high price. And there I found Geordie Sutherland—dancing with one of my Dolly Sisters.

Lord Beaverbrook, The Decline and Fall of Lloyd George, 1963

243

Soft Option

On 14 January 1918, Field Marshal Sir Douglas Haig wrote to his wife from the Front about the War Secretary, Lord Derby:

D. IS a very weak-minded fellow, I am afraid, and, like the feather pillow, bears the marks of the last person who had sat on him! I hear he is called in London 'Genial Judas'.

Private Papers of Douglas Haig, ed. Robert Blake, 1952

244

An Editor's Vanity

Charles Prestwich ('CP') Scott (1846–1932), editor of the Manchester Guardian *from 1872 to his death—one of the longest editorships in British history—was often hailed as a paragon of journalistic integrity.*

THE fact was there was a streak of vanity in CP, on which Lloyd George was not slow to play. Whenever Lloyd George spoke in Manchester, CP must always be given a seat on the platform close to him, and Lloyd George would never miss referring to his presence as that of 'the world's greatest living journalist'. During the final somersaults of the Coalition in 1922, he was hard put to find a saving word for Lloyd George, and I remember H. W. Massingham, at that time Editor of the *Nation*, saying at lunch at the Club one day, 'To me there are few spectacles more melancholy than that of dear old C. P. Scott wearily dredging in a foul pond for the soul of Lloyd George.'

Vivian Phillipps, *My Days and Ways*, 1943

245

[CP was remembered] only as a symbol of good, noble journalism as distinct from the sensational kind instituted by Northcliffe. 'CP would never have agreed to that,' people would say, shaking their heads, and recalling his refusal to allow racing news, or liquor advertising, or the publicising of the Irish Sweep in the *Guardian*. Why, in the early days, he even, it seems, on one occasion turned down a full-page advertisement for corsets, worth £260, because it showed a picture of a lady wearing the advertised product. What was conveniently forgotten was that the *Guardian* subsisted on the profits of its sister-paper, the *Manchester Evening News* (does, indeed, to this day) in whose columns racing, the Irish Sweep, liquor advertising and uncorseted bosoms got the fullest play. Every now and again someone would write in to the effect that the malicious rumour was circulating in Manchester that the great C. P. Scott had some connection with that odious sheet the *Manchester Evening News*, and might this lie please be nailed. Such letters were put on CP's desk, whence they disappeared without trace. Northcliffe is alleged to have undertaken a special pilgrimage to Manchester to salute Scott as the man who had uniquely shown that truth could be made to pay. The encounter between them must have been interesting, revealing, I should imagine, that they had more in common than might superficially be supposed. If Scott had made truth pay, a lot of his truth was lies; whereas Northcliffe, in making his lies pay, sometimes told the truth. So the contest in a way evened out. [CP died on New Year's Day 1932 and] his office never was occupied by anyone else. When the Cross Street premises were finally evacuated in August 1970, having been sold for demolition, it was still empty, and just as when he had last used it. Now it has finally gone, along with the whole building, and the legend of CP with it.

Malcolm Muggeridge, *Chronicles of Wasted Time*, 1972

246

The Fatal Parrot

At the end of 1921, the Lloyd George coalition government triumphantly concluded the negotiations for an Irish settlement. Should the coalition cash in on its success by holding an immediate general election?

By the New Year Lloyd George had set his headquarters at Villa Valetta in Cannes. There we gathered—Churchill, Horne, Worthington-Evans and myself. The only subject for discussion was Election—

yes! or Election—no! The Prime Minister's reputation, temporarily
improved by the Irish Treaty, was again in swift decline. Without
doubt the sale of honours for the benefit of Lloyd George's personal
Political Fund had damaged his prestige and injured his standing in
Parliament and in the constituencies. Moreover the Tory Central
Office and the heads of staff there were extremely hostile to the
Coalition Liberal section, and most critical of the Prime Minister
himself.

The real grievances of the Tory managers did not turn on the sale of
honours but on the suborning by Lloyd George of their Tory
Treasurer, Lord Farquhar, known to his friends and intimates as
'Horace'. Large sums of Tory money contributed by their supporters
had been diverted by Lord Farquhar to Lloyd George's fund. The
danger to Lloyd George of publicity and also the menace to his future
relations with Tory leaders might disturb and possibly destroy the
whole structure of cooperation. What should he do? The decision was
final: 'After all, there was the money.' Thus at the Villa Valetta it was
an interesting and exciting moment when a parrot in a cage almost
unnoticed intervened in the midst of the words of greeting addressed
to the assembling company, crying 'Stop it, Horace!'

[One by one, Churchill, Horne and Beaverbrook gave their views on
the election.] Worthington-Evans spoke out vigorously in support of an
immediate appeal to the nation. Unless there was an election, he said,
a split in the Conservative Party was inevitable and could not be postponed for long. A Conservative split, he argued, would put an end to
Coalition. Sir Laming was the leading exponent of 'Election at once'.
He concluded his statement by hurling defiance at all opponents. He
claimed that immediate action would take the Tory candidates by surprise and leave them no time to bolt from the Coalition. With a deep,
resonant, most attractive voice, he put his case with such force that the
Prime Minister, who had the sole right to say the word 'Dissolution',
appeared to be readying himself for 'Action this Day'.

When Evans concluded his intervention with a stirring peroration,
silence fell upon the company. We awaited the pronouncement from
the source of all power, the Prime Minister of Great Britain: Election—Yes! or Election—No!

Then an inhuman, rough and exceedingly harsh sound fell upon the
company for the second time. 'You bloody fool! You bloody fool!' said
the parrot.

The company was shaken. The Ministers departed. I went off with

Churchill. We drove into the night, and along the way we laughed over the parrot.

Lord Beaverbrook, *The Decline and Fall of Lloyd George*

(No election was held. When it finally came, the coalition was defeated, Churchill lost his seat, and Lloyd George never held office again.)

247

Picking the Right Fellow

When Lloyd George and his brilliant coalition allies were ousted in 1922, the incoming Tory government found itself rich in magnates, of whom the Earl of Derby and the Duke of Devonshire were the most prominent, but short of parliamentary talent.

ONE evening while the Government was being formed, Derby went round to Devonshire House. This was only a few months before this splendid building in Piccadilly, with its galaxy of memories of political confabulations extending over two centuries, was to be pulled down and replaced by Lord Rootes's glittering automobile emporium. Devonshire expressed concern about the Government's lack of adequate representation in the Commons, and in particular as to who would be the Government's principal spokesman, Baldwin being at this time utterly unversed in Parliamentary technique.

Someone said: 'Let's get some clever lawyer'. 'I know the very man', said Derby. 'Someone was telling me about him the other day, a fellow called Pig.' 'The only Pig I know', said Devonshire, 'is James Pigge in Surtees.'

Thus did that able lawyer, Sir Douglas Hogg, who at that time was probably the leading Silk at the Bar and was destined as the first Viscount Hailsham to sit on the Woolsack, first come to the attention of the magnificoes of the Tory Party.

Randolph Churchill, *Lord Derby, 'King of Lancashire'*, 1959. [This account
is contested in R. F. V. Heuston, *Lives of the Lord Chancellors*, 1964]

248

An Establishment Operation

In 1931 the Liberal leader in the House of Lords, William Lygon, 7th Earl Beauchamp, was threatened with divorce proceedings by his wife, sister of the 2nd Duke of Westminster; his valet was to be named as co-respondent. The way in which the establishment dealt with this potential scandal was first revealed in the official life of a Liberal Lord Chancellor, Lord Buckmaster.

BUCKMASTER'S reputation in court circles was further shown in the following year when he was asked to undertake a mission of a peculiarly delicate and painful character. A former Liberal Cabinet Minister, a nobleman of ancient family, a Knight of the Garter, was in serious danger of criminal prosecution as a result of revelations arising out of contemplated divorce proceedings. There was a distinct feeling at Windsor that the matter should, if possible, be kept out of the Law Courts, and Buckmaster, together with two other peers, Crewe and Chesterfield, the former representative of the Liberal Party, the latter of the world of fashion, called upon the culprit in order to point out to him the necessity for speedy action on his part. Although he had already been warned by [Lord] Reading of his danger, they found him in a jovial mood, prepared to brazen the matter out, but in a few sentences Buckmaster revealed to him the terrible peril in which he stood and the disgrace which his folly was likely to bring upon his family and, indirectly, upon the monarchy itself. At the end of a distressing interview the nobleman signed a deed agreeing to leave the country and never return. The following week he duly surrendered all his public offices except one and went to live in the United States.

Heuston, Lives of the Lord Chancellors, 1885–1940

(Later he lived in Europe and became the model for Lord Marchmain in Evelyn Waugh's novel, Brideshead Revisited *(1945).)*

249

MacDonald's Birth

The Labour Party leader, James Ramsay MacDonald (1866–1937), was victimized for his wartime pacifism, especially by Horatio Bottomley's John Bull, *which wrote: 'We demand his trial by Court Martial, his condemnation as an aider and abetter of the King's enemies, and that he be taken to the Tower and Shot at dawn' (19 June 1915); three months later it published a sensational article, accompanied by a facsimile reproduction of MacDonald's birth certificate.*

FOR months past—ever since the man who calls himself James Ramsay MacDonald, but whose real name is James MacDonald Ramsay, has stood aloof from the almost unanimous response of the nation to the call of the King—we have persistently labelled him as a traitor and a coward; and we have called upon Leicester to rid itself of the stigma of having such a 'representative' in Parliament. But, despite all provocation, we have so far confined ourselves to criticising and exposing his words and deeds in the capacity of a public man—of a paid servant of the state. Even when we were recently described by him as having spent most of our time 'on the threshold of the gaol', we simply retorted that if he wished to push us through the door the machinery of the criminal prosecution for libel was available to him. For, whatever our knowledge concerning his antecedents, we felt that even in the case of a traitor, there was a recognised line beyond which journalistic revelation should not travel. So we have remained silent with regard to certain facts which have been in our possession for a long time. First of all, we knew that this man was living under an adopted name—and that he was registered as *James MacDonald Ramsay*—and that, therefore, he had obtained admission to the House of Commons in false colours, and was probably liable to heavy penalties to have his election declared void. But to have disclosed this state of things would have imposed upon us a very painful and unsavoury duty. *We should have been compelled to produce the man's birth certificate.* And that would have revealed what today we are justified in revealing—for the reason we will state in a moment. It would have revealed 'James Ramsay MacDonald', MP for Leicester, late 'leader' of the Labour Party; late member of a Royal Commission, under the seal of His Majesty; the leading light of the

'Union of Democratic Control'—libeller and slanderer of his country—it would have revealed him *as the illegitimate son of a Scotch servant girl*!

John Bull, 4 September 1915

250

ON the day when the paper with the attack was published, I was travelling from Lossiemouth to London in the company as far as Edinburgh of the Dowager Countess De La Warr, Lady Margaret Sackville and their maid. Breaking the journey at Aberdeen, I saw the Contents Bill of the paper announcing some amazing revelations about myself and when I rejoined the ladies at the station, I saw the maid had *John Bull* in her hand. Sitting in the train, I took it from her and read the disgusting article. From Aberdeen to Edinburgh, I spent hours of the most terrible mental pain . . . The first time I had ever seen my registration certificate was when I opened the paper at Aberdeen. Never before did I know that I had been registered under the name of Ramsay, and cannot understand it now.

Ramsay MacDonald, diary, 12 September 1915

251

A Besotted Prime Minister

While Prime Minister, MacDonald scandalized his Labour followers by forming a close friendship with the Marchioness of Londonderry, the leading Tory hostess; indeed, he was in love with her. Among the letters he sent her was this of May 1932:

MY DEAR: You were very beautiful, and I loved you. The dress, dazzling in brilliance and glorious in colour and line, was you, & my dear, you were the dress. I just touch its hem, & pray for your eternal happiness wondering at the same time what generous hearted archangel ever patted me on the back & arranged that amongst the many great rewards that this poor unwelcome stranger to this world was to receive was that he would be permitted before he returned to his dust to feel devotion to *you*.

Printed in David Marquand, *Ramsay MacDonald*, 1977

252

MacDonald in Decay

From about 1931, Ramsay MacDonald, while Prime Minister, began to suffer from chronic insomnia and delusions. Early in 1933 he was detected looking nervously over his shoulder while making a speech in the Commons; he later explained that he thought someone in the gallery was trying to shoot him. General Temperley, in the British delegation at Geneva, described the Prime Minister during a disarmament conference: 'At one moment I saw him reel backwards and start exhorting the audience to "be men, not mannequins", becoming completely irrelevant. He said afterwards that, for half a minute, he had completely lost consciousness and did not know what he was saying.' His speeches in the Commons became increasingly meaningless. In February 1933 he answered criticism by Lloyd George by saying: 'He thinks he is the only impatient man in this House to get things done. I will beat him 50 per cent any day he likes . . . No doubt he has a hawk-like desire for action, without bridle and saddle, across the Atlantic'. During the debate on the Address, November 1932, he said:

THE world cannot afford to wait. One is appalled sometimes when one reads articles as though the world is going at the rate of five miles an hour. (An Hon. Member: 'It is going quicker than that.') It is, and the Hon. Member will find it on this side, not on that. The reason is that the politicians, the direct representatives of this Government, that Government and the other Government, brought face to face, will much more quickly find an accommodation, a way out, and will be so minded knowing the larger issues outside, knowing the tremendous importance of getting an agreement—the direct representatives of the Government meeting the direct representatives of other Governments will much more quickly and much better, as a piece of workmanship, find the accommodation which will lead to a great world agreement.

Hansard, 1932

He told the House in April 1933:

THERE is a third point, or a third section of interest; it is more than a point. The stabilisation of the relative value of currency must be attempted by agreement. I doubt if anyone who has not gone through my experience of the last two or three weeks can appreciate the danger of unstable international values not only to trade—I take it that the Committee are fully acquainted with that—but to political relationships. While I was still at sea (Laughter.)—Hon. Members laugh; I think it is a very valuable point which I have conceded—the United States went off gold.

Hansard, 1933

253

MORE and more he dreaded the prospect of appearing at the dispatch box. The night before making a speech, he would lie awake worrying; after a bad performance, he would torture himself with the memory. 'Fit but with feeling of coming flop' he noted apprehensively, '. . . would I were a Winston Churchill so that I might express adequately my disgust with myself.' 'Trying to get something clear into my head for the H. of C. tomorrow', he noted. 'Cannot be done. Like man flying in mist: can fly all right but cannot see the course . . . Tomorrow there will be another "vague" speech impossible to follow & and as usual with these attacks of head & eyes no sleep tonight.' On the day of the speech he ended the story with an even sadder entry: 'Thoroughly bad speech. Could not get my way at all. The Creator might have devised more humane means for punishing me for overdrive & reckless use of body.'

Marquand, *Ramsay MacDonald*

254

On 17 February 1931, in the debate on the Trades Disputes Act, Winston Churchill told the Commons:

WHAT is the Prime Minister going to do? I spoke the other day, after he had been defeated in an important division, about his wonderful skill in falling without hurting himself. He falls, but up he comes again, smiling, a little dishevelled but still smiling. But this is a juncture, a situation, which will try to the fullest the peculiar arts in which he excels. I remember when I was a child, being taken to the celebrated Barnum's Circus which contained an exhibition of freaks and mon-

strosities. The exhibit on the programme which I most desired to see
was the one described as 'The Boneless Wonder'. My parents judged
that that spectacle would be too revolting and demoralising for my
youthful eyes. I have waited fifty years to see the Boneless Wonder—
sitting on the Treasury Bench.

Hansard, quoted in Martin Gilbert, *Winston Churchill*, 1976

255

17 March 1934. . . . Lady Londonderry told me of a strange anonymous letter she had recently received: it was dated AD 2035 and described the visit of a mother and daughter to 'Ulster House'
(Londonderry House) by that time, apparently, a museum. The child,
pointing to a portrait of 'The Duchess of Ulster' (i.e., Circe Londonderry) asks 'Who is that pretty lady? 'Don't look at it—she was an evil
woman who tempted the Labour Prime Minister, Ramsay Mac-
Donald, and turned him into a Tory. She ruined England and was very
wicked.' Circe L. is enchanted with the ingenuity of the malice and is
preserving the letter; but when she showed it to the Prime Minister he
was very annoyed. He has little sense of humour.

'Chips' Channon MP, diary

256

*On 7 June 1934 MacDonald resigned as Prime Minister and became Lord
President.*

FIRST thing of which awakening made me conscious was 'I die
today' . . . 3.50 audience with King which in end lasted for 50 minutes
and he was $\frac{1}{4}$ hour late in seeing Baldwin. He was most friendly. He
said again looking sadly down to the floor with his right elbow on the
arm of his chair: 'I hoped you might have seen me through, but I now
know it is impossible. But I do not think it will be very long. I wonder
how you have stood it—especially the loss of your friends & their
beastly behaviour.' Again: 'You have been the Prime Minister I have

liked best; you have so many qualities, you have kept up the dignity of the office without using it to give you dignity.' And so. He made me doubly & trebly sorry to lay down my office . . . My first duty as Lord President was to call up Malcolm to be sworn in (Note: his coat fitted badly.) New Government sworn and left to catch the 7.30 train for Lossiemouth—I left with feelings which mingled regret with relief, a sense of freedom with one of impotence. I might have been a memory disembodied. Dining with Lady Grant & Robbie & Malcolm in the train north I kept wondering who I was & how I would wake up next morning.

Ramsay MacDonald, diary, 7 June 1934

257

At the 1935 election, despite the government's triumph, both MacDonald and his son Malcolm lost their seats:

A HEART-BREAKING day. Arrived early at King's Cross & saw first results. Not at all good for the Labour Opposition. Very tired; hardly able to walk. Buck joined me at lunch. In the middle Mita opened door & sobbed 'Malcolm is defeated' & before we finished Dr Grant telephoned in a broken voice: 'I am heartbroken & have had to escape from the counting. You must be prepared for a defeat by at least 15,000.' Thus the cloud descended. My poor boy. Luck has been hard, & I cannot put my crushed feelings into thought. . . . The miners have done it to both of us. When I entered the fight for Seaham I knew that I could keep the seat only by a miracle, but I did not anticipate the bitterness and hysteria of the fight. I found myself up against an immovable wall. I talked to people whose minds had been poisoned by a previously conducted campaign of lies & calumny to regard me as the author of all their hardships. The Means Test applied to hundreds of families & the coal agitation did the rest . . . Very soon there developed a wild and hysterical rowdyism, the persistent interruption of meetings which forbade connected & built-up speeches and the actual break up of meetings. Some of the displays were absolutely bestial. Many of the faces of the women were lined with destitution; their eyes flamed & gleamed with hate & passion; their hair was dishevelled; their language filthy with oaths & some obscenity; they filled one with loathing & fear just like French Revolution studies. Night after night their misery was upon me.

Diary, 15 November 1935, quoted in Marquand

258

Baldwin and the Press Lords

In 1930, the two Press Lords, Rothermere and Beaverbrook, owners of the Daily Mail, Daily Express *and many other newspapers, made a determined effort to oust Stanley Baldwin from the leadership of the Conservative Party, over the issue of Empire trade. The crux came in March, at the Westminster by-election, when they put up their own candidate against the official Tory, Duff Cooper. On 17 March, flanked by Cooper and his wife Lady Diana, Baldwin counter-attacked at the Queen's Hall.*

OUTSIDE the doors were supporters of the Press Lords and sand-wichmen whose boards read: 'A vote for Duff Cooper is a vote for Gandhi.' The headline in Rothermere's own papers was 'Gandhi is Watching St George's'.

Baldwin explained why he was there, breaking 'my rule and a gener-ally accepted rule of leaders of parties, because of the exceptional cir-cumstances of this election (cheers). And it gives me an opportunity, as various observations have been made about me for many years (laughter) of making a few observations myself.' He said that the Press of Great Britain was the admiration of the world for its fairness, ability and high principles. But propaganda, stemming from the war, was 'a poison gas that poisoned men's souls', and it had left its mark on one section of the British press. 'The papers conducted by Lord Rother-mere and Lord Beaverbrook are not newspapers in the ordinary acceptance of the term. They are engines of propaganda for the con-stantly changing policies, desires, personal wishes, personal likes and dislikes of two men. What are their methods? Their methods are direct falsehood, misrepresentation, half-truths, the alteration of the speaker's meaning by publishing a sentence apart from the context, such as you see in those leaflets handed out outside the doors of this hall: suppression and editorial criticism of speeches which are not reported in the paper. These are methods hated alike by the public, by the whole of the rest of the press.' He gave one or two instances: the refusal of those papers, alone, to publish Mrs Baldwin's appeal for the provision of anaesthetics for mothers in confinement; and their reaction to his own use of the term 'insolent plutocracy', which had provoked the *Daily Mail* to write, 'Those expressions come ill from Mr Baldwin, whose father left him an immense fortune, which, so far as may be learnt from his own speeches, has almost disappeared. It is difficult to see how the leader of a party who has lost his own fortune, can hope to restore that of anyone else, or of his country.'

Baldwin now castigated the editor, who had signed the article simply 'Editor, *Daily Mail*', as no Prime Minister had ever turned on a journalist before. 'I have no idea of the name of that gentleman. I would only observe that he is well qualified for the post which he holds. The first part of that statement is a lie and the second part of that statement, by its implication, is untrue. The paragraph itself could only have been written by a cad. I have consulted a very high legal authority and I am advised that an action for libel would lie (a shout of 'Take it!'). I shall not move in the matter, and for this reason. I should get an apology and heavy damages. The first is of no value, and the second I would not touch with a bargepole. What the proprietorship of these papers is aiming at is power, and power without responsibility—the prerogative of the harlot throughout the ages.'

Lady Diana Cooper wrote: 'I saw the blasé reporters, scribbling semi-consciously, jump out of their skins to a man.'

Keith Middlemas and John Barnes, *Baldwin: A Biography*, 1969

259

Baldwin's Political Philosophy

In the early 1930s, Frank Pakenham (as he then was) worked in the Conservative Research Department, and was a fervent Tory; Stanley Baldwin was the party leader and Lord President in the National Government.

ONE Sunday afternoon, a guest of Lord and Lady Salisbury at Hatfield, I was told that Mr Baldwin wished me to go for a walk with him. I was flattered but surprised. He was not supposed to feel at ease with the young or with intellectuals of any age. . . . As we made our way across the countryside the conversation lagged painfully. Only once, when I mentioned his son Oliver (at that time a Labour MP and supposed to have caused his family a lot of anxiety) did Mr Baldwin brighten. 'Dear fellow,' he exclaimed, coming to life suddenly. Then we trudged on again in virtual silence. Finally, as the house came in sight, I grew desperate. Somehow I must find out a little of the profound political philosophy with which I unquestioningly credited my leader. I informed him that I was teaching political theory for the Workers' Educational Association in the Potteries, and asked him which were the political thinkers to whom he himself owed most. He reflected for a moment and then spoke quietly and emphatically: 'There is one political thinker who has had more influence on me than all others—Sir Henry Maine. When I was at Cambridge, his authority was complete and I never ceased to be grateful for all I learnt from him.'

I was, of course, all ears. After all, the walk had been anything but in vain. 'What,' I persisted, 'would you say was Maine's supreme contribution?' Mr Baldwin paused perhaps a shade longer and then said with conviction, 'Rousseau argued that all human progress was from contract to status. But Maine made it clear once and for all that the real movement was from status to contract.' He paused again, and this time for quite a while, and suddenly a look of dawning horror—but at the same time of immense humanity and confederacy—stole across his face. 'Or was it,' he said, leaning just a little towards me, 'or was it the other way round?'

Earl of Longford, *Eleven at Number Ten*, 1984

260

Fabiana

Sidney and Beatrice Webb were the couple around whom Fabian middle-class socialism revolved for the first four decades of the twentieth century. Kingsley Martin, who edited the New Statesman, *the paper they founded, in the years 1930–60, described life at their houses in London and the country:*

I ONCE or twice lunched with the Webbs at the famous house in Grosvenor Road. If the food was really as plain as H. G. Wells declared, it was quite good enough for me. It was true that Mrs Webb drank water and Sidney was allowed one glass of whisky, and only one. The rest of us, I think, had water or perhaps lemonade. My pride at being entertained by the Great, plus the importance of the conversation, would have satisfied me if the food had been bran and sawdust, instead of boiled mutton and rice pudding. After lunch I asked Webb, who looked a little surprised, if I could use the lavatory. Harold Laski and I walked away together. Harold declared that my request had been an extraordinary act of courage which no one had ever dared perform before in the Webb household. He said that the week before he had dined there with Ramsay MacDonald, and that he and the Prime Minister had had to make use of a timber-yard on the way home.

Kingsley Martin, *Father Figures*, 1966

261

THE Pilgrimage to Passfield Corner was sometimes exhausting. The Webbs had been working intensively all the week, and their immense fund of argument and conversation was bottled up inside them. You arrived for tea on Saturday. Mrs Webb met one very graciously at the door. Sidney gave you a rather perfunctory handshake. You were taken upstairs and your part of the house, including the bathroom, very firmly indicated. You went down to tea, where there were probably other guests. Serious talk began at once. The condition of the world and of the Labour and Socialist movements in particular, and immediate topics of the day, were systematically dealt with. One could almost hear Mrs Webb putting a mental tick after each item when it had been discussed and nothing more of importance was likely to be said on the subject. The long, meaty conversation would continue at night by the fire. At 10.30 you went to bed. At half past eight next morning you would be having breakfast, and Mrs Webb, who had already been up for several hours and done a lot of work, would be standing arms akimbo between you and the window, lecturing you—as I remember on one occasion—on the defects of the Douglas social credit system. You were released for an hour after breakfast, but you started promptly at eleven on the walk over the heather and through the lanes of Hampshire. Mrs Webb would usually remark that 'the English climate is the best in the world, because it is never too hot or too cold to work or to walk'. Since the Webbs did both tirelessly, and had no desire to ski or sunbathe, there was no point in arguing, you put on your raincoat and followed along.

There was always the strange and to me incomprehensible incident with Sandy, the terrier in Nicholson's portrait of the Webbs. Just before the walk started, he began to bark, as dogs do when a walk is in prospect. Mrs Webb knelt and hit the ground violently with a walking stick, while she shouted loudly and repeatedly, 'Sandy! Sandy!' Sidney stood silently by, watching. Perhaps, though she did not know it, she was really working off her feelings about Sidney; was she vicariously hitting him with her stick? Certainly her suppressed love of power was revealed in this extraordinary, regular ritual. She, and maybe the dog, found in it some mysterious emotional satisfaction. In the end Sandy made a final and tragic rebellion. I suppose he reached the end of his patience. He bit Mrs Webb and had to be destroyed.

Kingsley Martin, Editor, 1968

262

George V's Priorities

ONE summer morning (in 1935) Mr Anthony Eden, on his way to Geneva, had an audience with the King at Buckingham Palace. The King's Private Apartments were then under repair, and Mr Eden was received in the north-east corner room, hung with relics of the Royal Pavilion, and situated immediately above the band-stand in the fore-court. The King, on entering, apologised to Mr Eden for having to receive him in this unfamiliar drawing-room. 'It is all right however', His Majesty added, 'I have told the band not to play till I give the word.' The King then furnished Mr Eden with a *catalogue raisonné* of all the subjects which, at Geneva, he would have to discuss. At last he reached a conclusion, and Mr Eden, in the few minutes that remained, started to make some observations of his own. 'Just one second,' said the King, as he rang the small hand-bell at his side. A page appeared. 'Tell the bandmaster that he can start playing now.'

Harold Nicolson, King George V: His Life and Reign, 1952

263

At Mrs Greville's

Sir Austen Chamberlain was an unusually unselfish politician. It was said of him, 'Austen always played the game—and he always lost it'. He was accident-prone too. Lord Beaverbrook described an evening in 1921, when Chamberlain was Chancellor of the Exchequer, at Polesden Lacey, the home of the Tory hostess Mrs Ronnie Greville:

THERE it was in the house on the hill that political parties were held. The guests, drawn from the Front Bench, spent happy hours talking of

Lloyd George and Ireland. The food was good and the wine well-chosen. Mrs Greville was rich, generous, outspoken and sometimes rude . . . It was Sunday night, the dining table was laden with sparkling glass and shining silver. Pyramids of fruit and sweets scattered here and there in reach of everybody. Gay and happy conversation was exchanged from one neighbour to another and also across the wide table. Only one detail was going wrong. The butler was obviously tight.

Surely Austen was the most important and impressive guest! An effort to invite a discourse on the Empire policy failed. Instead in a pause in general conversation he casually mentioned that the Empire must not be wrecked on the Irish issue. He carried on with an interesting and informed monologue on Ireland and the difficulties confronting his Party. He had reached the story of the momentous decision of the Unionist group in 1886.

Mrs Greville's attention wavered. On a scribbling pad she was busily writing. Summoning her butler, well known for his intemperate habits, she handed him the written message. It read: 'You are drunk—leave the room at once.' The butler placed the note on a big and beautiful salver and, walking unsteadily to Austen Chamberlain, with a deep bow presented the message. Austen paused in his admirable exposition of the intransigence of the Irish race. He slowly fixed his monocle and read the startling message, 'You are drunk—leave the room at once.'

Lord Beaverbrook, *The Decline and Fall of Lloyd George*

264

A Brotherly Rebuke

Neville Chamberlain became Prime Minister in 1937 and immediately began playing an active role in foreign policy; the next year his Foreign Secretary, Anthony Eden, resigned in protest. In his memoirs he recalled dining with the Prime Minister, and his elder half-brother, Sir Austen Chamberlain, shortly before the breach:

THIS was one of the last occasions on which I saw Sir Austen before his death. Neville was a delightful host, and food and drink were always excellent at his table. I enjoyed my evening and Austen told us about his visits to Benes and what he thought of the dangers in Austria, while Neville and I listened, Neville in particular taking little part in the conversation. However, towards the end of the evening he did venture to make certain comments on the situation as he saw it, where-upon Austen said: 'Neville, you must remember you don't know any-thing about foreign affairs.' Neville smiled wryly and remarked that this was rather hard on a man at his own dinner table. Austen made one of his sweeping, depreciatory gestures, half-apologetic, and went on his way.

Anthony Eden, *Facing the Dictators*, 1962

265

Long Shot

Viscount, later Earl of, Halifax (1881–1959) was an immensely tall York-shire grandee, whom Neville Chamberlain promoted to Foreign Secretary when Anthony Eden resigned over Appeasement in 1938.

IMMEDIATELY after the Munich crisis, a journalist asked Halifax if he were not worn out by all the late nights. The Foreign Secretary replied: 'Not exactly. But it spoils one's eye for the high birds.'

Anon.

266

A Flogging Judge

Sir Gordon Hewart was appointed Lord Chief Justice by Lloyd George in 1922, serving for nearly twenty years, a fierce scourge of criminals.

IN February 1938 he was in the public eye when he heard the case of the 'Mayfair Boys' [public schoolboys who had beaten and robbed a jeweller]. One evening an elderly lady, well-upholstered and wearing ample jewellery, accosted the Chief as he was taking a cocktail at a public reception. 'Lord Hewart', said the Dowager reprovingly, 'it is dreadful, *dreadful*, to think of those nice boys being flogged. Imprison them, yes. But why did you have to order *public schoolboys* to be flogged?' The Chief flushed with anger. When he became Chief Justice

he made a rule never to discuss in public any case that was or had been
before the courts, and certainly he would never have thought of publicly or privately discussing a case he had heard, with someone he knew
slightly. The implied criticism of his judgment stung him, for he felt
deeply about the case. 'Scoundrels!' he said harshly to the woman.
'Scoundrels, all of them! They are lucky. They might easily have been
on the capital charge. The fact that they are public schoolboys makes
their crime all the worse. They should have known better.'

Robert Jackson, *The Chief: The Biography of Gordon Hewart*, 1959

267

Churchill and Amery

I FIRST went to Harrow in the summer term. The school possessed
the biggest swimming bath I had ever seen. It was more like the bend
of a river than a bath, and it had two bridges across it. Thither we used
to repair for hours at a time, and bask between our dips, eating enormous buns, on the hot asphalt margin. Naturally it was a good joke to
come up behind some naked friend, or even enemy, and push him in. I
made quite a habit of this with boys of my own size or less. One day
when I had been no more than a month in the school, I saw a boy
standing in a meditative posture wrapped in a towel on the very brink.
He was no bigger than I was, so I thought him fair game. Coming
stealthily behind, I pushed him in, holding on to his towel out of
humanity, so that it should not get wet. I was startled to see a furious
face emerge from the foam, and a being evidently of enormous
strength making its way by fierce strokes to the shore. I fled; but in
vain. Swift as the wind my pursuer overtook me, seized me in a ferocious grip and hurled me into the deepest part of the pool. I soon
scrambled out on the other side, and found myself surrounded by an
agitated crowd of younger boys. 'You're in for it,' they said. 'Do you
know what you have done? It's Amery; he's in the Sixth Form. He is
Head of his House; he is champion at Gym; he has got his football colours.' They continued to recount his many titles to fame and reverence, and to dilate upon the awful retribution that would fall upon me.
I was convulsed not only with terror, but with the guilt of sacrilege.
How could I tell his rank when he was in a bath-towel and so small? I
determined to apologise immediately. I approached the potentate in

lively trepidation. 'I am very sorry', I said. 'I mistook you for a Fourth Form boy. You are so small.' He did not seem at all placated by this; so I added in a most brilliant recovery, 'My father, who is a great man, is also small.' At this he laughed, and after some general remarks about my 'cheek' and how I had better be careful in the future, signified that the incident was closed. . . . We were afterwards to be Cabinet colleagues for a good many years.

Winston Churchill, *My Early Life*, 1930

268

Churchill's Cuticle

CLEMMIE . . . told me that Winston was most extravagant about his underclothes. They were made of very finely woven silk (pale pink) and came from the Army & Navy Stores and cost the eyes out of the head. This year according to her calculations he had spent something like eighty pounds on them. When I taxed him with this curious form of self-indulgence he replied: 'It is essential to my well-being. I have a very delicate and sensitive cuticle which demands the finest covering. Look at the texture of my cuticle—feel it (uncovering his forearm by rolling up his sleeve). I have a cuticle without a blemish—except on one small portion of my anatomy where I sacrificed a piece of skin to accommodate a wounded brother-officer on my way back from the Sudan campaign.'

Bonham Carter, *Winston Churchill as I Knew Him*

269

Churchill Excluded

When, in December 1916, Lloyd George ousted Asquith and made himself Prime Minister, Churchill expected office; but L. G. felt he was too unpopular with the Tories, and asked Max Aitken (Lord Beaverbrook) to break the news to him gently.

SO when I came back to Birkenhead's party that night with Lloyd George's information stowed away in my pocket, I smiled on Churchill as a senior colleague might on an aspiring junior. I still, so to speak, walked warily—but I walked. Churchill also had every reason to suppose that he was sure of high office. We discussed as allies and equals the personnel of the new Government. Churchill suggested that I might be made Postmaster-General—a task suitable to my abilities.

Then I conveyed to him the hint Lloyd George had given me. I have a reason for saying that these are the exact words I used: 'The new Government will be very well disposed towards you. All your friends will be there. You will have a great field of common action with them.'

Something in the very restraint of my language carried conviction to Churchill's mind. He suddenly felt he had been duped by his invitation to the dinner, and he blazed into righteous anger. I have never known him address his great friend Birkenhead in any other way except as 'Fred' or 'F. E.' On this occasion he said suddenly: 'Smith, this man knows that I am not to be included in the new Government.'

With that Churchill walked out into the street.

Lord Beaverbrook, *Politicians and the War*, 1932

270

Silence

Max Aitken had played an indispensable role in the formation of the Lloyd George cabinet and expected a place in it.

I WAS so sure of the Board of Trade that I told the Conservative Chairman at Ashton-under-Lyne my expectations, and warned him to be ready for a by-election on my accepting an office of profit under the Crown. . . . And then on that Wednesday afternoon something strange happened. It was as though a curtain had suddenly fallen between me and the busy active world of politics in which I had been living for days. At one moment everything had been excitement—the abyss of despair or the exhilaration of triumph. The day had been all too short to fit the events into it. Only by staying up late and rising early could one deal with the constant stream of letters, telephone messages, notes by hand, which poured in unceasingly in the intervals of private and vital conferences. The whole world seemed to turn round Whitehall or Kensington. The strained nerves felt that this racket would be unending, and now came tranquillity in a most disturbing fashion.

A quietude like death settled on the Hyde Park Hotel. There were no more calls from politicians—no more agitated interviews. No

special messengers arrived with notes. Even the telephone bell ceased
to ring. The reaction was tremendous. It is said that people in a balloon
do not feel any sensation of motion, but simply think the earth is drift-
ing past them. There came to me this same curious sense of detachment—passing by degree into boredom and then into anxiety, and
finally into a kind of desperation. I had been in the centre of affairs and
now I found myself translated to the extreme circumference.

I had waited in all afternoon and evening, expecting a message from
the Prime Minister which never came. The dark drew down and no
one came near me. There was no news of friend or foe. At last I could
bear it no longer and walked out into the street. As by a magnetic
impulse I was drawn towards the War Office, where all things must be
settled. There the Prime Minister must be allotting the offices after his
sensational and almost miraculous triumph. What I really wanted was a
sight of Lloyd George. I reached the War Office, but a sense of propriety restrained me from going in. In that dark December night I
walked round and round the square stone walls of the War Office like
a lost soul.

As I was coming away I ran into Sir Reginald Brade, who told me in
the most casual manner that Albert Stanley would be the new President of the Board of Trade.

Ibid.

271

Churchill and Lloyd George

ONE day, after I had become his Parliamentary Private Secretary
[1926], Churchill said to me: 'I know you are a great friend of Lloyd
George. I am now writing the last volume of *The World Crisis* and there
are certain questions that he alone can answer. Do you think you could
persuade him to come and see me ?' I said: 'It is not a question of persuasion. He would be delighted.' I then went to see Lloyd George and
said: 'Winston wants to see you.' He replied: 'Splendid. Fix up an
appointment.' I did, for the following evening at six o'clock. Lloyd
George arrived punctually and I showed him into Winston's room.
They were alone together for about an hour. After that I heard Lloyd
George leave by the outside door, down the corridor. I sat alone in the
secretary's room. Nothing happened. No bell rang. After about ten

minutes curiosity overcame me and I went in to find the Chancellor sitting in an armchair, gazing into the fire, in a kind of brown study. I said to him: 'How did it go?' He looked up and replied: 'You will be glad to hear that it could not have gone better. He answered all my questions.' Then a hard look came into his face and he went on: 'Within five minutes the old relationship between us was completely re-established. The relationship between Master and Servant. And I was the Servant.'

Lord Boothby, *Recollections of a Rebel*, 1978

272

2 April 1915. Winston had a bad throat. Lloyd George gave an amusing account of Winston's interview with a throat specialist at which L. G. was present. Winston ended the interview by saying, 'I entirely disagree with your diagnosis.'

Lord Riddell's War Diary 1914–18, 1933

273

Churchill and Baldwin

5 November 1924. I was shown into the Prime Minister's office. After a few commonplaces I asked him whether he minded the smoke of a cigar. He said 'No', and pulled out his famous pipe. Then he said 'Are you willing to help us?' I replied guardedly, 'Yes if you really want me.' I had no intention of joining the government except in some great position, and I had no idea—nor had anyone else—what was in his mind. So when he said, 'Will you be Chancellor of the Exchequer?' I was astonished. I had never dreamt my credit with him stood so high. I replied at once, 'What about Horne?' (who was a great friend of mine). 'No', said the Prime Minister, 'I offered him that post a year ago when I needed him, and he refused. He will not have it now . . . ' There was another pause. Then he said: 'Perhaps you will now tell me what is your answer to my question. Will you go to the Treasury?' I should have liked to have answered, 'Will the bloody duck swim?' but as it was a formal and important conversation I replied, 'This fulfills my ambition. I still have my father's robe as Chancellor. I shall be proud to serve you in this splendid Office.'

Quoted in Martin Gilbert, *Winston S. Churchill*, 1976

274

17 November 1935. In a letter to Davidson, Baldwin gave his own comment on Churchill's exclusion from the Cabinet. 'I feel we should not give him a post at this stage', Baldwin wrote. 'Anything he undertakes he puts his heart and soul into. If there is going to be war—and no one can say that there is not—we must keep him fresh to be our war Prime Minister.'

Ibid.

275

Churchill Grim

5 November 1940. The Prime Minister makes a statement after Question Time. He is rather grim. He brings home to the House as never before the gravity of our shipping losses and the danger of our position in the Eastern Mediterranean. It has a good effect. By putting the grim side foremost he impresses us with his ability to face the worst. He rubs the palms of his hands with five fingers extended up and down the front of his coat, searching for the right phrase, indicating cautious selection, conveying almost medicinal poise. If Chamberlain had spoken glum words such as these the impression would have been one of despair and lack of confidence. Churchill can say them and we all feel, 'Thank God that we have a man like that!' I have never admired him more. Thereafter he slouches into the smoking-room and reads the *Evening News* intently, as if it were the only source of information available to him.

Harold Nicolson, *Diaries and Letters, 1939–45*, 1971

276

Churchill Cruel

I THINK that the first time I ever deeply disliked Winston and realised the depths of selfish brutality to which he could sink, was when he told me, not only that he was getting rid of Wavell from the Middle East, but why. He walked up and down his room, chin sunk on chest, glowering ferociously, and muttering, 'I wanted to show my power!' over and over.

Churchill and Morton: Correspondence between Major Sir Desmond Morton and R. W. Thompson, ed. R. W. Thompson, 1976

277

Churchill Decisive

In the closing stages of the 1939–45 war, Churchill's most decisive act was to save Greece from a Communist takeover:

CRUCIAL decisions today over Greece. The climax not reached till after dinner. We discussed a statement to be made by the PM in the House the following day, and while this was going on, telegrams came in from Rex [Leeper], saying the situation was deteriorating and Papandreou about to resign. We drafted a telegram and a statement which I then took over to Number Ten, and showed [Churchill] the Greek telegrams and our proposed instructions to Leeper. He thought them not nearly strong enough and held that the time had come to order General Scobie to take over law and order and disarm ELAS by force. He cleared this on the telephone with Anthony, who was going to bed, and then settled down to draft his instructions, sitting gyrating in his armchair and dictating on the machine to Miss Layton, who did not bat an eyelid at the many blasphemies with which the old man interspersed his official phrases. He was in a bloodthirsty mood, and did not take kindly to suggestions that we should avoid bloodshed if possible.

Sir Pierson Dixon, diary, 4 December 1944

278

Churchill Bathed

Churchill contrived to meet nearly all the great wartime leaders while bathing himself, Stalin being the only notable exception; the CIGS, Sir Alan Brooke (later Lord Alanbrooke), described the procedure:

26 March 1943. The PM sent for me. By the time I . . . reached him in the Annexe he was in his bath. However, he received me as soon as he came out, looking like a Roman centurion with nothing on except a large bath-towel draped round him. He shook me warmly by the hand in this get-up and told me to sit down while he dressed. A most interesting procedure. First he stepped into a white silk vest, then white silk drawers. Then a white shirt which refused to join comfortably round his neck and so was left open with a bow-tie to keep it together. Then the hair (what there was of it) took much attention, a handkerchief was sprayed with scent and then rubbed on his head. The few hairs were then brushed and finally sprayed direct. Finally, trousers, waistcoat and coat, and meanwhile he rippled on the whole time about Monty's battle and our proposed visit to North Africa.

A. Bryant, *The Turn of the Tide*, 1957

279

Churchill Yearning

20 August 1944. . . . A clock struck two, but the PM had no intention of going to bed. It is not what Alex [General Alexander] says that wins the day. He is not so foolish as to suppose that anyone has ever got his way with Winston by argument. Winston likes a good listener; he is always ready to do the talking. And Alex seems to wait on his words. He will listen attentively until half the night is over. Like a woman, he knows intuitively that listening is not just a question of keeping silent, but it can be a means of communication of a more subtle kind. Besides, when Alex does open his mouth he is always so reassuring, always so sure that the PM's plans are right, and that there will be no difficulty at all in carrying them out. That is what Winston wants; he dislikes people who are forever making trouble. 'Anyone can do that', he snorts

impatiently. Soon he found himself confiding to Alex his most intimate
thoughts. 'I envy you', he said, 'the command of armies in the field.
That is what I should have liked.'

Lord Moran, The Struggle for Survival, 1966

280

Churchill in Twilight

THE last years were sad, but not as sad as some make out. He knew
very well that his place in history was secure. The few friends he had
were gone. The only person he ever loved, his wife, didn't like the
Riviera, and liked Lord Beaverbrook still less; so he often went there
alone. Once he rang up a friend of mine, who had a villa in Monte
Carlo, and said that he would like to come to lunch. My friend was
rather apprehensive, and invited Mrs (Daisy) Fellowes, the Singer
sewing-machine heiress, who had known him for many years, to help
him out. Soon after lunch began, he closed his eyes and appeared to
pass out. Mrs Fellowes then said to her host: 'What a pity that so great
a man should end his life in the company of Onassis and Wendy
Reves.' Suddenly, to their horror, one eye opened and Churchill said:
'Daisy, Wendy Reves is something that you will never be. She is young,
she is beautiful and she is kind.' Then the eye closed again.

Lord Boothby, Recollections of a Rebel

281

Magnanimity and Bile

RATHER late at night, Mr Churchill was leaving the Smoking Room.
As he passed a little group of us—all parties—we said: 'Good night,
Sir.' He stopped and beamed upon us, that wonderful, genial beam!
His glance fell on my friend Richard Stokes, the Socialist member for
Ipswich. All the war he had attacked Mr Churchill fearlessly, continuously, about tanks (among other things). I never knew enough about
tanks to know whether he was talking sense or not; but certainly he was
a formidable enemy to Mr Churchill and his Ministers. Now Winston
came back and put a hand on his shoulder and said: 'Of course I have

forgiven you. Indeed I agree with very much that you are saying about the Germans. Very good.' He moved away a few paces and said: 'Such hatred as I have left in me, and it is not much, I would rather reserve for the future than the past.' He beamed again, and moved off a pace or two, but stopped once more and made that inimitable sound of his, half-grunt, half-chuckle, and said: 'H'mm. A judicious and thrifty disposal of bile.'

A. P. Herbert, *Independent Member*, 1950

282

Churchill and God

RAB [BUTLER], whom I meet at dinner, is worried about the Korean situation . . . He says that Winston gives fortnightly luncheons at the Savoy to his Shadow Cabinet. At luncheon yesterday Winston said: 'The old man is very good to me. I could not have managed this [Korean] situation had I been in Attlee's place. I should have been called a war-monger.' 'What old man?' asked David Maxwell Fyfe innocently. 'God, Sir Donald', replied Winston. It seems he always calls David 'Sir Donald'.

Nicolson, *Diaries*, 28 June 1950

283

Winston Churchill and his Son

DIANA [COOPER] read me a letter from June Churchill describing a gruesome evening at Chartwell, Randolph drunk at dinner calling Soames a shit, enraging Winston by diatribes against Jerk Eden. Winston so shaken with fury that June and Clemmie feared another seizure. Randolph storming up saying he would leave at once and never see his father again. June, already in bed, forced to dress and start packing. Then at one a.m. Sir Winston padding down the passage in pyjamas, saying: 'I am going to die soon. I cannot go to bed without composing a quarrel and kissing them both.'

Evelyn Waugh, 21 July 1955, *Diaries*, 1976

284

Churchillian Fortitude

Randolph Churchill (1911–68) was a political failure, but not without some of his father's robust characteristics.

March 1964—Randolph Churchill went into hospital (Sister Agnes's, thus keeping me away who had arranged to go for two days' examination as the result of being taken ill at Mentone) to have a lung removed. It was announced that the trouble was not 'malignant'. Seeing Ed Stanley in White's, on my way to Rome, I remarked that it was a typical triumph of modern science to find the only part of Randolph that was not malignant and remove it. Ed repeated this to Randolph whom I met on my return from Rome, again in White's. He looked so pale and feeble and was so breathless that we there and then made up our estrangement of some twelve years.

Waugh, *Diaries*

285

DEATH itself did not frighten him. In hospital for the operation on his lung, it was a treat to see him refuse to be reduced to a vegetable, as most people are, ticking off the eminent surgeons for talking about doctor's orders: 'I'm paying. It's my lung. I give the orders. I take advice, but I give the orders.' He instructed the formidable matron on how to make a decent cup of tea. He insisted on seeing what had been removed before allowing it to be disposed of. 'It was rather nasty-looking, really,' he told me, 'like a fat mutton chop you wouldn't even give to the dog. Well rid of that, I'd say.'

Alan Brien in *Randolph Churchill, the Young Unpretender* ed. Kay Halle, 1971

286

DERBY was distressed by the way King George V bullied his children, and he ventured one day at Knowsley when they were walking up and down the terrace, to raise the subject, justifying his remarks on the ground that he was the King's oldest friend. He said what delightful companions his own children had become for him when they grew up, and begged the King to realise that the royal children were on the verge of manhood and that he was missing very much in life by frightening them and continuing to treat them as if they were naughty schoolboys. Lord Derby told me that the King remained silent for some four minutes after this and then said: 'My father was frightened of his mother; I was frightened of my father, and I am damned well going to see to it that my children are frightened of me.'

> Harold Nicolson, quoted by Randolph Churchill, *Lord Derby*. [The story has been repeatedly contested]

287

Royal Manners

3 December 1951. After dinner on Sunday Ben Nicolson . . . told an interesting story about the ten days he spent at Windsor Castle as Deputy Keeper of the King's Pictures. On four of those days parlour games were played after dinner and the Queen chose her favourite game. The master of ceremonies took all the male guests outside and provided them with brass pokers, shovels, etc. After ten minutes practice they were then made to parade as a squad, with the shovels and pokers on their shoulders, in slow goose step down the long drawing room past the King, the Queen and the Princesses, who found it exquisite fun seeing Sir Stafford Cripps, Lord Ismay and Anthony Eden doing 'Eyes right'. Nicolson said he hadn't seen anything like Stafford Cripps, who had been forced at two hours' notice to spend a weekend at Windsor and who humbly obeyed the Royal command but suffered the full humiliation which Royalty seemed determined to extract from its Commoner guests.

> *The Backbench Diaries of Richard Crossman*, ed. Janet Morgan, 1981

288

The Attlee Style

THE day after the coalition ended [1945], the new Labour Party chairman, Harold Laski, wrote a long letter to Attlee about the widespread feeling in the party 'that the continuance of your leadership is a grave handicap to our hopes of victory in the coming election'. Attlee would 'draw the inference that your resignation of the leadership would now be a great service to the party. Just as Mr Churchill changed Auchinleck for Montgomery before Alamein, so I suggest you owe it to the party to give it the chance to make a comparable change on the eve of this greatest of our battles.'

Attlee replied:

Dear Laski,

Thank you for your letter, contents of which have been noted.

C. R. *Attlee*

Kenneth Harris, *Attlee*, 1982

289

[WHEN visitors to his room at Number Ten came through the door] Attlee would put down his pen, raise his head with his nose pointed to the sky and take a long sniff, like a fox-terrier about to bark. Then he'd stare at the visitor and say nothing. If he wanted to encourage a visitor to leave, which was rarely necessary—they were usually ready to go— he'd take his pipe from his mouth and put it carefully on his blotter, lift himself out of his chair slightly, look across at the clock, and give a little grunt. It never failed.

Lord Moyne, quoted, ibid.

290

JOHN STRACHEY wished to publish some poems. A colleague pointed out to him that cabinet ministers could not publish a book without the Prime Minister's prior consent. Strachey wrote to Attlee that he proposed to publish a book, but that he did not think the PM would wish to see the book since it would consist of poetry. Attlee asked to see it. Strachey complied. He heard nothing of the book for three weeks, so he made a telephone call to Downing Street. Attlee came to the phone: 'Can't possibly publish. The lines don't scan.'

Ibid.

291

ONE junior minister . . . was summoned precipitately to Number Ten, to be congratulated on the work of his department, he thought. 'What can I do for you, Prime Minister? he said as he sat down. 'I want your job,' said Attlee. The minister was staggered. 'But—why, Prime Minister?' 'Afraid you're not up to it,' said Attlee. The interview was over.

Ibid.

292

Praising Attlee's modesty, Churchill added: 'But then, he has a great deal to be modest about.' And when Attlee showed unexpected Prime Ministerial authority, Churchill commented 'Feed a bee on royal jelly, and it becomes a queen.' Attlee's own feelings were expressed in a verse he composed on the eve of his installation as KG at Windsor:

> FEW thought he was even a starter.
> There were many who thought themselves smarter.
> But he ended PM
> CH and OM
> An Earl, and a Knight
> Of the Garter.

Ibid.

293

A Sartorial Point

BEVAN had the presence and poise of a natural aristocrat but he had never owned a dinner jacket in his life. In January 1946, after he had been a cabinet minister six months, he was summoned to a royal banquet at St James's Palace, and the invitation, issued by the Lord Chamberlain, bore in the left-hand bottom corner the words: 'Dress: Dinner Jacket; Day Dress: Service Dress.' Bevan saw the dinner jacket as the hated symbol of the old ruling class, now in process of being superceded by the people's representatives—he always held that democracy did not come to Britain until 1945. He told Number Ten that he had no such garment and would not buy one specially. Thus he became the first man to attend a royal dinner wearing a lounge suit, the Sunday best of his class. No one took any notice, but the Attlees, or at any rate Mrs Attlee, were disturbed. A message—several messages—came from Number Ten that the offence should not be repeated. Eventually, Bevan acquiesced. He would not buy the hated suit himself but his wife Jennie Lee, who knew his measurements, went to Peter Jones in Sloane Square and got one off the peg, a week before the next royal dinner. But word of the surrender had reached Violet Attlee, who exulted the next time she met Jennie Lee and congratulated her that her husband had at last 'shown sense'. When he heard of this encounter, Bevan swore a great oath that no power on earth should ever get him to don the dinner jacket. So he put on his old blue double-breasted best lounge suit again, and the dinner jacket remained, unworn, in his closet to the end of his days.

Michael Foot, *Aneurin Bevan 1945–60*, 1973

294

The Nemesis of Harold Laski

Professor Laski of the London School of Economics was for many years the Labour Party's leading intellectual propagandist and in 1945 was its Chairman. Following a speech he made in Newark on 19 June, he sued the Newark Advertiser *for suggesting, in its report, that he had advocated the use of violence to promote the political aims of socialism. The case was heard before Lord Chief Justice Goddard and Laski's colleague, Sir Patrick Hastings, a former Labour Attorney-General, appeared for the defence. Arthur Smith, Goddard's clerk, describes Hastings's famous cross-examination of Laski on the subject of violence:*

'Do you believe that if achievement of political aims cannot be arrived at without the use of violence, then violence is justifiable?' Sir Patrick asked.—'Not in all circumstances', replied the Professor. 'In circumstances where a burden is intolerable, violence may be inevitable because that burden is intolerable, but not otherwise.'

'In the circumstances which existed on the 16 June 1945, the date you made this speech, did you then believe that if the aims of the proletariat could not be achieved without the use of violence, then violence was justifiable?'—'No.'

'Do you agree that anyone who preached that doctrine would be a public danger?'—'Yes.'

'And you have preached it for twenty years?'—'No.'

'We shall have to see. If you had preached it for twenty years, you agree you would be a public danger?'—'If I had preached to the proletariat the inevitability of violence for twenty years, I should certainly be a public danger.'

'You have written many books in which the word revolution is contained, and you define it in your books. Have you preached the doctrine that this revolution may be brought about in one of two ways, either by consent—you call it revolution by consent—or else a revolution by violence?'—'That is so.'

'And by a revolution by consent, do you mean this—because the enemies are always capitalist, are they not?'—'Broadly.'

'Do you mean that the enemy, if there is to be a consent, must in the very nature of things, consent to their own elimination—that is to say, they have to consent to go?'—'They have to consent to great changes.'

'I have in front of me, and I have read, some twenty, thirty or forty different publications of yours, so I know something about them. I want you to answer this question if you will: have you stated that what you mean by a revolution by consent is that the capitalists must consent to their total erosion—that is your word—I thought it might have meant elimination, but you say "erosion"?'—'No, I did not mean by what I have said the elimination of the capitalists.'

'What do you mean by your word "erosion"?'— 'Erosion means rubbing away.'

'Rubbing away, do you say?'—'Rubbing away.'

'How do you consent to rub yourself away?'—'By fading out of the picture in which previously you have been the most prominent part.'

'By disappearing?'—'Yes.'

'Consent to their own disappearance?'—'To their loss of power.'

'And you have pointed out that is unlikely if not impossible?'—'No, not impossible: I have said it is historically unlikely.'

Sir Patrick's cross-examination of the Professor lasted for two days. Laski was a dreadfully bad witness. He seemed incapable of answering yes or no to a question. He was evasive, hair-splitting and sometimes plainly offensive.

'It may be difficult for you to be courteous, but do not be rude', said Sir Patrick. 'You are rude to everyone, everybody, are you not?'—'I do not think so.'

'You know that some people in this country possess religious beliefs, do you not?'—'Yes.'

'I want to read one short sentence which is the most offensive thing, I suggest, that you have ever said: it is in a book, I think, called *Threat to the Constitution*, or something of that sort. Just listen to this, it is only four lines. "Nor was it an accident that no influence was more persuasive than that of Wesley"—Wesley was the Nonconformist Minister and reformer was he not?—"in inducing the masses in England to adopt the grim discipline of the factories in return for the dubious consolation of an unproved and unprovable eternal bliss".

'By that passage, addressed to people who had some religious beliefs, you meant that it was rubbish, and that Wesley blackmailed the workers to accept conditions in the factories by promising them eternal life?'—'That is a fantastic rhetorical exaggeration, Sir Patrick. What I meant by that was that, as is well known to all historians, at the time of the Industrial Revolution, Wesleyism deflected the sense of men's indignation with their conditions in the new factories to religion as a consolation for the sorrows of this life, and that I thought that, in the light of the historical problem presented by Wesleyism, that was an unjustified thing to do.'

'Of course, when you are rude to other people, Mr Laski, you think that it is argument. When people say something about you, you bring actions for libel. That is your view of fairness, is it not?'—'Not in the least, Sir Patrick.'

The cross-examination now ranged over more than a dozen of Laski's other books. Sir Patrick read passages from them in which the Professor had referred to revolutionary change and asked for Professor Laski's comments. Finally, he turned to the actual meeting at Newark.

'You have, of course, I suppose, read many times the article of which you complain of being libellous?'—'Yes.'

'In so far as the report of the meeting is concerned, was I right in understanding that the part of which you really complain of here is the sentence: "We shall have to use violence, even if it means revolution?" '—'Yes.'

'That is really the whole of your charge here?'—'That is the essence of the allegation, that I advocate revolution.'

'Leave out the headlines, everything else is substantially accurate?'—'I think it is substantially accurate.'

'I am now going to read what you admit to be substantially accurate and see how far it differs, firstly, from anything that I have put to you as to your writings, and secondly from the one passage of which you complain. I am reading from the pleadings, and this is what you complain of: "As for violence", he continued, "if Labour could not obtain what it needed by general consent," and then are these words of which you complain: "we shall have to use violence even if it means revolution." I now pass from this and I am going to read the rest which you say is substantially accurate and ask you to tell me where it differs. "When people felt that was the moment of great experiment, for innovation, because when war is over people so easily forget—especially those who had the power in their hands—that was the time for experiment." In substance that was what you said. Now listen to this: "Great changes are so urgent in this country."—You said that and that meant changes in favour of the Socialist regime?'—'That meant changes in favour of the working class.'

'But am I not putting it accurately when I say it is the principle?'—'Changes operated on Socialist principles.'

'If you please, "Great changes are so urgent in this country, and if they were not made by consent"—now those were the changes to be made by consent and you have described in your books so often what you mean by consent—"they would be made by violence." You said that?'—'I think so.'

' "They would be made by violence"—by whose violence?'—'By the drift of events in the country.'

'Who was going to drift?'—'The whole country would drift into a situation where agreement between parties would be suspended.'

'Very well. Let us assume all that. Who would use violence to bring about these changes?'—'My view is the view I have consistently affirmed, that a Labour government would obtain the power, would be challenged and would have to suspend the Constitution, that the outcome of its suspension would nevertheless be its successful government, and by the successful government it would operate the changes for which it was elected.'

'I do wish you would try if you could, Mr Laski, to answer my questions a little more shortly.'—'I am doing my best, Sir Patrick, but you are trying to confine me in a narrower compass than is justified by the fact.'

'Just read the whole passage, Mr Laski, beginning "When people felt it was the moment of great experiment . . . ",' interposed the Lord Chief Justice. 'You are being asked, in view of that, when you say that if they are not made by consent, they will be made by violence, you mean it would be made by violence by the people who would make the experiment?'—'Certainly.'

'That is all I am asking you,' continued Sir Patrick. 'Now let us see what that means, Mr Laski. This is what you are saying, what you admit you are saying: If these Socialistic changes are not made by consent they will be made by the violence of those who believe in Socialism?'—'Yes.'

After that answer Professor Laski could not possibly retrieve his position. A few more questions and he retired, extremely white and shaken, from the witness box. He was a little, frail-looking man, with steel-rimmed spectacles. Had it not been for his insufferable arrogance, I should have felt very sorry for him at that moment . . .

[After his summing-up] the Lord Chief Justice sent the Jury to their room. After less than forty minutes they returned. They had found that the report in the *Newark Advertiser* was a fair and accurate report of the public meeting, dealing with a matter of public concern and published for the public benefit. Therefore it was privileged and therefore the far more difficult question which had been posed them relating to the accusation that Professor Laski had advocated sedition, did not have to be considered. Judgment was entered for the *Newark Advertiser* with costs. These, which amounted to nearly £13,000, were paid by public subscription. Poor Professor Laski lapsed into obscurity.

He quarrelled with the Labour government, and in two years he was dead.

Arthur Smith, Lord Goddard: My Years with the Lord Chief Justice, 1959

295

A Mighty Fall

The Chancellor of the Exchequer, Hugh Dalton, together with Bevin and Morrison, composed the Big Three of Attlee's post-war government. On 12 November 1947 he introduced his fourth budget.

THE next day, 13 November, the cabinet met. Debate ran tediously on secondary issues. Just before noon a messenger handed Morrison a note. He was sitting on the Prime Minster's left, and on my right. These were our usual places at the cabinet table. The note was from Maurice Webb. It said that a very serious situation had arisen. There had been a bad budget leak yesterday evening in the *Star*. The Tories were in full cry and one of them had put down a Private Notice Question for me this afternoon. Morrison passed the note to me and I wrote on it: 'Discuss when we adjourn.' And then, for the first time since yesterday afternoon, I remembered that, on the way to the Chamber to make the budget speech, I had had a few words with John Carvel, the *Star's* Lobby Correspondent, about the contents of my budget. This I had completely forgotten until I read Maurice Webb's note. The cabinet adjourned soon after, and I took Morrison and Maurice Webb to my study at Number Eleven. Webb had a copy of yesterday's *Star*. I told them I had spoken to Carvel and I added: 'This means I must resign my office.' Morrison and I then went back to the Cabinet Room to dicuss with Attlee how I should answer the Private Notice Question. I asked Cripps, who was coming to see me on another matter, to join us. And Willy Whiteley, the Chief Whip, whose office was next door to my study, came too.

We five were alone in the Cabinet Room. We all agreed that I must make full and frank admission of my responsibility and express my deep regrets and apologies to the House. This was a case where anything short of a hundred per cent would be wrong. We then drafted a reply on these lines. I then repeated what I had previously said to Morrison: 'This means that I must resign my office.' The first reaction of those present was to brush this aside. Whiteley in particular said that this was quite out of the question. But I said to Attlee: 'Prime Minister, I now offer you my resignation.' [After the afternoon session of the Commons] about five o'clock I left the Bench and went again to see the Prime Minister. It was a sad and short conversation. I began by reminding him that it was now nearly four hours since I had offered him my resignation. I hoped that he would now accept it. He replied that he felt he must, but I was moved to see that he was much more deeply moved than I was at this moment. He said he hated—hated—he repeated the word several times—hated to lose me. He thanked me for what I had done as a minister in several successive departments, and he hoped that I should be able to rejoin the government later, in some other department, as an 'elder statesman'.

Hugh Dalton, *High Tide and After: Memoirs 1945–60*, 1962

296

Attlee's private comment on Dalton after the indiscretion:

'ALWAYS was a loud-mouthed fellow.'

Harris, *Attlee*

297

An Amorous Secretary of State

Ernest Bevin, once boss of the Transport workers, became Foreign Secretary in 1945. He conceived a robust affection for Lady Diana Cooper, a former actress and wife of Britain's Ambassador in Paris, Duff Cooper.

IN March 1947, he was again dining at the Embassy and as his private secretary, Pierson Dixon, had temporarily vanished, Diana [Cooper] took him to the lift: 'What was my surprise when he suddenly clasped me in his arms with the strength and immobility of a bear and buried his pudgy face in my neck. So we stood for a full minute, or an eternity: then, with a very slow, utterly relentless gesture, he shifted his mouth to mine. No struggles could have affected the situation, as well stand against the mountain weight of lava. I was agonised at the thought of Bob Dixon coming in and writing me down as an office-hunter seducing the boss, but as far as I know he didn't see anything, unless it was the lipstick that transformed poor Ernie into an end-of-the-evening old clown Joey. He asked me to stay the night. Could he have thought I would?'

Philip Ziegler, *Diana Cooper*, 1983

298

Gaitskell's Ablutions

During the harsh winter of 1947, in an attempt to save ten per cent of electricity consumption, the Minister of Fuel and Power, Hugh Gaitskell, told a municipal election meeting at Hastings to wash less:

'IT means', he said, 'getting up and going to bed in cold bedrooms. It may mean fewer baths. Personally I have never had a great many baths myself, and I can assure those who are in the habit of having a great many baths that it does not make a great deal of difference to their health if they have fewer. And as far as appearance [goes] most of that is underneath and nobody sees it.'

As he wrote later, it was meant and taken simply as a joke. But Winston Churchill could not resist the opportunity. He said in the Commons: 'When Ministers of the Crown speak like this . . . [they] have no need to wonder why they are getting increasingly into bad odour. I had even asked myself whether you, Mr Speaker, would admit the word "lousy" as a Parliamentary Expression in referring to the Adminstration, purely as one of factual narrative.'

Sensitive though he was, Gaitskell was not worried at first. But the publicity convinced him he had been unwise. He received a few anonymous letters and a protest from a remote relative, while his old nurse, from whom he had not heard for thirty years, sent an indignant denial. Even a quarter of century later, a school friend told the author: 'He washed well!'

Philip M. Williams, Hugh Gaitskell, 1979

299

Massacre of Bartholomew

During the 1930s, Guy Bartholomew made the Daily Mirror *the most successful tabloid in Britain, and in the 1940s it became the chief Press supporter of the Labour Party. It was popularly credited with winning Labour the 1945 election. But by 1951 he was under threat from Cecil Harmsworth King, Northcliffe's nephew, and the rising star of the Mirror Group board:*

THOUGH Bart was amusing and at times brilliant, he was a dreadful man to work with or for. He enjoyed spying on people, and so our telephones were tapped and our letters read. Any critical remark about any member of the staff would be passed on by Bart to create mischief. If no critical remark was made he would often concoct one. Setting different members of the staff—or the board—at each other's throats was a real pleasure for him. This, of course, is the reverse of the proper role of a chairman. Towards the end of his reign I got more and more involved in our West African papers, and Bart's spirit and influence became more and more perceptible in the paper. Eventually his drunkenness reached such proportions that something had to be done.

He had got to the point of insulting distinguished guests at lunch, repeatedly alleging, for instance, to the head of the Australian Radio Control Board, Sir Lionel Hook, that 'all Australians were crooks', mercifully said so incoherently as to be barely intelligible. Eventually I collected the votes of my colleagues, who said I would never succeed in shifting Bart, but that I had their vote. Then early one morning (he was usually incoherent by 9.30 am) I told him he had lost the confidence of his board and must vacate the chair. He rang one of the other directors, Bolam, the editor, and found he was supporting me, so his reign was over. He lingered on that morning, weeping maudlin tears into his whisky in the company of the hall porter.

Cecil King, *Strictly Personal*, 1969

300

Regicide

King succeeded Bartholomew as chairman of the Mirror, *and built it into IPC, the largest publishing corporation in the world, wielding as was supposed enormous political power. But in 1968, aping his uncles Northcliffe and Rothermere, he tried to replace the Prime Minister, Harold Wilson, and was destroyed in his turn. His deputy, Hugh Cudlipp, told the story of how King tried to get Earl Mountbatten to head a government of national safety:*

I ARRANGED a meeting between King and Mountbatten and myself for 4.30 Wednesday 8 May 1968 at his London residence, No. 2 Kinnerton Street, SW1. [Mountbatten] phoned on the day to mention he would be accompanied by Sir Solly Zuckerman, then Chief Scientific Adviser to HM Government; there had been no sort of conversation with King on any previous occasion and the move was obviously a precaution. Cecil and I had known Solly for a number of years and the choice seemed felicitous from King's point of view.

Cecil had given me no indication in advance of how far he proposed to go at the meeting; he always gave great thought to what he would say on important occasions, but did not on this occasion rehearse the part with me. He awaited the arrival of Sir Solly and then at once expounded his views on the gravity of the national situation, the urgency for action, and then embarked on a shopping-list of the Prime Minister's shortcomings. He spoke with his accustomed candour. He did the talking and I sat back in my chair to observe the reactions, detecting an increasing concern on the part of the two listeners. He explained that in the crisis he foresaw as being just around the corner the government would disintegrate, there would be bloodshed on the streets, the armed forces would be involved. The people would be looking to somebody like Lord Mountbatten as the titular head of a new administration, someone renowned as a leader of men who would be capable, backed by the best brains and administrators in the land, to restore public confidence. He ended with a question to Mountbatten—would he agree to be the titular head of a new administration in such circumstances?

Mountbatten turned to his friend: 'Solly, you haven't said a word so far. What do you think of all this?'

Sir Solly rose, walked to the door, opened it, and then made this statement: 'This is rank treachery. All this talk of machine-guns at street corners is appalling. I am a public servant and will have nothing to do with it. Nor should you, Dickie.' Mountbatten expressed his agreement and Sir Solly departed. Only a minute or two elapsed between Zuckerman's departure and King's. Lord Mountbatten was, as always in my experience, courteous but firm: he explained explicitly but briefly that he entirely agreed with Solly and that that sort of role, as far as he was concerned, was 'simply not on'.

Two days later Cecil King announced on the front page of the *Daily Mirror* that Mr Wilson and his government had lost all credibility, all authority, and demanded a fresh start under a new leader . . .

(*For Cudlipp and his colleagues on the board, this was the last straw and at a secret meeting on 29 May 1968, the board decided to demand King's resignation as Chairman, and a letter to this effect was delivered to him early the next morning. At 9.35 he summoned Cudlipp and two of his colleagues, Don Ryder and Frank Rogers, to the chairman's room in the IPC building.*)

On the way in the directors' private lift from the fifth floor to the ninth I said to my colleagues, 'You can be sure that though three of us are expected there will be only one chair in front of the William Kent [desk] as usual. I'll take that, but won't start the proceedings until you have settled in your pews.' I anticipated long pauses from Cecil, designed to promote in the unhappy delegation a sense of discomfort, doubt or guilt, and asked my colleagues not to imagine I had suddenly become inarticulate and rush to my aid if I, too, fell in with the long pause technique.

There was one chair in front of the octagonal desk, and there was a long pause. I felt that Cecil should open the meeting, giving his reaction to the letter. He thought otherwise but eventually offered, 'Well?' I said he had received our letter, that it was necessary under the Articles of Association for it to be written stating the vote at the meeting the night before, and I therefore thought he would wish to give his reactions to it. Was he prepared to resign? There was another long pause, with Cecil's eyes focused firmly and accusingly on me. Frank Rogers, sitting on my right, broke the silence: 'I would like to say Cecil that—' (King's head turned slowly to Frank to give him the benefit of the formidable glare I had received for the previous minute) 'all your colleagues hold you in high esteem and affection. You should not doubt this. We have done what we think is right for the Corporation, and that is our duty as directors. But the affection—'

Cecil King: 'An odd way of showing it.'

There was another long pause, and the beam from the lighthouse turned again on me. 'Resign? Resign today? Certainly not. It would look as if I had been found with my hand in the till. Certainly not.'

Pause.

Cudlipp: 'I'm sorry you take that view, Cecil. You leave me with no alternative but to go back and consult the board.'

King: 'You can go and consult anybody you like.'

Pause.

It seemed to me, nevertheless, that he had not yet said his ultimate piece and had carefully considered in advance just what he would say and when he would say it. That was his style. Don Ryder spoke next, as the glare revolved accusingly to him: 'I would like to say something that Hugh will probably not say for himself, but I think should be said. You should know that this is in no way, and has not at any time been, a revolt led by Hugh against you.' Don said more on these lines, but the expression on Cecil's face was not encouraging to a dissertation on the subject of loyalty.

'I think', said King, 'we have had enough insincerity for one morning.'

Cecil turned to me with the same matchless slow-motion: 'If you wish to say to me that the time has come for me to go, I don't want to outstay my welcome. Far from it. In two or three months' time, or something like that . . . '

Pause.

Cudlipp: 'I will discuss this suggestion with our colleagues and, of course, will let you know within an hour or so what their reply is. Will you be in the office all day?'

Cecil, opening his arms in a gesture of lofty patience and a hint of resigned boredom, said 'I am at your disposal.'

Don Ryder, Frank Rogers and I withdrew for a talk in my room. It was obvious to anybody who had worked with Cecil as long as we had, and who knew his methods, that he would employ such a period of respite not to clear up his affairs and gracefully retire, but to conduct a subtle campaign to dominate his colleagues one by one, selecting first the weakest or most emotional or most gullible, and to hold rigidly and triumphantly to his original intention to retire at seventy and not a day or an hour or a minute sooner . . . I called a meeting of the directors in Orbit House where we had met the night before. . . . It was unanimously decided by the thirteen directors present that since a resignation that day with an agreed statement was spurned by King, there was no alternative to his dismissal but a degrading retreat by his colleagues. The second letter was signed and delivered to Cecil's room:

May 30 1968

Dear Cecil,

Frank Rogers, Don Ryder and I reported back to all members of the board after our discussion with you this morning. All your remarks were conveyed in full.

The unanimous view of the board is that the decisions which were made last night cannot be revoked or altered in any way.

The letter of request which was delivered to you this morning stands. Accordingly, therefore, you have ceased to be the Chairman and a director of IPC.

An announcement will be made later today.

All the directors regret that the announcement cannot, as things stand, be made in the form of a resignation.

Sincerely,
Hugh Cudlipp

Hugh Cudlipp, *Walking on the Water*, 1976

301

A Pair of Eggheads

Richard Crossman (1907–1974) and Anthony Crosland (1918–1977) were the two leading Socialist intellectuals of the post-war period. Crossman eventually became Secretary of State for Social Services and Crosland Foreign Secretary, but neither left much mark on politics, though Crosland's The Future of Socialism *(1956) was widely read at one time. Both were inclined to arrogance and, in Crosland's case, to extreme rudeness, especially to women.*

WHEN Crosland was in the second Wilson cabinet, he attended a party in Kensington. He wore shirt, trousers and a pair of carpet-slippers. He was bored by the company and, though not particularly drunk, lay at full-length on the floor, just outside the room which was serving as the ladies' cloakroom. Any lady wishing to retrieve her coat had to circumnavigate or stride across his recumbent form. A tall, plain and very shy girl did this with some difficulty, and reactivated the Minister in the process. The supine Crosland looked up, focused on her, and announced: 'Hello, ugly face!' Later, in tears, the girl asked 'Who is that horrible man?' and was told 'That is Her Majesty's Secretary of State for Education.'

Anon.

302

THE late Francis Hope's mother once had a dream about Richard Crossman. She was seated in a dentist's chair and he, attired in a white coat, was about to attend to her teeth. 'Don't be silly, Dick,' she said, 'you know you're not a dentist.' 'I know I'm not, you fool,' Crossman replied, 'but I can work it out quite easily from first principles.'

Hugh Gaitskell, who was staying in the same house and to whom this dream was related at breakfast, said that it perfectly expressed the reason he would not give Crossman any post in a Government formed by him.

Alan Watkins, Brief Lives, 1982

303

Libel or Perjury?

In November 1957 three Labour leaders, Aneurin Bevan, Richard Cross-man, and Morgan Phillips, the party's General Secretary, sued the Specta-tor for libel. The magazine's correspondent Jenny Nicholson had suggested they were drunk at a Socialist meeting in Venice. Its proprietor, Sir Ian Gilmour, later a Tory cabinet minister, had unsuccessfully tried to arrange an out-of-court settlement and the case brought together a cast of famous legal personalities: Arnold Goodman, who advised the plaintiffs, Gilbert Beyfus QC, who represented them, W. Fearnley-Whittingstall QC, who appeared for the defence, and the Lord Chief Justice, Lord Goddard, who presided.

So the case began, with quite a good presentation by Beyfus, after which Nye and I went into the witness box before lunch. Nye, I thought, was extremely good and Fearnley-Whittingstall, who I had been told was one of the bitterest Conservatives and who had been boasting that he was looking forward to cross-examining Mr Bevan and dressing him down, seemed to me to get very little out of him. I fancy I was all right, although I was always a danger to my own side, owing to a streak of voluble candour, which works usually but can of course also undo you if the candour lets a cat out of the bag.

In this case it didn't. Indeed I am fairly sure that the impression I created—that I was genuinely, sincerely and, as a journalist, pro-fessionally determined to try to get Gilmour to print an apology—was a completely decisive element in winning the case. Or, to put it another way, Nye wanted to fight (until he got cold feet at the last moment, a fact he will certainly forget) and get big damages; but the man who won him his big damages was the man who didn't want to fight and genuinely wanted to settle, because what got us damages was our ability to disprove the other side's assertion that we had turned down all their draft apologies.

At the end of the morning we were told that the other side were offering to settle for our terms of £1,000 etc. I at once turned this down, since it was clear to me that, once the case had started and the first evidence about the drinking had been printed, it was essential to get right on and have the Lord Chief Justice's comments, which I knew would be favourable, at the end. For, even after half an hour, it was clear that this astonishing old monster of eighty had made up his mind that we were in the right and that the *Spectator* had behaved outrageously. He was quite friendly to me when I was standing in the box. Indeed at one point he said *sotto voce*, 'Do remember you're not in the House of Commons', not in a rude but in a helpful way, to stop one talking too much; and at another point he commented, when I said I wanted to settle, 'Of course. Dog does not eat dog.'

But Lord Goddard really came into his own after lunch. First we had to endure the cross-examination of Morgan Phillips. At lunch Goodman had said that whether a witness is good or bad depends on his self-confidence and quickness of wit. That is why a man like Fearnley-Whittingstall is so surprised when he is confronted with Nye or me, because the usual witness can be hectored or bullied and made to take the attorney's line, whereas we gave a great deal better than we got. But directly Morgan got into the box, it was clear he was a subnormal witness—shifty, fearful, sweating with panic (legitimately, for he'd been dead drunk most of the conference)—and within ten minutes the cross-examiner was exploiting his inferiority complex and forcing him to admit things he'd never thought of admitting an hour before.

However, Morgan didn't do much harm. Then came the cross-examination of Gilmour . . . It became clear very soon that I had guessed right when in my original telephone conversation I had warned him that, in order to satisfy us, he would have to disown Jenny Nicholson. I managed to get this into my evidence and thereby to tip off Beyfus who had the sense to extract from Gilmour the admission that he couldn't disown the truth of the story completely for fear of an action from Miss Nicholson! Since Gilmour had previously made a complete fool of himself by saying that he'd published the article, seeing nothing libellous in it, this finally finished him with the jury. That concluded the first day.

This morning Gilmour's examination went on. I thought Beyfus rather exceeded himself by calling him a liar for saying in the *Spectator* that no draft apology had been offered to us and defending the statement on the grounds that I had specifically stated that our communications were off the record. I would have called this disingenuous, dishonest, dishonourable and pointed out that, though one certainly can't be blamed for not *mentioning* what is off the record, it's quite a different thing when one says the *opposite* of what happened off the record. Beyfus put it more crudely and, I thought, enabled Gilmour to get a little sympathy. Then we had the speeches of the two leading QCs, both stock speeches, Fearnley-Whittingstall working up all the emotion he could against our insistence on a grovelling apology, and Beyfus replying with some fine fustian about the lies of Gilmour and his scurrilous newspaper. I didn't think either of them very good and thought they both missed some important points.

But as soon as lunch was over, the Lord Chief Justice changed all that by making the speech on our behalf that I had hoped Beyfus would make. It was a devastating exposure of Gilmour's disingenuousness, incompetence and weakness and it was an instruction to the jury. Looking at the jury, I couldn't believe that they could understand much of what was going on, particularly the question of what was a real and what was a spurious apology, and I don't think they would have given us adequate damages if they hadn't been ordered to in the precisest detail by the Lord Chief.

The only thing which scared us in the summing-up was his advice that the jury should not give extravagant but moderate damages. After all, by this time the size of the damages was all-important. From the morning press account of the first day, it was clear enough that, unless we got swingeing damages, we should be turned into a laughing-stock, and the *Daily Mail* had already tried to do this on its front page. Did these twelve jurymen have the same idea of moderate damages as the Lord Chief, or would they think that £500 was moderate?

I also had my own private worry, since Beyfus, who obviously didn't like me, and did like Nye, has in his winding-up speech carefully distinguished between Nye and Morgan, with their international reputations, and me, whom he left out altogether as a mere journalist. After that it was possible that the jury would give distinct damages to each person. I was unutterably relieved when the LCJ specifically advised them that it would be fair to give each of us the same.

We had twenty minutes waiting outside. Then came the judgment— £2,500 each. Afterwards, after a few words outside, we each went our separate ways, escaping from the photographers. When I told Sydney Jacobson the result, he remarked 'If I could get £2,500 tax-free for being called an alcoholic, I would gladly submit myself to the libel!' George Wigg was delighted, especially for the effect it would have on the Labour Party that somebody was fighting at last. I was relieved, though not surprised after today, but I still think the risk we took was appalling. If it hadn't been the Lord Chief Justice but a more moderate judge, the damages might have been quite small. If Gilmour hadn't been such an appalling bad witness, the *Spectator* could have sustained its case far better. Finally, if I hadn't preached moderation and genuinely tried to get an apology without damages, there would have been no damages for Nye or Morgan. So altogether you can say it was a very satisfactory result. I'm sure of one thing—that Mr Goodman, whom I regard as a pleasant villain, will sleep easier in his bed tonight now that he's got his verdict, despite the disparate and discordant views of his three clients.

The Backbench Diaries of Richard Crossman

304

A Canny Crofter's Grandson

Harold Macmillan was Minister of Housing, 1951–4, his junior ministers being Ernest Marples and Reginald Bevins.

HE is careful. In the narrow financial sense he always seemed to enjoy receiving hospitality. During a visit with me to Liverpool he was handed a silver spade in order to plant a tree. A few days later I found a note on my desk: 'What has happened to the silver spade I got in Liverpool? Tell them to send it to Birch Grove.' He was most insistent about it. Some days later Marples's bike was stolen from New Palace Yard and a manufacturer offered to replace it. The transaction was vetoed.

Reginald Bevins, *The Greasy Pole*, 1965

305

Harold Macmillan's press secretary, Sir Harold Evans, went to see his sick Master immediately after his resignation in 1963.

HE was in a very small room (when the Queen came, they took him to the Matron's room), but brisk and cheerful, with only occasional references to his dotage. Chiefly he talked about why Rab (Butler) had never made the final ascent. Quite simply it was because ultimately the fire and determination were lacking . . . He had one complaint, he said. Within twenty-four hours of his ceasing to be Prime Minister, the

Post Office had taken out his line to Number Ten. Now he was having to pay a penny-halfpenny a call. So please would I call him, rather than wait for him to call me?

Sir Harold Evans, *Downing Street Diary*, 1981

306

A Vague Foreign Secretary

The 14th Earl of Home, Foreign Secretary 1960–3, was inclined to eccentricity. He confided to one interviewer that he did his sums by using matchsticks, and to another that his favourite pastime was arranging flowers. His brother related he was also a little vague:

'PEKING, Alec, Peking, Peking,' his devoted wife Elizabeth would constantly repeat to him while walking behind him down the steps of the aeroplane, when he was Foreign Secretary. 'Peking, Peking, Peking,'—in order to prevent him saying to his hosts, as he stood up before the microphone, 'I'm very happy to be back in Montreal' (or Rome or Washington or Moscow).

William Douglas-Home, *Mr Home Pronounced Hume*, 1979

307

A Disputed Succession

Immediately after his operation for prostate in October 1963, Harold Macmillan decided to resign, and he managed the procedure to choose his successor from his hospital sickbed.

ON the Monday afternoon Macmillan dictated a memorandum for his deputy, R. A. Butler. It was of a magisterial character but since officially it is a Cabinet paper it cannot be quoted here. Macmillan indicated that he was out of touch and in no position to render advice if he should be asked. In these circumstances he recommended: (1) Lord Dilhorne shall poll the cabinet. (2) The Chief Whip shall sound the opinion of Members of the House of Commons including junior ministers. (3) Lord St Aldwyn, Chief Whip in the House of

Lords, shall sound opinion in the House of Lords: namely those who regularly take the Whip including junior ministers. (4) Lord Poole and Mrs Shepherd and Lord Chelmer shall sound the constituency parties as best they can. Next day, Butler presided at the Cabinet. He read out the Prime Minister's letter and the Cabinet unanimously approved of what the Prime Minister had proposed.

. . . By the morning of Thursday 17 October the party soundings had been completed. Shortly before 10 o'clock Macmillan was taken down in a lift, in his bed, from his hospital bedroom to the matron's sitting-room on the ground floor. The Prime Minister received each report separately. The first to be received at 10.22 were Poole, Mrs Shepherd and Chelmer. They had been sounding the constituency organisations and had polled as many constituency chairmen as they could.

The three party officials reported that they could give no actual figures but that they could give a fair and accurate impression of feeling in the constituency associations. At Blackpool they had sought information and found that some 60 per cent were for Hailsham and 40 per cent for Butler. It turned out, however, that there was immense bitterness among the rival adherents against their adversaries. The soundings they had taken since the Conference only served to confirm this bitterness of feeling and point to the fact that only Home could avoid a split in the party. But at this time Home was considered a non-starter. They further added that many people were volunteering the name of Home, particularly as their second choice.

Dilhorne arrived at the hospital at 10.56 and he reported to the Prime Minister that most of the Cabinet were very strong for Home. Whereas originally there had been six adherents of Butler and six of Hailsham, Dilhorne had to report that the overwhelming consensus now pointed to Home. Home had the best chance of uniting the Cabinet if he could be persuaded to disclaim his peerage. At 11.30 Redmayne and Major John Morrison, Chairman of the 1922 Committee, called. Their combined report of feeling among junior ministers and Conservative backbenchers showed that Home led in popularity among them, but only narrowly. There was no clear-cut overall majority for him . . . Finally at noon, St Aldwyn came to speak for the Tory peers. All who normally take the Whip, including junior ministers, had been consulted. St Aldwyn was able to report that the peers were overwhelmingly for Home.

Ill though he was, the Prime Minister was determined to neglect no method which could ensure a smooth and successful transference of power. He was taken upstairs again to have his luncheon, and decided that he would now see representatives of the four groups together. Accordingly, after luncheon, he came down once more to the matron's room and there received, at three o'clock, Dilhorne, Redmayne, St Aldwyn and Poole. The Prime Minister asked each of them in turn to repeat to the others the advice that they had given to him in the morning. By so doing he made sure that there could be no recriminations afterwards and that everybody would know what everybody else had advised. From their advice it once again became clear that those who wanted Hailsham were violent against Butler and those who wanted Butler were equally violent against Hailsham. Everything pointed to Home.

. . . A good example of the care the Chief Whip, Redmayne, took to sample all opinion in the parliamentary party is a cable he sent to Aidan Crawley, member for West Derbyshire, who was at the time in South Africa. Crawley, in a remote part of the Northern Transvaal, happened to telephone to the South African Trust in Johannesburg—it was his accommodation address—on some matter connected with his tour. They read him a telegram: 'Welcome your views on leadership – Redmayne.' Crawley dictated over the telephone his answer: 'Strongly favour Lord Home.' The South African papers had scarcely adverted to Home's chances; so when Crawley reached Johannesburg a few days later he was hailed as a king-maker.

No less assiduous was the Chief Government Whip in the House of Lords, Lord St Aldwyn. He contacted all those peers who take the Tory Whip and whom he could reach. After considerable difficulty he reached Field Marshal Lord Montgomery in Manchester. Asked his views on the leadership Montgomery said: 'What do you want: the best PM or a man to win the election?' St Aldwyn replied: 'We want both.' 'You can't have that,' said Monty in his brusque, staccato fashion. 'Home'd make the best PM, Hailsham's the best man to win the election.'

[The next day Macmillan resigned and the Queen, accompanied by her secretary, Sir Michael Adeane, came to the hospital.] Adeane waited in another room, since Ministers and ex-Ministers always see the Queen alone on such occasions. This unique royal audience at a bedside was of memorable character. The Queen expressed her regret at Macmillan's departure and asked him whether he could offer any advice as to whom she could entrust the formation of a new Government. Macmillan explained that he did not feel well enough to speak to

her spontaneously and asked permission to read her the memorandum
he had prepared the night before. The Queen assented. After spend-
ing half an hour with her former Prime Minister, she took a copy of it
with her. It was of a most detailed character incorporating all the four
reports on which Macmillan had based his advice. On arrival at the
Palace the Queen immediately sent for Lord Home and at 12.56 the
following announcement was made: 'The Queen has received the Earl
of Home in audience and invited him to form an administration.'

Randolph Churchill, *The Fight for the Tory Leadership*, 1964

308

Another View

*Disgusted with the way Macmillan had handled the succession problem,
Enoch Powell and Iain Macleod refused to serve in Lord Home's administration. Macleod went further, and published his own version of how it was
decided:*

THE truth is that at all times, from the first day of his premiership to
the last, Macmillan was determined that Butler, although incom-
parably the best qualified of the contenders, should not succeed him.

Iain Macleod, *Spectator*, 17 January 1964

309

The 14th Earl and TV

*Lord Home did his best as premier, and came within an ace of winning the
1964 election, but he was not entirely happy in his job.*

I FEAR that I could not conceal my distaste for the conception that the
political leader had also to be an actor on the screen. In 1963 I had an
unpromising start when I was being made up for some Prime Ministerial appearance; for my conversation with the young lady who was
applying the powder and tan went like this: 'Can you make me look

better than I do on television?' 'No.' 'Why not?' 'Because you have a
head like a skull.' 'Does not everyone have a head like a skull?' 'No.'
 So that was that.

Lord Home, The Way the Wind Blows, an Autobiography, 1976

310

The Woman Minister

*As Social Services Secretary, Barbara Castle had to visit the scene of a disas-
trous fire at an old folks' home.*

17th December 1974. The alarm didn't go off and I had a wretched rush
to catch the 8 am train, arriving at St Pancras half-dressed to find a
photographer lurking in the gloom. Getting up in a rush always jangles
my nerves and I nearly hit him. Besides, I had had nothing to wear (all
my clothes seem to need a stitch, a press or a clean) and my hair was a
mess. I knew that cameras would be there in force, so in despair I had
slammed on 'Lucy' [her wig]. After a leisurely breakfast on the train I
began to feel that my exhaustion might be containable. I retired to the
loo, finished making up my face and adjusted Lucy carefully. So when
we arrived at Nottingham I was ready for anything that might come—
or so I thought. The discussion with the County Council and my
experts went well and then we got into cars for the visit to Fairfield. TV
and press cameramen and journalists came climbing over the charred
ruins in full cry after me, as the Chief Fire Officer and others took me
round, helping me over twisted girders and ash-strewn mud. Lucy
rocked uneasily on my head in the strong wind, but I managed to cope,
looking—and feeling—appropriately subdued. Cameras peeped at me
through every aperture as I went through the ruined home, watching
my feet in case I tripped. Alas, I did not watch my head and suddenly
to my horror I felt Lucy snatched from it by a piece of wire trailing
from the roof. The officer said 'Oh', I snatched Lucy back and somehow pulled her on my head again, askew—and carried on. It was one
of those nightmares one dreams about and I froze inside with embarrassment. No doubt some wretched camera had caught the whole
thing! But some inner grimness of will always comes to my rescue in
these crises and I walked on, looking, questioning and *willing* my

entourage to believe they had imagined it. No one dared to imagine it
and so, somehow, I got through the dreadful day and back again. . . .
What a life!

The Barbara Castle Diaries, 1974–6, 1980

311

Band of Brothers

*The 1964–70 Wilson government began to break up in 1969 on the issue of
how to reform the trade unions.*

8 May 1969. The main thing at Cabinet was the Industrial Relations
Bill . . . I finally got irritated with Callaghan [Home Secretary] and
said, 'But look, we are not facing the real issue, which is that Douglas
Houghton has lined himself up with people who are trying to get rid of
the Prime Minister. That is the meaning of his speech. He is prepared
to see the Prime Minister go because he hopes to get another Prime
Minister who will drop the Bill. As I tried to say last Friday at Yardley
this is totally unrealistic and it would not be credible unless it was
believed there was somebody in the Cabinet who held the same view. I
know and you all know that Roy Jenkins and Barbara Castle are as
deeply committed as the Prime Minister and that there is no sense in
suggesting that the Prime Minister could be got rid of. I detest these
rats who are leaving our sinking ship to climb on to another sinking
ship. We have got to sink or swim together.' At this point Callaghan
said from the other side of the table, 'Not sink or swim, sink or sink',
and I said, 'Why can't you resign if you think like that? Get out, Jim, get
out!' We had never had such a scene in Cabinet before (I was told later
on it was a phenomenally dramatic moment) and there was an awkward
silence. Then Jim muttered, 'Of course, if my colleagues want me to
resign I'm prepared to go if they insist on my going.' He had been
punctured. He hadn't responded, he had crawled, and it was quite a
moment.

Richard Crossman, *Diaries of a Cabinet Minister*, 1977

312

Sacked!

In April 1976 Harold Wilson retired as Prime Minister and handed over to James Callaghan. Mrs Barbara Castle, Secretary of State for Social Services, was summoned to see him at 10 Downing Street.

8 April 1976 . . . Jim was sitting tense in the study . . . He waved me to a seat and said quickly: 'I don't want to soft-soap you, Barbara. I must reduce the average age of Cabinet and I want to ask you for your portfolio.' I felt detached. 'Did someone tell you that I wanted to retire at Easter?' I asked. He shrugged. 'It was Harold', I went on. He replied: 'Whoever it was this isn't the reason.' I paused and then said: 'I never intended to hang on indefinitely. But I did see Harold about a month ago to tell him I wanted to see my pay beds Bill through parliament. Then I would wish to retire—with dignity. You do realise that I am due to introduce that Bill on Monday?' He shrugged again and looked miserable. . . . Another pause, then Jim burst out, 'Harold said to me that the worst thing about this job would be the Parliamentary Questions. It isn't that: it is this.' 'Harold thought that too,' I replied sweetly, 'that's why he didn't do it.' Another pause, and Jim said with a semblance of briskness: 'So you will let me have a letter saying that you are putting your job at my disposal in order to make way for someone younger.' 'Oh no', I replied, even more briskly. 'So you are going back on what you have just said', replied Jim with a show of nastiness. 'Not at all', I replied. 'What I have said is that I have no choice. But I am not doing this voluntarily. I want to stay to finish my legislation. And that is what I shall say in my letter to you. And I shall hold a press conference to spell this out. I shall go on to the Standing Committee on the Bill and shall defend it line by line.' 'Heaven help your successor', he replied mournfully. . . . I got up to go and Jim held out his hand: 'Wish me well, Barbara.' I shook his hand and said 'Good luck.' He said almost desperately: 'You should know that Mike [Foot] has fought for you very hard. I had to tell him this was one thing I could not give him. Perhaps this is the first mistake I have made but, as Harold said to me, I must make my own mistakes.' I said nothing and Jim said to me impulsively: 'Will you let me do this?' and kissed me on the cheek. I said 'Cheerio' and walked out of the room.

The Barbara Castle Diaries, 1974–6

ACKNOWLEDGEMENTS

THE editor and publisher acknowledge with thanks permission to reprint the following copyright material:

Lord Alanbrooke: reprinted from *The Turn of the Tide* by permission of Collins Publishers.

Lord Beaverbrook: reprinted from *Politicians and the War* (Thornton Butterworth, 1932), and from *The Decline and Fall of Lloyd George* (1963) by permission of Collins Publishers.

J. R. Bevins: reprinted from *The Greasy Pole* (Hodder, 1965), by permission of the author.

Earl of Birkenhead: reprinted from *F.E.*, by permission of Methuen, London and Hughes Massie.

Robert Blake: reprinted from *Disraeli* and from *The Unknown Prime Minister*, by permission of Eyre & Spottiswoode (Publishers) Ltd.; (ed.), reprinted from *The Private Papers of Douglas Haig*, by permission of Earl Haig.

Lady Violet Bonham Carter: reprinted from *Winston Churchill As I Knew Him*, by permission of Eyre & Spottiswoode (Publishers) Ltd.

Lord Boothby: reprinted from *Boothby: A Rebel Remembers* (Hutchinson, 1978) by permission.

James Boswell: reprinted from *Boswell in Extremes 1776–8*, by permission of the Boswell Editorial Committee (Yale University Library), William Heinemann Ltd. and McGraw-Hill Book Company.

William Camp: reprinted from *The Glittering Prizes* (MacGibbon & Kee, 1960), by permission of the author.

Barbara Castle: reprinted from *The Barbara Castle Diaries 1974–6* (1980) by permission of David Higham Associates Ltd.

Lady G. Cecil: reprinted from *Life of Lord Salisbury* (Hodder, 1931), by permission of A. P. Watt Ltd., on behalf of Lady Cecil.

Lord David Cecil: reprinted from *Lord M.: The Later Life of Lord Melbourne* (1954), by permission of Constable Publishers, and of David Higham Associates.

Randolph S. Churchill: reprinted from *Winston S. Churchill* (Heinemann, 1967), Vol. II, © 1967 C. & T. Publications Ltd., by kind permission of Curtis Brown Ltd., on behalf of C. & T. Publications Ltd.; from *The Fight for the Tory Leadership*, © Randolph S. Churchill 1964, and from *Lord Derby: King of Lancashire*, © Randolph S. Churchill 1964, by permission of Curtis Brown Ltd., on behalf of the Estate of Randolph S. Churchill.

Winston Churchill: reprinted from *Great Contemporaries*, by permission of Curtis Brown Ltd., on behalf of the Estate of Sir Winston Churchill; from *Lord Randolph Churchill* by permission of Macmillan, London and

Basingstoke; and from *Marlborough: His Life and Times* (1933), copyright George G. Harrap & Co., Ltd., All Rights Reserved, by permission of Harrap Ltd.; from *My Early Life* (Hamlyn 1930).

Brian Connell: reprinted from *Regina v. Palmerston* (Evans Bros., 1962), by permission of the author.

Richard Crossman: reprinted from *The Backbench Diaries of Richard Crossman* (ed. Janet Morgan, 1981), and from *Diaries of a Cabinet Minister* (1971), by permission of Hamish Hamilton Ltd.

Hugh Cudlipp: reprinted from *Walking on the Water* (1976), by permission of The Bodley Head Ltd.

Sir Pierson Dixon: reprinted from a diary entry for 4 December 1944, by kind permission of Piers Dixon.

Mrs Edgar (Blanche) Dugdale: reprinted from *Arthur James Balfour* (Hutchinson, 1939).

Anthony Eden: reprinted from *Facing the Dictators*, by permission of Times Books, a Division of Random House, Inc.

John Ehrman: reprinted from *The Younger Pitt* (1969), by permission of Constable Publishers and of Stanford University Press.

D. H. Elletson: reprinted from *Maryannery: Mary Ann Lincoln and Mary Anne Disraeli* (1959), by permission of John Murray (Publishers) Ltd.

Sir Harold Evans: reprinted from *Downing Street Diary* (1981), by permission of Hodder and Stoughton Ltd.

John Evelyn: reprinted from *The Diary of John Evelyn*, ed. E. S. de Beer (Oxford Standard Authors, 1959), by permission of Oxford University Press.

Sir A. Fitzroy: reprinted from *Memoirs* (Hutchinson, 1929).

A. G. Gardiner: reprinted from *Life of Sir William Harcourt* (1923), by permission of Constable Publishers.

Martin Gilbert: reprinted from *Winston S. Churchill*, Vol. V, © C. & T. Publications Ltd., 1976, by permission of Curtis Brown Ltd., on behalf of C. & T. Publications.

Edward Gregg: reprinted from *Queen Anne* (1980), by permission of Routledge & Kegan Paul.

Wilson Harris: reprinted from *J. A. Spender* (Cassell, 1946), by permission of Macmillan Publishing Company.

A. P. Herbert: reprinted from *Independent Member* (2nd edn., Methuen 1950), by permission of A. P. Watt Ltd., on behalf of Lady Herbert and Methuen London Ltd.

G. Huehns (ed.): reprinted from *Selections from Clarendon* (World's Classics Series 1955), by permission of Oxford University Press.

R. F. V. Heuston: reprinted from *Lives of the Lord Chancellors 1885–1940* (1964), © OUP 1964, by permission of Oxford University Press.

Alec Douglas-Home: reprinted from *The Way the Wind Blows: An Autobiography* (1976), by permission of Collins Publishers.

William Douglas-Home: reprinted from *Mr Home Pronounced Hume* (1979), by permission of Collins Publishers.

George Hutchinson: reprinted from *The Last Edwardian at Number Ten: an Impression of Harold Macmillan* (1980), by permission of Quartet Books Ltd.

Montgomery Hyde: reprinted from *Carson* (Heinemann, 1953).

Earl of Ilchester: reprinted from *Hervey and His Friends* (1950), and from *Henry Fox, First Lord Holland* (1920), by permission of John Murray (Publishers) Ltd.

Robert Jackson: reprinted from *The Chief: The Biography of Gordon Hewart*, © Robert Jackson 1959, by permission of Harrap Ltd.

Roy Jenkins: reprinted from *Sir Charles Dilke* (1958), by permission of Collins Publishers.

B. R. Jerman: reprinted from *The Young Disraeli* (Princeton, 1960).

J. M. Keynes: reprinted from *Essays in Biography* (1933), by permission of Macmillan, London and Basingstoke.

Cecil King: reprinted from *Strictly Personal* (Weidenfeld & Nicolson, 1969).

Anita Leslie: reprinted from *Edwardians in Love* (Hutchinson, 1978).

Anthony Lincoln and Robert McEwen (eds.): reprinted from *Lord Eldon's Anecdote Book* (Stevens & Sons, 1960), by permission of the publisher.

Earl Lloyd George: reprinted from *Lloyd George* (1960), by permission of Muller, Blond and White Ltd.

John Locke: extract from his diary, reprinted from Maurice Cranston, *John Locke* (Longman, 1959) pp. 151-2.

Elizabeth Longford: reprinted from *A Pilgrimage of Passion: A Life of Wilfrid Scawen Blunt*, copyright © Elizabeth Longford 1979, and from *Wellington: Pillar of State*, copyright © Elizabeth Longford 1972, by permission of Weidenfeld & Nicolson Ltd., and Curtis Brown Ltd., London.

Frank Longford: reprinted from *Eleven at Number Ten*, copyright © Frank Longford, by permission of Curtis Brown Ltd., on behalf of the Patrick Morris Pakenham Trust, and Harrap Limited.

Mary Lutyens: reprinted from *The Lyttons in India* (1979), by permission of John Murray (Publishers) Ltd.

Iain Macleod: reprinted from *The Spectator*, 17 January 1964, by permission of Baroness Macleod of Borve.

Harold Macmillan: reprinted from *The Past Masters* (1975), by permission of Macmillan, London and Basingstoke.

Philip Magnus: reprinted from *Gladstone: A Biography* (1954), and from *Burke: A Life* (1936), by permission of John Murray (Publishers) Ltd.

Leslie A. Marchand (ed.): reprinted from *Byron's Letters and Journals* (1974), by permission of John Murray (Publishers) Ltd.

Joyce Marlow: reprinted from *Mr & Mrs Gladstone: An Intimate Biography* (Weidenfeld, 1977).

David Marquand: reprinted from *Ramsay MacDonald* (Cape, 1977), by permission of David Higham Associates Ltd.

Kingsley Martin: reprinted from *Father Figures* (Hutchinson, 1966); and from *Editor* (Hutchinson, 1968).

Keith Middlemas and John Barnes: reprinted from *Baldwin: A Biography* (1969), by permission of Weidenfeld & Nicolson Ltd., by permission of A. D. Peters & Co. Ltd.

Lord Moran: reprinted from *The Struggle for Survival* (Constable, 1966).

Nicholas Mosley: from a letter from Lady Desborough to A. J. Balfour reprinted from *Julian Grenfell* (Weidenfeld, 1976), used with permission.

Malcolm Muggeridge: reprinted from *Chronicles of Wasted Time* (1972), by permission of Collins Publishers.

David Newsome (ed.): reprinted from *Edwardian Excursions: from the Diaries of A. C. Benson, 1898–1904* (1981), by permission of John Murray (Publishers) Ltd.

Harold Nicolson: reprinted from *Diaries and Letters 1939–1945* (1971), by permission of Collins Publishers; reprinted from *King George V: His Life and Reign* (Constable, 1952), from *Curzon: The Last Phase* (Constable, 1934), and from *Some People*, by permission of Nigel Nicolson.

Sir Charles Petrie: reprinted from *Bolingbroke* (1937), by permission of Collins Publishers and Curtis Brown Ltd.

Thomas Pinney (ed.): reprinted from *Letters of Thomas Babington Macaulay*, Vol. II (1974), by permission of Cambridge University Press.

Reginald Pound and Geoffrey Harmsworth: reprinted from *Northcliffe*, originally published by Cassell & Co. Ltd. (1959), copyright Sir Geoffrey Harmsworth 1959, by permission of Macmillan Publishing Co.

Robert Rhodes James: reprinted from *Rosebery* (Weidenfeld, 1963) © Robert Rhodes James 1963; and from *Lord Randolph Churchill* (Weidenfeld, 1959) © Robert Rhodes James 1959, 1986, by permission of Anthony Sheil Associates.

Kenneth Rose: reprinted from *The Later Cecils* (Weidenfeld, 1975); and from *Superior Person* (Weidenfeld, 1969), by permission of the author.

Arthur Smith: reprinted from *Lord Goddard* (1957), by permission of Weidenfeld & Nicolson Ltd.

Peter Smithers: reprinted from *The Life of Joseph Addison* (2nd edn. 1968), © OUP 1968, by permission of Oxford University Press.

Earl of Stanhope (ed.): reprinted from *Notes on Conversations with the Duke of Wellington 1831–51* (World's Classics Series 1938), by permission of Oxford University Press.

A. J. P. Taylor (ed.): reprinted from *Frances Stevenson's Diary* (Hutchinson, 1971).

R. W. Thompson (ed.): reprinted from *Churchill and Morton: Correspondence Between Major Sir Desmond Morton and R. W. Thompson* (1976), by permission of Hodder & Stoughton Ltd., and David Bolt Associates.

G. M. Trevelyan: reprinted from *Grey of Fallodon* (1937), pp. 73, 266, by permission of Longman Group Ltd.

J. R. Vincent (ed.): reprinted from *Disraeli, Derby, and the Conservative Party: the Political Journals of Lord Stanley, 1849–67* (1978) pp. 89, 90, 106, 228–9, 341, 331 with permission from The Harvester Press Ltd., Brighton.

Alan Watkins: reprinted from *Brief Lives* (1982), by permission of Hamish Hamilton Ltd.

Evelyn Waugh: reprinted from *The Diaries of Evelyn Waugh*, ed. Michael Davie (1976), by permission of A. D. Peters & Co. Ltd., and Little, Brown & Co.

Philip M. Williams: reprinted from *Hugh Gaitskell: A Political Biography* (1979), by permission of Jonathan Cape Ltd., and A. P. Watt on behalf of the Estate of the late Philip Williams.

John Wilson: reprinted from *C.B.: Life of Sir Henry Campbell-Bannerman* (1973), by permission of Constable Publishers.

Trevor Wilson (ed.): reprinted from *The Political Diaries of C. P. Scott* (1970), by permission of Collins Publishers.

A. S. Woodhouse (ed.): reprinted from *Puritanism and Liberty, from the Clark Manuscripts with Supplementary Documents*, (2nd edn. 1975), by permission of The University of Chicago Press, and J. M. Dent and Sons Ltd.

Philip Ziegler: reprinted from *Diana Cooper* (1981), by permission of Hamish Hamilton Ltd.

While every effort has been made to secure permission, we may have failed in a few cases to trace the copyright holder. We apologize for any apparent negligence.

INDEX OF AUTHORS

INDEX OF NAMES MENTIONED